THE PATH

ACCELERATING YOUR JOURNEY TO FINANCIAL FREEDOM

BY

PETER MALLOUK

WITH

TONY ROBBINS

RANKED THE #1 INDEPENDENT FINANCIAL ADVISOR IN
THE U.S. FOR 3 CONSECUTIVE YEARS BY BARRON'S˙

WORLD-RENOWNED LIFE AND
BUSINESS STRATEGIST

Post Hill
PRESS

A POST HILL PRESS BOOK
ISBN: 978-1-64293-701-5
ISBN (eBook): 978-1-64293-702-2

THE PATH:
**Accelerating Your Journey
to Financial Freedom**

Cover Design by Damin Sterling, BLVR

Interior Design by Brett Burner, BLVR

Post Hill Press
New York • Nashville
posthillpress.com

Published in the United States of America

CONTENTS

PART IV
THE CLIMB

PART V
THE SUMMIT

THE PATH

INTRODUCTION

The financial services industry is broken. You may be surprised to hear this from someone who has made his living in the financial industry, but it's true. Financial advice and services are traditionally delivered through a system that requires relationships with a variety of professionals: an accountant, an attorney, an insurance agent, a financial advisor, a banker, and many others. These individuals rarely talk to one another, leaving you stuck in the middle, fighting to make sure everything is done correctly. The problem with this model[1] is that your finances don't operate in a vacuum. The investment decisions you make with your portfolio are affected by income tax, estate planning, charitable giving, income needs, debt management strategies, business planning, financial independence goals, and many other factors. Of all of these people acting on your behalf, only you see the full picture. How can others help you achieve your desired investment outcome if your desired outcome wasn't even considered before you started?

To make things worse, the individuals sought for guidance in these matters are not necessarily legally required to meet the highest standard of care with your money. Instead, many professionals in the finance industry operate in a manner that's confusing to the average investor or, worse, purposefully misleading. Traditional brokerage firms can offer any product they think is appropriate for you, even if it arguably benefits their company more than it benefits you. You have insurance companies that

---

1   As if it didn't already sound terrible enough.

package investment products inside annuities and insurance products that often generate huge commissions for their agents at your expense. And other firms can be "dually registered," and alternate at will between acting in a manner that meets the strictest responsibility for client care and in a manner that does not. Finally, independent firms, which are legally required to act in their clients' best interests at all times, often lack the size, scale, and resources to effectively address the full scope of their clients' needs. And who is stuck in the middle of all this mess? It's you, the average investor, having to make some of the most important decisions of your life! Asking questions like: How do I create a path that maximizes my financial opportunities, avoids potential pitfalls, and leads me to the "right" investments for my financial goals? How can I find the right guide to help lead me down this path?

I started my career in this industry largely focused on estate planning, financial planning, and investment management advice, primarily for other advisors' clients. From this vantage point, I could see it all, and I didn't like what I saw. I saw that many advisors are excellent, but they work in conflicted environments. I saw advisors who would force their clients to sell all of their existing holdings before implementing a new strategy, regardless of the tax consequences for the client or the amount of damage done to the portfolio. I saw other advisors push their own products or a generic portfolio model on unsuspecting clients. I saw expensive insurance products sold instead of very low-cost investments that would have been better aligned with the client's goals. In short, people were often entrusting their life's savings to a professional, only to later discover that individual did more harm than good.

I realized there had to be a better way of doing things. When I took over Creative Planning, a small, independent investment firm in Overland Park, Kansas, I saw it as an opportunity to change the way financial advice is given in this country. I vowed to operate a firm that would not sell its own proprietary investment products, would create portfolios tailored to each client's needs, and could provide advice across key areas of a client's financial life, including taxes, law, financial planning, and investments. I am proud to say that we have not wavered from that commitment since I started in 2003. We are, however, able to do so much more for clients today than we ever dreamed of back then.

Since I started at Creative Planning, the assets under our management have grown to nearly $50 billion. We have been repeatedly recognized as a top wealth management firm by various media outlets, including the #1 Independent Advisory firm in America by *Barron's* (2017), twice named the #1 Wealth Management Firm by CNBC (2014 & 2015), and *Forbes* has listed Creative Planning #1 on its ranking of the fastest-growing independent firms in the country (2016).[2] This success is largely due to the incredible team we have built and their passion to deliver on our promise to clients. As our team has grown, we've been able to add specialized services and expertise well beyond the reach of most other independent firms. An equally important reason for our tremendous growth is that average investors increasingly expect more from their advisors. Tony Robbins for many years has been a vocal advocate in promoting the fiduciary standard, helping to educate millions on the importance of working with an advisor who has a legal obligation to act in their clients' best interests. In 2017, he and I wrote *Unshakeable: Your Financial Freedom Playbook* to answer some of the most pressing questions in investing today.

If the past seventeen years have taught me anything, it's that Americans are yearning for a clear and concise way to receive financial advice that is free from conflicts. They want a portfolio customized to their unique circumstances and goals. They are looking for a guide who can show them the path that leads to financial freedom. Creative Planning has been that guide for tens of thousands of families by creating customized plans, tailored portfolios, and comprehensively addressing any risks that

---

2   See disclosure on page v for information about rankings and recognitions.

might take them off their path to success. My goal in this book is to share my experiences with you and help eliminate the complexities you face in creating your own path. I look forward to being your guide, helping you to articulate your financial goals, avoid dangerous mistakes, and maximize the opportunities available to you along the journey. Together, we can chart your path to financial freedom.

PART I

———

THE JOURNEY AHEAD

CHAPTER ONE

THE PATH TO FREEDOM

by Tony Robbins

The only thing we have to fear is fear itself.
PRESIDENT FRANKLIN DELANO ROOSEVELT

We all want to be truly free. Free to do more of what we want, when we want, and share it with those we love. Free to live with passion, with generosity, with gratitude, and with peace of mind. This is financial freedom. It's not an amount of money; it's a state of mind. And regardless of your stage in life or your current financial picture, the goal of financial freedom can indeed be reached – yes, even in times of crisis. In fact, many fortunes have been made during times of "maximum pessimism."

Everyone has their own definition of financial freedom. For you, it might mean spending more time traveling, more time with your kids and grandkids, or more time giving back to a meaningful cause. Maybe you desire to work because you want to, not because you have to. Whatever your definition of financial freedom, you might be wondering: Is it *truly* possible?

After interviewing over 50 of the world's greatest financial minds, I can tell you with certainty that there is indeed a path to get there. But there are clear rules that you must follow if you want to make the summit. There are pitfalls and obstacles you must avoid. There are numerous bad actors who can lead you astray with self-interested advice. **This book addresses all of these in detail.** Becoming financially independent isn't rocket science, but there is also no magical black box to becoming financially free (despite those who would tell you otherwise). Your future self can't afford to climb without the groundwork of ropes and solid anchors. If you are committed to your personal vision of financial freedom, you must protect yourself and participate in your own rescue.

Depending on where you are today, financial freedom might sound like a pipe dream or you may be right on track but don't *feel* a sense of freedom. You might be millennial with burdensome student debt. You might be a baby boomer who needs to play some serious catch-up. You may be even wealthy by most standards yet have tremendous fear about losing all that you have worked hard to create. Regardless, this book will give you the proven tools, strategies, and peace of mind you need not only to achieve financial freedom but have a true sense of fulfillment on the journey.

IT TAKES DECADES TO BECOME AN OVERNIGHT SUCCESS

Let me fill you in on the biggest secret of financial freedom: you probably won't earn your way to it. For the vast majority, even those making great money, saving enough to become financially secure is nearly impossible. Isn't it funny how the more we make, the more we seem to spend? In thousands of conversations on the topic, most people say their plans involve hitting a financial home run: selling a business, winning the lottery, getting a huge raise or promotion or a surprise inheritance. But let's be honest: hope is not a strategy. There are simply way too many variables outside our control for many of these scenarios to fall perfectly in place. We must tap into the power that Albert Einstein called the eighth wonder of the world: compound interest.

In *The Tipping Point*, Malcolm Gladwell describes the tipping point juncture as *"the moment of critical mass, the threshold, the boiling point."* **This is most certainly true when it comes to the power of compounding.** So you want to be a millionaire? It's doable, especially if you start early. **The chart shown in Figure 1.1 is perhaps one of the most important charts you will ever see** (however, you can plan on seeing a bunch more in a financial book like this!). This shows the amount of money you need to invest each year to have $1 million saved by age 65. This assumes a 7% earning rate and investing in a tax-deferred account like a 401(k) or IRA. If you start young, it's astonishing the amount you can save by the time you retire. At age 20, you only need to save $3,217 per year, or $272 a month. But if you wait until you are 50, you need to plunk down $37,191 per year, or $3,099 a month.

Figure 1.1

ANNUAL SAVINGS TO BECOME A MILLIONAIRE BY 65

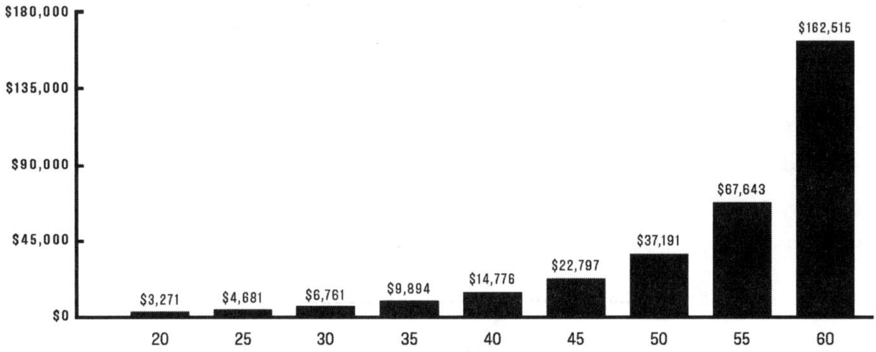

Now, is this chart an oversimplification? Sure it is. There's no magical account where you can get a 7% return year after year. In fact, from 2000 through the end of 2009 (a full ten years), the S&P 500 produced a whopping 0% return; this became known as the "Lost Decade." But smart investors don't just own US stocks. During my own journey to financial freedom, I had the opportunity to sit down with investment legend Burt Malkiel, who authored the famous book, *A Random Walk Down Wall Street.* He explained that if during the Lost Decade, you were diversified in US stocks, foreign stocks, emerging market stocks, bonds, and real estate,[3] you would have averaged 6.7% annually—all during a period that included the tech bubble, 9/11, and the 2008 financial crisis.

As I write this, we are in the middle of the COVID-19 pandemic, and fears of a global recession are mounting, with the length and severity being anyone's guess. The important thing to remember is that these economic "winters" are actually some of the best wealth-building opportunities. If you can discipline your fear and manage your emotions, major market pull-backs can present the opportunity of a lifetime. Why? Because everything is on sale! During the Great Depression, Joseph Kennedy, Sr. dramatically increased his fortune by investing heavily in real estate that was selling at a fraction of its previous value. In 1929, Kennedy's fortune was estimated to be $4 million (equivalent to $59.6 million today). But by 1935, just six years later, his wealth had ballooned to $180 million (equivalent to $3.36 billion today)!

Are economic winters challenging? To be sure; however, winters don't last forever! They are always followed by spring. And even during winter, not every day is a snowy, dark blizzard. There are still sunny days that are there to remind us that winter won't last forever. As you will learn in this book, how you choose to navigate the continuously changing investment "seasons", both emotionally and financially, is going to be crucial.

---

3   Broken down this way: 33% fixed income (VBMFX), 27% US stocks (VTSMX), 14% developed foreign stocks (VDMIX), 14% emerging markets (VEIEX), 12% real estate investment trust (VGSIX), rebalanced annually.

So, in order to make the summit of financial freedom (and stay there), there are questions you must answer:

- What investments are available to you, and which will be right for your goals?
- What mix of investments will you include in your account(s), and how will they be managed throughout the year?
- What strategy will you use to legally minimize taxes (the largest single "expense" in your lifetime)?
- How will you eliminate excessive fees or unnecessary commissions and, by doing so, greatly increase your future nest egg?
- How will you navigate, and even take advantage of, market corrections and crashes?
- How can you pick an advisor who is legally required to meet the highest standards of care with your money? (spoiler alert: most aren't)?

These are the questions that my friend and coauthor, Peter Mallouk, address in this incredibly rich book. Peter has nearly two decades of experience running Creative Planning (www.creativeplanning.com), a nearly $50 billion independent investment advisory firm that offers comprehensive wealth management services for thousands of families across the United States. In this book, Peter has generously taken his years of wisdom and hands-on experience and offered it up to anyone who wants to know what it truly takes to achieve financial security and freedom.

But having the tools necessary to achieve financial freedom and taking action are two different things. Execution trumps knowledge every day of the week. If achieving financial freedom isn't rocket science, why is it that we are living in the most prosperous time in history and yet so many fail to secure even basic levels of financial security? Frighteningly, 60% of

Americans don't have even $1,000 saved for retirement. And less than 40% could handle a $500 emergency.

We are a nation of consumers, but if we are to collectively prosper, we must make the shift to becoming owners. Many Americans own iPhones, but why not own Apple? Many Americans find Amazon boxes on their doorstep every day, but why not own the powerhouse retailer?[4] Nothing prohibits us, regardless of our socioeconomic status, from benefiting from the power of innovative capitalism. Anyone, with just a few dollars, can own a piece of the top US companies and be an owner of arguably the most prosperous and profitable economy in world history.

MOVING BEYOND

The relationship we have with money is undoubtedly an emotional one. The strategies and information we all need to achieve financial freedom are readily available, so why is it that so many are wandering aimlessly, financially stressed, or unaware that a path forward even exists? And why are so many people financially successful yet entirely unfulfilled and emotionally bankrupt?

The reason is the worst four letter word one could imagine . . .

F-E-A-R

Fear is the invisible force that keeps us from creating the life we truly deserve. It is the greatest obstacle on the path and, left unchecked, encourages us to make incredibly poor investing decisions.

As you will learn in the pages ahead, our brain is hardwired to focus on what is wrong—on what can harm or threaten our way of life. We often want certainty above all else. But guess what? Becoming a great investor

---

4   Not a specific stock pick. Just making a point here.

involves embracing uncertainty! Becoming financially free is certainly about having the right strategy, but if you don't have mastery of your mind, your strategy will likely fail due to your own misguided intervention (e.g., selling during volatile times and putting your cash under your mattress).

REPETITION IS THE MOTHER OF SKILL

In 2014, I wrote *Money: Master the Game*, which was the compilation of everything I had learned from years of interviews with true money masters like Carl Icahn, Ray Dalio, and Jack Bogle. Around the same time, Peter wrote a book, *The 5 Mistakes Every Investor Makes & How to Avoid Them*. Two years later, Peter and I wrote *Unshakeable: Your Guide to Financial Freedom* as a way for people to truly understand how markets work and remove the fear around corrections and crashes. Now, we are in the middle of the "Great Pause", where the world has come to a halt, and there will surely be winners and losers when we emerge to normal life again.

Compared to the previous books, Peter takes a much deeper dive into the fundamentals of how to build your plan and win the game. This book is about mastering the strategy of investing, not just the concepts. But I have also included two chapters on self-mastery. In Chapter 3, we explore understanding the "6 human needs" that each one of us has and how they influence your path in life, business, and money. The insights we unpack will transform the quality of your life. In Chapter 12, we tackle the issues of why those with financial abundance are often still not happy and how you can have the feeling of abundance today. Each of us is prone to live in suffering states (fear, anger, frustration) if we surrender to an undirected mind. We must learn to rescue our thoughts from the hostage taker between our ears. In doing this, you can experience the true promise of *real* wealth: a life that is filled with joy, happiness, generosity, excitement, and peace of mind.

If you have read my previous books, these two chapters may offer some repetition; however, the principles are worth repeating. I have learned from my own mentors that repetition is the mother of skill. You don't become LeBron James or Stephen Curry by shooting a few shots during practice. Even though they know how to make a free throw, they still shoot thousands of practice shots a week so it's embedded in their nervous system and they can execute under pressure. This is the path to mastery! So as you read, look for important nuances as to how these principles are showing up in your life and relationships now. When we see a movie or hear a song we have heard before, we are at a different place in our life and we get something new out of it. I suggest the same is true here.

COURSE CORRECT

We are living in a time when our fear is magnified and exploited by both the media and social media. Add a pandemic to the mix, and fear becomes heightened to extraordinarily unhealthy levels. Tidal waves of information hit us daily with the goal of getting our attention, hence the term *click bait*. Good news takes a back seat to the latest tragedy, threat, or swarm of murder hornets that is coming to a town near you. The fear part of our brain is continuously stoked and our anxiety levels are at record highs.

But let's face the truth. If we don't learn to control our fear, to master our mind, we will never truly execute on the great principles in this book. Remember that courage doesn't mean you don't experience fear. It means consistently taking action and moving forward in spite of the fear. You may read this book and get some great information, but never take the steps to achieve the goal that you and your family deserve. But I know this isn't you. If you've purchased this book and are still reading, I know you're of the few who "do," not the many who talk.

The first step in taking our minds back from the tyranny of terror is to recalibrate our perspective. As I pass the baton to Peter Mallouk, I am thrilled for you to dive into this next chapter. You will have a full appreciation for the incredible times we are experiencing now and the exponential, unimaginable future we have in store IF we can arm ourselves with the right education and learn to conquer our fears.

Let the journey begin!

As with our previous books, 100% of the profits are being donated to charity. For this book, Peter and I have committed to donate 100% of the profits of this book to *Feeding America*.

CHAPTER TWO

THE WORLD IS BETTER THAN YOU THINK

On what principle is it, that when we see nothing but improvement behind us, we are to expect nothing but deterioration before us?

THOMAS BABINGTON MACAULAY

London, 1858. It was a beautiful morning—that was, until Queen Victoria opened her balcony door at Buckingham Palace. A stench quickly invaded her nostrils and overwhelmed her to the point of nausea. In what came to be known as the "Great Stink," London had been completely overcome with the gut-wrenching, oppressive smell of human and animal feces. For the better part of the previous 50 years, two and a half million London residents had been dumping waste directly into the streets and the river Thames. The situation had finally reached a proverbial tipping point. There were now over 200,000 steaming cesspits beneath the city's homes and businesses that, in futility, were routinely shoveled by "night soil men." Cholera breakouts became common as sewage overflowed into cisterns and rivers, contaminating the drinking water and causing all manner of sickness.

SURVIVAL WAS THE GOAL

We all seem to wish for a return of the good old days when, in fact— let's face it—the good old days weren't all that good. Four hundred years ago, nearly 30% of the European population was wiped out from a single disease: the bubonic plague. Just 200 years ago, during the time of the stink bomb in London, 45% of children died before reaching the age of five. Having your children survive to adulthood in Victorian England was a relative coin flip. Imagine the morale of a society that routinely lost nearly half of its offspring.

And we don't need to go as far back as Victorian England. Just 100 years ago, 20 million people were killed in the four years of World War I. In 1918, the Spanish flu tore through Europe, infecting 500 million people—one-third of the world's population—and killing over 50 million.

Okay, I promise I'm done with this tour through depressing events in human history. I recall this history only because it's important for us to recalibrate our brains to the blessing of the here and now. Our brains trick us into loving narratives of nostalgia, but these narratives contain a real flaw: they rarely capture the whole picture. History is riddled with war, disease, and famine, and these past times are brutally sobering when compared to our present day. Even with modern pandemics, like the COVID-19 coronavirus, humanity's prognosis is vastly superior to that of previous generations.

Today, only about 4% of children worldwide die by the age of five, and overall pediatric and maternal health is at an all-time high. We haven't had a major war in a generation, and most illness can be treated with modern medicine. Furthermore, sanitation is *greatly* improved (for which I am grateful). We struggle to remember this, because we are often limited by our day-to-day experiences. Not only is our view of history mistakenly labeled a "golden age"; our view of the future is mistakenly pessimistic.

Dr. Hans Rosling, the late scholar of international health, wrote in his book *Factfulness* that "every group of people thinks the world is more frightening, more violent and more hopeless—in short, more dramatic—than it really is." Despite the facts, we are predisposed to a deterministic fate of doom and gloom. This darkened point of view is often apparent when I sit down with people regarding their personal finances. When we are imagining their future and mapping out their plans, the conversation will take a sharp turn from optimistic saving for a comfortable retirement to a quick-cash, survivalist mentality. They reveal a fatalistic view of society coming unraveled (supported, I'm sure, by websites and YouTube videos committed to perpetuating that narrative). Nobody knows what the future has in store, but a look at our recent past should allay our worries. In his book *The Rational Optimist*, Matt Ridley waxes eloquent on the rapid acceleration of human progress and expansion over just the past 50 years:

> In 2005, compared to 1955, the average human being on Planet Earth earned nearly three times as much money (adjusted for inflation), ate one-third more calories of food, buried one-third as many of her children and could expect to live one-third longer. She was less likely to die as a result of war, murder, childbirth, accidents, tornadoes, flooding, famine, whooping cough, tuberculosis, malaria, diphtheria, typhus, typhoid, measles, smallpox, scurvy or polio. She was less likely, at any given age, to get cancer, heart disease or stroke. She was more likely to be literate and to have finished school. She was more likely to own a telephone, a flush toilet, a refrigerator and a bicycle. All this during a half-century when the population more than doubled . . . by any standard, an astonishing human achievement.

THE ANTIDOTE

Consider the five charts that follow to be the visual antidote for our susceptibility to worrying about the future. Based on research that charted spending, life expectancy, global well-being, poverty, and education, these graphs are comforting reminders of where our world is headed. As a father, I am hopeful about the future of humanity and the quality of life my children and grandchildren will enjoy. And as we will get to shortly, as an investor, I am licking my chops at the opportunities ahead. I suspect you will be too.

Figure 2.1 shows the precipitous drop in how much of our income we use in this country to survive. In other words, we are living at the peak of disposable income. College tuition, Disney cruises, luxury cars that drive themselves, date nights out on the town, movie theaters with giant leather recliners, and, of course, our ability to save for a comfortable retirement: these are all relatively new phenomena when viewed through the arc of history.

Among many other factors, not having to spend every dollar we make on the bare necessities has dramatically increased our global population's sense of happiness and well-being. (Figure 2.2) No surprise there! We are now free to move beyond survival in our own hierarchy of needs and begin asking the more existential questions around purpose, what it means to be fulfilled, and how we want to spend our precious time. Without the day-to-day struggle of figuring out how to pay for housing and food, we are able to spend more time on what matters—and be happier doing it.

Figure 2.3 is astonishing! Life expectancies around the world are continually on the rise. Get this: someone born this year is projected to have a life expectancy three months longer than someone born in 2019. Earlier in my career, when my senior clients faced serious health challenges, they often asked for hospice planning or quotes on the price of end-of-life care. Now, they are looking to stay alive as long as they can and are quick to look for experimental treatments or the latest breakthroughs in global medicine. These clients know that the longer they can stay alive, the more likely there will be an innovation that can help their condition.

Figure 2.1

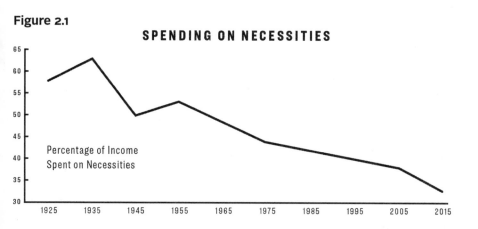

SPENDING ON NECESSITIES

Percentage of Income
Spent on Necessities

Figure 2.2

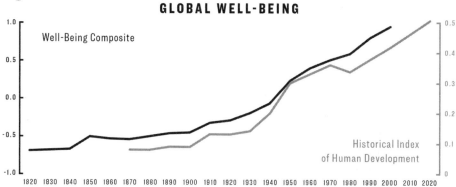

GLOBAL WELL-BEING

Well-Being Composite

Historical Index
of Human Development

Figure 2.3

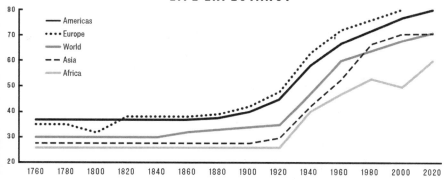

LIFE EXPECTANCY

— Americas
•••• Europe
— World
– – Asia
— Africa

Figure 2.4

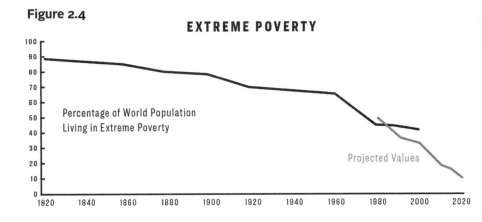

Figure 2.5

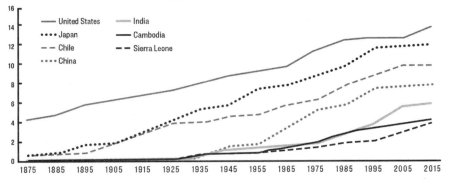

Figure 2.4 is perhaps the most eye-opening. Assuming you aren't a royal descendant, you probably don't have to go back too far in your family tree to find lives defined by struggle and survival. Until the 1950s, the vast majority of human existence on this planet was experienced in extreme poverty. "Extreme poverty" is defined as living on less than $2 a day (adjusted for inflation). In the 1980s, 44% of the world's population still met the definition of extreme poverty. Now, a mere four decades later, fewer than 10% of the world is living in such dire conditions. What changed? Technological and economic growth have pulled hundreds of millions of people up into the middle class. Want more good news? The

World Bank estimates that we can be completely rid of extreme poverty within 20 years!

Finally, education is the great equalizer. (Figure 2.5) If families are focused on survival, children will often have to drop out of school early to work. Children, forced to stack bricks, shepherd animals, and lug heavy jugs of water for hours each day, begin to view education as an unattainable luxury. But if economic forces take hold, children can be released from survival tasks and spend more time in school. The longer children are able to stay in school, the better chance they have at building the skill set needed to overcome their circumstances and pursue new opportunities. Education can allow children to get a better job, earn more money, send their own children to school, and end the cycle of poverty in their family, once and for all.

CHORUS OF CHAOS

So with all the good news, why doesn't it feel as if we are making progress? Why does it feel as if we are swimming in a tumultuous tide? In part, I think we have the news to thank for this. Your brain has one primary function: survival. It's designed to focus on what is wrong, what is dangerous, and what threatens your way of life. News producers know this, and with a steady flow of fear, crises, countdowns, and suspense, they get you addicted to staying tuned in.

To get viewers, shows often overdramatize events. Many events are packaged into stories with a tagline and a three-step story arc. Often they are accompanied by what screenwriters call "putting a clock on it.[5]" Just as a movie will create tension and a sense of urgency with a ticking clock ("If Sandra Bullock doesn't get to the space station in 90 minutes, she will get

---

5   Thanks to my brother, Mark, a screenwriter, for sharing this concept with me. For free.

hit by space junk and die!"),[6] so too the media match many of these stories with a clock in the lower-right-hand corner of the screen. Tick, tick, tick.

When the media depict finance and the economy, they employ these same tactics. Just think of terms like "the sequester" and "the fiscal cliff." These terms are developed to invoke a sense of danger into news stories that are far from life and death. For a recent example, recall the clock winding down, by the minute (really, we need by the minute?), to the 2019 debt ceiling limit. What happened when the clock struck zero? Politicians compromised, papers were signed, and the debt ceiling was raised with little fanfare. Similarly, it seems that no matter in which direction the market is heading, there is always a chorus of vocal fatalists that dominates the financial channels. Of course, this is nothing new. The financial media have been selling fear dating back to the market panic of 1907. Many books have been written about the inaccuracy of the media's more recent financial predictions, such as the 1970s stagflation, the 1987 crash, the tech bubble (which took hysteria to an entirely new level since it accompanied the rise of 24-hour televised news), the 2008 crisis, the European debt crisis, the 2019 debt ceiling . . . the list goes on.

So what do we have so show for such mania? Investors panic unnecessarily and make preventable mistakes. Many retirement plans were compromised when investors sold everything and cashed in during the 2008 financial crisis, the government shutdown, and the debt ceiling talks. These sellers suffered permanent losses by missing out on gains that occurred once the crisis subsided. In other words, they took the elevator down, got off, and missed the ride back up (usually to new highs!).

And what about the toll on their physical health? Investors get completely stressed out by financial discussions in the media. In "Financial

---

6   This is a reference to the 2013 blockbuster *Gravity,* and not to be confused with, "If Sandra Bullock doesn't help disarm a bomb on this bus before it drops below a certain speed, everyone will die!" which would reference the 1994 blockbuster *Speed.*

News and Client Stress" (2012) Dr. John Grable of the University of Georgia and Dr. Sonya Britt of Kansas State University showed that an individual's stress level increases substantially while viewing financial news, regardless of what the news was about. When the market is down, people worry about their accounts. When the market is up, they are upset that they're not more aggressively positioned. In fact, 67% of people watching financial news showed increased stress levels. Even when the financial news was positive, 75% exhibited signs of increased stress.

I am not suggesting there is not real volatility and market corrections (and we will explore more how to navigate these times later), but let's look at the reality. Every US bear market has given way to a bull market. Every economic contraction has given way to economic expansion. As I write this, investors are grappling with a bear market brought on by a global pandemic. However, as with every bear market in history, the market will fully recover and go back to its normal upward trajectory. But you wouldn't know it watching the news.

A large part of the issue with financial media is that many people misunderstand the purpose for its existence. Media are businesses, and businesses exist to make a profit. The primary purpose of media is not to inform; it's to make money. Media outlets make money by selling advertisements, and news channels can charge higher prices for advertising placement if they have high ratings. Because of this, the primary purpose of any news outlet is to get as many viewers as possible (they call them "eyeballs") to tune in and to get those viewers to watch for as long as possible. The rough math is:

More viewers = higher prices for advertising =
larger profit = happier shareholders

On the Weather Channel, nothing gets more viewers than coverage of a hurricane or tornado. But most of the time, weather reporting is pretty boring. Partly sunny, 30% chance of rain, possible thunderstorms. These headlines don't draw in viewers. Similarly, there's often not much to report in the world of financial news. The market goes up, the market goes down, companies go public with an initial public offering. This really isn't revolutionary stuff. To make things interesting, media reporting often spins average stories about the dip in one day of the stock market into tales of financial crisis, but there is often little to no effect on the long-term success of the market, which is why Figure 2.6 is one of my favorites. It's aptly titled "Human Innovation Always Trumps Fear." On the graph, you'll see that there's barely enough space to pack in all the "crises headlines" going back to 1896. And what does the market do? The market shrugs. And it goes on to make new highs, rewarding long-term investors.

Figure 2.6
THE DOW JONES INDUSTRIAL AVERAGE 1896–2016
HUMAN INNOVATION ALWAYS TRUMPS FEAR

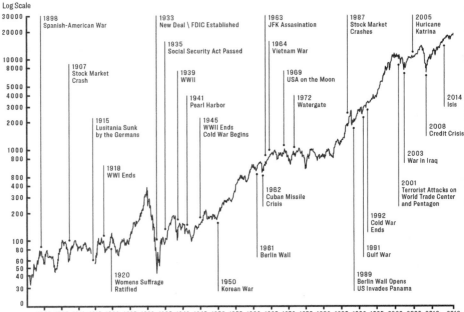

WHO CARES?

Although it's easy to forget sometimes, a share is not
a lottery ticket . . . it's part ownership of a business.
PETER LYNCH

If a business does well, the stock eventually follows.
WARREN BUFFETT

People often ask, What makes the stock market move up or down? Some are confident that they know the answer, but they are almost always wrong.

Investors often cite one of the following as being the primary driver of stock prices: unemployment, housing, economic policy, monetary policy, the strength of the dollar, consumer confidence, retail sales, and interest rates. All are popular choices. In fact, the stock market cares about only one thing above all else: anticipated earnings (i.e., future profits). If companies make more money, their shares become more valuable and their share prices eventually rise. The stock price is simply a reflection of a company's earning power. Everything else is noise.

Assume for a moment that you are going to buy a sandwich shop. What do you care about? As a newly minted small business owner, the most important factor you care about is anticipated earnings. If you buy the shop, you are doing so because you believe the profits earned will justify the purchase price with a good return. To arrive at this conclusion, you would likely look at every factor that could affect your ability to make money from this sandwich shop. For example, if interest rates are low, you could make lower payments on your loan, thus making the shop more profitable. In this case, interest rates matter only because they affect your anticipated earnings. Commodity prices will also likely matter, as oil, cheese, ham, and bread are all commodities that vary in price. If oil prices go up, you will pay more to have the food delivered to your shop every day. Rising food costs will also increase your expenses. While low interest rates could increase your bottom line, increases in commodity prices could eat away at your bottom line, and both affect your anticipated earnings. Consumer confidence matters too because if consumers think their financial world is collapsing, they will forgo your $8 sandwich and make the kids a PB&J at home. That will drive down sales, which would lower your earnings. You get the idea.

Note, however, the important word here is *anticipated*. No one cares about yesterday's earnings. Let's go back to that sandwich shop you have your eye on. You are talking to the owner, reviewing his financials, and you can see he made $100,000 each of the three previous years by selling about 20,000 sandwiches a year. This sounds pretty stable, so you are thinking about offering him $200,000 for his business, knowing that you can make $100,000 per year once you pay off the debt it takes to buy it. By year three, you'll be in the black. But you're too smart to take these sales at face value. You notice that the owner has sold 5,000 of his sandwiches each year to a large corporate client and that client just went out of business. If you take those sales out of the equation, the sandwich shop would be much less profitable and the anticipated earnings of the store would be lower than first estimated. As a savvy negotiator, you would no longer offer the same price for the shop. You are focused on the only thing that really matters: anticipated earnings.

The bottom line is this: all of the other factors in the economy matter only because people buying and selling stocks are trying to determine how the changes in various "indicators"—unemployment, interest rates, and so on—will ultimately affect a company's anticipated earnings. No one cares how much health care companies made in the past. They want to know how new health care reform laws will affect the future earnings of these companies. No one cares if Starbucks made a million or a billion dollars last year. They want to know if their earnings will be hurt now that McDonald's is selling gourmet coffee. No one cares how much money General Dynamics made selling military supplies to the government in the past. They want to know if worldwide military conflicts will persist, driving up future sales.

That's why, when the 2008 US bear market was in full swing, investors bought Walmart stock. The thought was that Walmart's anticipated earnings would increase as consumers scaled down to buy everything as inexpensively as possible. The same reasoning drove Nordstrom's stock price down. McDonald's stock held up relatively well because investors figured consumers would want to eat out on the cheap. The same logic drove down the stock price of higher-end restaurants like the Cheesecake Factory. And, of course, companies selling alcohol did just fine because people tend to drink when they are depressed (and when they are happy, which is why alcohol is considered recession proof).

Another interesting fact? The stock market as a whole tends to move up well before a recession is over. The market doesn't care what's going on today. It's anticipating the earnings of companies in the future. If the stock market drops, it's because investors believe future earnings will get worse. If the market moves up, it's because investors believe the economic climate is changing to enable companies to become more profitable in the future.[7]

Of course, so many variables go into predicting anticipated earnings that the market is not always right in the short run (although it is almost always right in the long run). For example, you can buy the perfect sandwich shop under perfect conditions and have a multitude of surprises derail your profits, like rising crime in the area, unforeseen road construction blocking access to your shop, or a new fad diet that prohibits any consumption of bread. And we can have a nearly perfect economic environment, and someone can fly a plane into a building and turn everything upside

---

7   Of course, it can get a little more complicated than that because investors will always be comparing their future earnings against earnings they can get elsewhere. For example, if the ten-year Treasury is paying 10%, that big swooshing sound you hear might just be money flying out of the stock market and into the bond market.

down overnight. However, unlike your sandwich store, which can lose all of its value, the stock market itself is resilient.

Throughout history, no matter how bad things have appeared, the top US companies (the S&P 500) have ultimately found a way to not only make money, but to make more money than they did before. Every single time. And, as always, the stock market continues to follow the earnings.

WHERE IN THE WORLD ARE WE HEADED?

It's my opinion, and the opinion of many experts, that humanity's best days are ahead of us. As we have already seen in this chapter, humanity is certainly trending upward. It is also why this could potentially be one of the best times in history to be an investor.

Human progress is an unstoppable force: our future is not linear; it's exponential. Case in point: In 1975, a 24-year-old engineer named Steven Sasson developed the world's first self-contained digital camera while working at Kodak. It weighed eight pounds and took 23 seconds to shoot a 0.01 megapixel photo that could be viewed only on a large television. His bosses were unimpressed. "They were convinced that no one would ever want to look at their pictures on a television set," Sasson told the *New York Times*.

Sasson kept plugging away, and each year, the resolution of his photos doubled. Blurry became fractionally less blurry. But it was still not impressive to the executives, who failed to understand the power of compounding:

Double something 10 times, it's a thousand times better.
Double it 20 times, it's a million times better.
Double it 30 times, it's a billion times better.

This is how technology works. This is how pictures taken on your iPhone now rival that of a professional photographer. It took 18 years after Sasson invented the digital technology for Kodak to pivot from film to digital. By that point, it was far too late. Companies like Sony and Apple were quicker to embrace the technology and got out ahead of their competitors. The rest is history.

Right now, we are on the cusp of many transformative "exponential" technologies. They may seem to the untrained eye to be the equivalent of an early-stage digital photograph, but make no mistake: they are changing the game for investors and, in fact, humanity itself.

For example, we have learned more about the human body in the last 20 years than in all of human history combined. That knowledge is being translated into dramatic advancements in tools available to fight the spread of disease and radically reimagine health care. Advancements in gene editing show the potential to eliminate the transmission of diseases like malaria, which would save the 1 million lives (mostly children) needlessly lost each year and prevent over 300 million additional infections. Similar advancements in the field of stem cell research are powering regenerative medicine, allowing doctors to use your own genetic material to rebuild diseased or damaged organs for your use when needed, offering the potential to dramatically extend the length and quality of our lives.

Exciting innovations are also improving the ways the world has access to food and water, while simultaneously reducing our ecological footprint. Americans consume 26 billion pounds of meat per year. One cow consumes about 11,000 gallons of water, and cattle account for 15% of all greenhouse emissions. Livestock take up nearly 80% of global agricultural land, yet produce less than 20% of the world's supply of calories. As much as I love a good steak, it's easy to see how our current model is unsustainable, both economically and environmentally, in meeting the needs of the 7 billion people (and growing) who inhabit the planet. Companies are already developing "lab grown meat" (and the marketing folks are surely working on a better name), which will allow for the creation of an unlimited amount of optimally nutritious, perfectly textured, and delicious cuts of meat from one small piece of the original source. The possibility of a sustainable and humane food chain is drawing near.

Similar innovations are impacting the fresh food market. The fruits and vegetables supplied to your local supermarket and restaurants, in many cases, have travelled hundreds if not thousands of miles to ultimately reach your plate. It's estimated that nearly half of a meal's cost in a restaurant is the transportation of the food. Imagine being able to have your community's fresh produce needs met locally year round, even in places like Anchorage or Albuquerque, with everything in season all the time. Companies are making this a reality with new technologies that allow 30 acres of food to be grown in an enclosed, fully-autonomous, climate-proof warehouse encompassing just 1 acre. Not only that, but these "farms" use just 5% of the water normally used in growing crops. This technology is about more than just providing variety and convenience to the developed world; these kinds of innovations have exciting applications for food shortages world-wide, especially in brutal climates where traditional farming is challenging.

Food shortages are not the only threat facing a large portion of the world today. Despite great progress, over a billion people still lack access to safe water, and millions die each year from water-borne illness. Access to clean water has a ripple effect across all aspects of life; clean water means improved health, time for education, and time for other activities. In Africa alone, women spend 40 billion hours a year walking to retrieve water. Imagine the increased productivity if clean water was four minutes rather than four hours away. Companies are working to revolutionize access to water by eliminating the traditional need to dig wells or improve filtration systems, but rather by using the water vapor present in the air. The technology now exists to draw over 500 gallons of freshwater each day from the air around us! And what happens when people have water? They are free! Free to go to school, find work, use a toilet that flushes, start a business, and free from preventable disease and death. And free to contribute to the global economy (which increases productivity and wealth for all).

Much has been made of the ever-increasing speed of cellular data communication, with advertisements for 5G technology rolling out across the country. These new networks promise wireless speeds to your handheld devices faster than DSL or cable speeds that are hardwired to homes or offices. The impact of this technology goes far beyond being able to stream classic episodes of *Friends* while you're on vacation. Entire continents will have immediate and rapid access to the Internet and all that it has to offer, and in some cases, for the first time ever. Children will have access to information and educational resources like never before. Entrepreneurs will gain access to markets and digital tools that will remove the barriers to joining the global marketplace. And these high speeds will allow for the proliferation of new technologies such as augmented reality, virtual reality, 4K streaming, and more. It will also enable the widespread deployment of artificial intelligence (AI), the promising use of machine learning to enhance our lives. Google CEO Sundar Pinchai says that "AI is one of the most important things humanity is working on. It is more profound than [the development of] electricity or fire."

Right now, we're living in a period of science fiction come to life. Consider what noted science-fiction writer Jules Verne would think. In the 1800s, he envisioned submarines, newscasts, solar sails, lunar modules, skywriting, videoconferencing, tasers, and aircraft landing in the ocean, all of them realities today.

I have only scratched the surface of the incredible and exponential future that lies before us. A number of others technologies, such as robotics, autonomous cars, passenger drones, 3D printing, and blockchain, are equally profound. The point is that the future that lies before us and our children is exciting. Innovation has never before occurred at such a rapid pace in human history! If you want to read further on these topics, I recommend *Abundance* by Peter Diamandis and *The Rational Optimist* by Matt Ridley.

At this point, you might find yourself asking, "What do all of these innovations have to do with my financial freedom?" The answer is "everything"!

Remember, what does the market care about? Future anticipated earnings! An estimated 1.2 billion people are coming out of poverty and moving into the middle class. An estimated 3 billion people who are yet to be online will soon have high-speed access to the Web and all it has to offer. We are on the cusp of a tidal wave of new consumers entering the marketplace. They will want to buy iPhones, wear Nike shoes, eat at McDonald's, shop at the Gap, buy a Volkswagen, post on Instagram, watch Netflix, and use Uber. They will want products and services from companies that don't yet exist! The next Google, the next Apple, and the next Facebook are just waiting to be developed to chart the course of human development.

When you consider these astonishing demographic trends and combine them with the exponential technologies we touched on in this chapter, you have what I believe is one of the best times in history to be a long-term, globally diversified investor. You won't have to pick companies blindly in hopes of investing in the next billion-dollar startup (often referred to by investors as a "unicorn"). You can own a piece of *all* the top companies that naturally rise to the top (more on this later). What you *can't* do is allow yourself to be paralyzed by a manufactured fear of the future. This will serve nobody, especially you.

So let's begin the journey and chart a course for your path to financial freedom. Let the excitement of the future be your fuel!

CHAPTER THREE

THE DRIVING FORCE
BEHIND EVERY DECISION

by Tony Robbins

The mind has a mind of its own.

OLD SAYING

A good friend of mine, let's call him Jason, gave me permission to tell his roller-coaster story in hopes that it would serve you. Let the ride begin . . .

Jason was, and is, an incredibly smart man. In the early 2000s, he had built an extremely successful advertising business from the ground up. He had immense pride in what he had created, and as the leader of his company, he was crystal clear about his vision and capabilities. Said another way, he had tremendous "certainty" as the captain of the ship, and his team put great confidence in him. In 2004, Jason sold his business for approximately $125 million, a validation of his business acumen and skills. He was just 40 years young. Sure, he was now immensely wealthy, but the sale was much more meaningful to Jason. He had crushed the competition, crossed the finish line, and proved to himself (and everyone else) that he was indeed the persona he portrayed. It wasn't long after that Jason moved from New York to Las Vegas, a town tailor-made for a young mega-millionaire. Everywhere he went, they rolled out the red carpet, and Jason felt he had "arrived."

Before long, Jason's entrepreneurial itch flared up, and he decided to try his hand at real estate. But instead of flipping a few houses, Jason decided to push all his chips to the middle of the table and develop not one, not two, but three high-rise luxury condominium towers right off the strip. In Jason's mind, it didn't matter that he had never been in real estate before. He was a mogul, and moguls are always successful, right?

Within 12 months, development was well underway, and his no-money-down condos were selling fast. Extravagant launch parties brought A-list celebrities who plunked down millions to buy penthouse units. It was now 2006, and the economy was booming along with Jason's net worth, which had ballooned to approximately $800 million . . . on paper.

Jason and I had a chance meeting at one of my events. I recall sitting down with him and pleading for him to diversify and take steps to protect himself. Sadly, he was less interested in listening and more interested in selling me a unit that "would only go up in value."

"Take a few chips off the table. Save some for a rainy day. Don't put all your eggs in one basket." I was running out of analogies, and Jason would have none of it. He was clearly intoxicated—not on alcohol or drugs but on "emotional needs." Jason felt bulletproof. He was "the man" approaching closer to $1 billion—a stratospheric milestone that would signify his ultimate arrival. "Every day was filled with incredible excitement: new choices, new experiences, new high-profile relationships, new sales, new opportunities to grow and expand," he explained.

You can probably guess the ending of this story. The financial crisis of 2008 decimated the Las Vegas real estate market more than any other city in the United States. By 2010, 65% of homes were worth less than what was owed. This was "underwater" of titanic proportions. The Great Recession chased away nearly all of Jason's buyers, leaving him with empty towers under construction. Jason was now worth negative $500 million. That's right. He owed approximately half a billion dollars to various banks that now were circling like frenzied sharks.

I share this story you with not just because it's a painful anecdote about the importance of diversification. There are plenty of those. More importantly, this is a story about how our brain works and how our emotional needs can take us off the path of wisdom—the path to financial freedom. As Jason would attest, it's much clearer in hindsight how his emotional needs had hijacked the decision-making abilities of an otherwise brilliant businessman. It would be easy to write off Jason's story as one of blinding greed, but I assure you that the human mind, yours and mine included, is far more complex than that. If we don't understand how our emotional needs work, we will always live in the backseat of our journey, never fully taking the wheel.

YOUR SOFTWARE IS HARD-CODED

My mission of helping people transform their lives has now spanned nearly four decades. I have had the privilege of working with over 4 million people in live events across the globe. The tapestry of humanity that I have experienced and interacted with is both broad and deep. From presidents to professional athletes to stay-at-home moms. From titans of industry to teenagers living in projects. My unique position has allowed me to see patterns of human behavior that transcend age, geography, culture, and socioeconomic status. To put it simply, we humans are all running the same software. Sure, each one of us is unique in our own desires and story, but what drives people, what moves people to action, what calls people, is simply the brain's attempt to meet one or more of the "6 Human Needs." My friend and co-author, Peter Mallouk, says he references these needs frequently when helping his clients think through what may really be motivating them and their decisions.

These 6 Human Needs are what make us tick. They are universal and serve as the fuel behind our actions, our compulsions, and even our addictions. They can be a force for good or a force for destruction. We all have the same six needs and prioritize them differently. We also go about meeting them in entirely different ways. And how you go about meeting those needs is what will ultimately determine whether you will live a life of fulfillment.

My hope is that this chapter will open your eyes to this simple yet powerful framework so that you can see which of your needs are prioritized in your life and if you are going about meeting your needs in productive ways. You will also discover how your pursuit of financial freedom will be helped or hindered by your own 6 needs.

SOME PEOPLE ARE SO BROKE, ALL THEY HAVE IS MONEY

You might be asking, "What do my emotional needs have to do with financial freedom? Let's just stick to making money, Tony!" Well, let me ask you this: Why exactly are you building wealth? We can all agree it's not to accumulate pieces of paper with pictures of dead presidents. Are you looking to feel certain and secure? Do you desire freedom to do what you want, when you want? Are you chasing wealth to feel special or unique? Or are you looking for a sense of contribution—to do things for others in need and make a lasting impact? Maybe it's all of the above. These are all feelings that you seek. Feelings that are driven by needs.

In order for you to feel successful on the journey to financial freedom, you must understand a bit more how this software of ours really works and, ideally, set up the code so you can win! As we go through each of the 6 Human Needs below, I will share some short, real-life anecdotes from my experience working with people in the arena of personal finance. These various scenarios illustrate how people's needs are running their financial decisions—for better or for worse.

LET ME INTRODUCE YOU TO YOUR NEEDS

Need #1 : Certainty

For my part I know nothing with any certainty,
but the sight of the stars makes me dream.
VINCENT VAN GOGH

Our need for certainty is perhaps the most deeply rooted survival mechanism in the human brain. Self-preservation is a backdrop of our operating system, and avoiding unnecessary risks is "Priority #1" in your million-year-old software. However, when it comes to investing, taking risk is an inherent part of the game, so you can see how an overwhelming need for certainty could drive you to make really poor choices (e.g., hiding your life savings under your mattress, selling all your stocks at the first sign of volatility).

When certainty takes the driver's seat in our journey to financial freedom, its hands can wrap a bit too tightly around the wheel. Its motivation to avoid all risk can go too far and actually hurt our chances at success. But with the right balance and context, certainty can be a game changer. Once you have certainty about how markets work and what exactly you need to do to stay on the path, you will experience true freedom in both the journey and the destination.

Consider how CERTAINTY is working itself out in these financial scenarios:

- The baby boomer who was scared out of the market in 2009 and is still sitting in cash in hopes of a "better time" to get back into the market. She has missed out on the longest bull market in history, and her chances for a long retirement are now in jeopardy.

- The newly married couple who wisely plans for their future, funds their retirement accounts in full, sets aside money for their child's college, and is protected with a financial and estate plan. They feel grounded while many of their friends are spending everything they make and have no plan at all.
- The man who will invest only in CDs and Treasury bonds to satisfy his obsession with "guarantees." Ironically, without taking greater risks for higher returns, his probabilities of reaching his retirement goals have plummeted. His psychological needs supersede his actual financial needs.
- The middle-class couple who forgo luxuries, shop frugally, and have saved 25% of their annual income since they began working (the husband chose a government job to ensure a guaranteed pension). Now in retirement, they have a seven-figure retirement portfolio.
- The couple who has more than they could ever possibly spend in retirement but refuse to take that vacation, buy a $4 latte, or lease that luxury car they always wanted. Ironically, they will leave it all to their kids, who will have no problem spending liberally!

So my question to you is, How does certainty show up in your journey to financial freedom? Do you have enough, not enough, or way too much?

Life Tip: Although certainty is healthy in the right "dosage," letting this need for it to take over is a quick path to paralysis because only one thing is for certain: life is uncertain.

Need #2 : Variety/Uncertainty
Variety's the very spice of life, that gives it all its flavour.
WILLIAM COWPER

Variety is what keeps life interesting! It's also what helps you build emotional muscle so you know you can deal with whatever life throws at you. Spontaneity is another aspect of this need, which can invigorate our sense of wonder and adventure. As I said, we each have all of the 6 Needs, but you already might be able to tell if you tend to be more certainty or variety oriented. Are you a gypsy at heart who wants to wander? Do you hate schedules and to-do lists? Or are you a bit of control freak who demands structure, predictability, and clear rules of the game?

Consider how the need for VARIETY is the primary driver in these situations:

- The man who always wants to find the next "sexy" investment that nobody else is aware of so that he can talk about it endlessly at the next dinner party. He loves researching and reading articles for his next idea.
- The couple who spends countless hours planning the details of their next vacation or weekend getaway, but won't spend one hour per year on their personal finances. They are paying only interest on their credit cards and put away a relatively paltry amount in their 401(k) plan because they'd rather spend their money now.
- The gambler who feels he needs to always swing for the fence in order to achieve financial freedom. He takes huge, unnecessary risks for the rush of the bet.

Life Tip: If you have an overwhelming need for variety, where this becomes the core driver of your daily life, you could find yourself untethered to anything and/ or anyone meaningful.

Need #3: Significance

What counts in life is not the mere fact that we have lived.
It is what difference we have made to the lives of others that
will determine the significance of the life we lead.

NELSON MANDELA

We all want to feel important. We all need to feel unique. We all want to know we matter and that we are making a difference. This can show up in numerous, beautiful ways, like the way our partner or friends can make us feel like a million bucks. Significance can show up in our life's mission, in the jobs we choose, or the titles we aspire to. We can feel significant as a wonderful parent, a loving soulmate, an important friend, or simply as a child of our Creator.

There are also the more obvious, and usually less fulfilling, ways of demanding significance. The most glaring example is the items we choose to purchase. One person buys an orange Lamborghini that howls at stoplights, while another will buy the more socially conscious Toyota Prius (both want a form of significance for their choice and what it says about them). Some want to stand out with tattoos and piercings, while others will choose an approach involving red-bottomed heels and a $2,500 monogrammed handbag.

Some people derive significance in more subtle and destructive ways, such as always having more or bigger problems—also known as a "victim mentality." I have often said that our biggest addiction as a society is not a substance; it's our problems. We all know the folks who want to one-up a conversation about how crappy their lives are and fail to see the gifts that are right in front of them. They often stack their victimhood with feelings of entitlement and judgment of others. Social media amplify these toxic traits more than ever before. Sadly, many never redeem their wounds for something empowering and meaningful. We all have wounds, but the most interesting and powerful people are those who choose to believe that life is happening *for* them, not *to* them. The wounds aren't their identity; they are their fuel.

The bigger point here is that significance is a need that must be handled with care. How we go about achieving a feeling of significance is crucial to our long-term fulfillment, our relationships, and our financial success.

Consider how SIGNIFICANCE is showing up on the financial path of these individuals:

- The guy who wants to be smarter than everyone else, so he consumes massive amounts of financial media and then attempts to be a stock picker (a losing proposition for nearly every investor, including the professionals). He loves to tell his golf buddies about his winners but fails to disclose his losers.
- The millennial who chooses not to participate in the markets. He demonizes the "capitalist pigs" and Wall Street, which conveniently allow him to neglect his own financial security.
- The person who conflates her spirituality with financial wisdom and decides that money is the root of all evil (and, thus, so is everyone who has it). She decides she will not worry about money, and ironically, all she ends up doing is worrying about not having enough. Side note: it's the LOVE of money that is root of all evil, not money itself.
- The guy who despises the general population as "sheep" who are deluded by the government. He puts his entire savings into a cleverly named cryptocurrency because he is convinced it's the way of a "decentralized future" and evangelizes to his friends incessantly.

Life Tip: Make no mistake: temporal and dysfunctional approaches to feeling significant are a fool's errand—an unquenchable thirst. Like all the other needs, when they are met in unhealthy ways, they can become a prison. Unchecked, the need for significance can transform a person into a full-blown egomaniac, blind with pride and too selfish for the self-sacrifice required for lasting relationships.

Need #4 : Love and Connection

The best and most beautiful things in this world cannot be
seen or even heard, but must be felt with the heart.

HELEN KELLER

Love is the oxygen of the soul. This is what we truly crave. We're made
for selfless and unconditional love, and we know this intuitively (hence
the endless appetite for love songs and romantic movies). It can be the
love of a partner, a family member, or a close friend. It can also be the
power of connection—a subtly different feeling. Feeling connected to
nature, to a moving story, or to your favorite song can make all feel right
in the world. The most important connection is of course, to yourself.
Staying in tune with your needs is your God-given duty as the keeper of
your soul.

So how in the world would a need for love or connection show up in
our financial journey? You may be surprised . . .

- The two best friends who ritually shop together and rack up
tremendous debt from buying haute couture brands. Their
codependency has found a dangerous and expensive outlet.
They even take pride in the color of their credit card because it
distinguishes them from the rest of the shopaholics. (Note: You
can see how the need for significance is also very much present
in this behavior.)
- The couple who wisely planned their financial freedom goals
together and surprise each other with vacations and fun luxuries as they hit certain milestones.
- The man who chose his college buddy as his broker and
knows that he sells him financial products to make substantial
commissions. He can't bring himself to move on to a "fiduciary"
advisor for fear of losing a friendship.

Life Tip: Love is what we crave the most, and we often go about getting it in the most interesting of ways. Some people are afraid of being truly known and loved and will often settle for a counterfeit, like "friends" on social media or intimacy with a relative stranger.

The first four needs are what I call the "needs of the personality." The final two needs come as we evolve and begin to recognize the deeper needs of the soul.

Need #5 : Growth

Growth begins when we being to accept our own weakness.

JEAN VANIER

The law of life says that if we aren't growing, we are dying. Financial freedom is useless if we aren't feeling a sense of growth in our lives. Our relationships need to grow, our businesses need to grow, our spirituality and beliefs need to grow, our minds need to grow, and, of course, our wealth should grow. And the reason we grow is so that we have something to give. Sure we can give money, and we should, but we can also give of ourselves, our wisdom, our love, and more.

I think a story from my personal life is the perfect anecdote. As I have written about before, I grew up in a relatively poor home. One Thanksgiving, when I was around 11 years old, we didn't have enough food in the cupboards for the holiday. We were stretched thin, and the tension between my parents was palpable. A surprise knock at the door, and there stood an angel: a deliveryman held bags of groceries with every possible thing we could need. He said they were a gift from a friend. My siblings and I were ecstatic, but my father's pride nearly turned the food away as he "doesn't accept charity." The deliveryman was quite forceful, so my father reluctantly accepted the bags. That night, we ate a wonderful meal because a stranger cared. The message was clear: if strangers care about me, I should care about strangers. Fast-forward to when I was 18. I found two local families that were in need, and I returned the favor on Thanksgiving Day. They were so grateful, and the hugs were endless even though I told them I was only the deliveryman.

As I sat in a borrowed van after making the final drop, I broke down in tears. I looked back on that earlier Thanksgiving, which could have been one of the worst days of my childhood, but instead, it became one of my best days and shaped me for this very moment. Life happened *for* me, not *to* me. I bet you could say that about a moment in your life as well. Each Thanksgiving, I began to feed more families in need and recruit my friends to fill up giant baskets of food and supplies. We coined our mission the "basket brigade," and today, millions of people are fed annually with the help of my foundation.

In 2014, I found out that the government was cutting food stamps (a.k.a. the SNAP program). The cut enacted was the equivalent of taking away 21 meals per month for a family of four. Said another way, a family would have to go without food for one week out of each month unless private citizens, food banks, and nonprofits stepped up. It was time for me to grow and expand my generosity. I partnered with Feeding America to set a massive goal, the "100 Million Meals Challenge." By donating the profits of two previous books and making some additional donations personally, we have blown the roof off our previous goal and have now surpassed 400 million meals! We've officially renamed it the "1 Billion Meals Challenge" and are on our way to meeting that ambitious goal. Yes, this is about contribution, but it's more about expansion. Expanding our vision, expanding our goals, expanding our capacity for generosity and much, much more.

Life Tip: Some of the most financially successful people I have met have everything they could ever want, but their belief that they have "arrived," that there is nothing left to conquer, has stunted their growth, and they inevitably find themselves unfulfilled.

Need #6: Contribution

We make a living by what we get. We make a life by what we give.

WINSTON CHURCHILL

As I just shared, I believe with my whole heart that the secret to living is giving. Getting beyond one's self is where the juice of life really is. Think about it this way: your life is really about the meaning you are able to create. When your life is meaningful, regardless of how much you have in the bank, your soul will be full. But meaning doesn't come from navel gazing. It comes come from giving, and giving generously. Giving of your time, your love, your resources—and with no expectation of anything in return. When your cup runs over, you become a blessing to all those around you, but, in a wonderful twist, the biggest recipient of blessing is you!

Here are a few beautiful anecdotes about the power of CONTRIBUTION:

- The couple who planned diligently and spent wisely, which gave them the ability to give liberally to their church and their grandkid's college fund, and volunteer their time at a local children's hospital. Their retirement is filled with deep, meaningful purpose.
- The family of four that sits together to decide where their annual giving should be directed and gives everyone a voice. Each child is responsible for selecting his or her favorite charity and gets to report back all the good that is being done with their family's donation. They are cultivating a heart of generosity that will last generations.
- An older man who had his mind set on having his fortune donated after he died, and not until then. Peter convinced him that "it's better to give with a warm hand than a cold one." He

began giving to local charities and visiting to see the fruit of his generosity. He was deeply touched and realized how much more fulfilling life can be when one's hands aren't clenched.

Life Tip: Giving is a discipline. If you won't give a dime out of a dollar today, you will never give $1,000 out of $10,000 or $1 million out of $10 million. Begin the discipline and cultivate a joyful and generous spirit!

JASON, TAKE THE WHEEL!

Remember the story about Las Vegas Jason? Negative net worth of $500 million Jason? Before we judge too quickly, let's look at how the 6 Human Needs were working within Jason's mind. Was Jason blinded by a driving need for significance? No doubt! You couldn't cook up a better recipe than being the hottest new developer in Sin City. He had a massive amount of certainty about his capabilities in business after selling his company for nine figures (albeit entirely misplaced since he had never been a real estate developer before). His new hometown of Vegas, the excitement and challenges of being a new developer, and the parties and promotional events gave Jason immense variety. He was also getting connection through a thriving social environment and interaction with potential buyers.

I often see that when three or more needs are met at once, you have the ingredients for addiction (be it positive or negative). In each of the anecdotes in this chapter, one or more of the 6 Human Needs was in full display. I could write an entire book on how these needs interact with one another and how they shape-shift over time and through various stages of life. There are endless examples of how our needs shape our stories, but the better question is, How are they currently shaping your story? What is driving your desire for financial freedom? What needs could be holding you back? What needs might need to be prioritized? What needs might need to move to the back seat?

Understanding what is driving you allows you to eliminate the self-imposed roadblocks and prioritize your needs in a more fulfilling and impactful way. In my own life, I have found that true freedom is moving beyond the core needs and working to fulfill the higher needs of growth and contribution. Sure the trappings of wealth (cars, homes, etc.) can be fun for a moment, but when I set forth to conquer a challenge that's bigger than myself, I find infinite fuel and an increasing capacity to experience true joy. When I set the goal to provide 1 billion meals (currently at 400 million) to those in need, it was a daunting task that would demand an incredible effort. Same is true when I committed to provide 250,000 people with clean water for the rest of their lives. I feel the heavy reality that children would die if not for my support. These audacious goals of contribution have made me look at my finances and my investments with fresh eyes. They have become more than numbers on a screen. They represent the opportunity to give, to support, to feed, to bathe, etc. They are tangible expressions of my love for others and my deep gratitude for a life beyond my imagination.

In your journey to financial freedom, don't forget why you are pursuing it: you're trying to meet your emotional and psychological desires. I have met numerous folks who are financially secure but don't possess financial freedom. They are rich in money but live in emotional poverty. They don't experience joy, growth, or contribution. They have plenty but live in scarcity.

So while you should certainly target measurable financial goals, the key is to decide which emotions you want to experience as part of your journey (e.g., gratitude, excitement, generosity, passion) and decide that you will experience those now, not at some future destination defined by a number. Financial freedom is partly a state of mind and it's attainable now, regardless of where you are financially. Yes, you will need the right strategy (which is what the rest of this book is all about), but your mindset, your desire, and your will to take control of your emotional needs will ultimately define just how free you really are.

Now that Peter has given you a glimpse into the future, and I have given you a glimpse into your mind's priorities, it's time to consider selecting a partner for your journey.

PART II

CHARTING YOUR PATH

CHAPTER FOUR

CHOOSING A GUIDE FOR YOUR JOURNEY

No road is long with good company.

TURKISH PROVERB

The road to financial freedom is long. It begins with your first job—yes, that job as a summer lifeguard counts—and ends with the financial legacy you're able to pass on to your descendants. Whether you decide to take this journey alone or with an advisor is entirely dependent on you and your financial needs. That said, every experienced climber knows that climbing Everest without a guide is inadvisable; the stakes are too high. Those with a passion for long-term planning, who are knowledgeable and informed about the market and have the time to devote to investing may choose to take the journey on their own. Others may decide to work with an advisor for a variety of reasons. As we will learn, selecting the right advisor can mean the difference between reaching the summit or wandering aimlessly around base camp.

About half of Americans use a financial advisor. You might assume that someone with a higher net worth is more likely to be financially savvy and confident enough to go it alone. In fact, the higher a person's net worth is, the more likely he or she is to seek financial advice. People with a high net worth are likely to know just how much they don't know. They're also more likely to know how important investing is to their long-term financial success.

In dealing with thousands of high-net-worth families, I can tell you that most believe one or more of the following:

- They value their financial advisor and believe the right advisors can pay for themselves many times over.
- They know the importance of avoiding major investing mistakes.
- They value access to investments they may not be able to invest in on their own.
- They are likely to substantially benefit from noninvestment planning advice and are more accustomed to using professionals like attorneys, consultants, and tax professionals.
- They are likely to value their time and don't want to spend time out of their "lane."
- They want their financial advisor to serve as a resource to them or their family for ongoing issues.
- They want their financial advisor to provide continuity of advice in the event of incapacity or death.

Many Americans wait until they have substantial assets, then look around for someone to help invest them. This is a critical mistake! Why climb halfway up the mountain only to discover you have to backtrack, when you could have just asked for directions from the wizened climber who has reached the summit countless times? Laying out a road map early in your financial journey will help you save time and money in the long run.[8] While it is true that the incremental benefits of an advisor don't have as much of an impact on someone with $100,000 to invest compared to someone with $1 million to invest, the right advisor can be the key factor in reaching your financial goals. Which debts should you

---

8   You may not see yourself as investor per se, but it's going to be important to embrace this as part of your identity.

pay off first? How much should you contribute to your retirement plans? How much should you be saving to send your children to college? These are just some of the questions that need to be answered at the beginning of everyone's financial journey. And these are questions that financial advisors love to answer.

For those with a high net worth, the decision to work with a financial advisor is often an easy one. Those with a modest net worth may be more reticent. At a minimum, get the quality[9] advice you need to put you on the right path to freedom.

MOST ADVISORS WILL DO
MORE HARM THAN GOOD

If you can, help others; if you cannot

do that, at least do no harm to them.

DALAI LAMA XIV

The choice of using a financial advisor is yours, and yours alone. If you are going to use one, be prepared to do your research to find a competent and trustworthy financial advisor. Because let me tell you a big secret in the financial services industry: most advisors do far more harm than good.

The vast majority of advisors fall into one of four camps:

1. They take custody[10] of your money as part of the regular course of business.

2. They are salespeople in disguise.

---

9   Note the emphasis on "quality." Sadly, many advisors offer up guidance that is better for them than you.

10   *Custody* is a fancy word for where/how the money is held and controlled. For example, Bernie Madoff had full custody.

3. They use strategies that are detrimental to their clients' financial objectives because they are trying to sell you something that you want to hear. They do this even though they know it won't work or because they don't know what they are doing.[11]

4. They describe themselves as "wealth managers" who consult on every aspect of your financial life, but they are really "money managers" who want to sell you a portfolio of funds and meet once in a while to discuss its progress.

There are many things to look for in an advisor, but if you can navigate the four core issues of conflict, custody, competence, and customization (I call them the "4 Cs"), you will eliminate about 90% of advisors from your search. Your odds of ending up with someone competent, who won't steal your money, sell you his or her own products, or lead you astray, will be much higher if you take the 4 C's into consideration when choosing a financial advisor.

ADVISOR SELECTION ISSUE CRITERION #1: CONFLICT

Conflict of interest: A conflict between the private interests and
the official responsibilities of a person in a position of trust.
MERRIAM-WEBSTER'S COLLEGIATE DICTIONARY, Eleventh Edition[12]

There are so many ways to be deceived by a financial advisor that it's shocking the profession is still in business. I am aware of no other industry where people go to a professional to get help and, more often than not, end up worse off than when they started. That will ruffle the feathers of quite a few in the industry, but the reality is that the financial services industry

---

11   I am so not looking forward to the hate mail I will receive from some financial advisors.

12   For example, the financial services industry.

is broken. Another statement that will ruffle some feathers: if you have a typical advisor, the odds are that you would be better off without one.

The reason is simple: the overwhelming majority of advisors are not on your side of the table. Many advisors get paid more if they sell you certain products, some do not have a fiduciary duty to act in your best interests, and a portion work for companies that sell their own "name-brand" funds. If any of these apply to your situation, it is time to look for a new advisor— and the sooner, the better. So how do you identify if your advisor, as nice as that person may be, might be conflicted? I'll break out this issue into three parts, to make it as easy as possible for you to determine if your advisor passes these critical tests.

Test #1: "Are You an Advisor or Broker?"

"Despite what many consumers have been led to believe, not all financial advisors have their best interest in mind when suggesting investment vehicles. They do not practice under a fiduciary standard."

NATIONAL ASSOCIATION OF PERSONAL FINANCIAL PLANNERS

Nine out of ten Americans agree—with 76% strongly agreeing—that when they receive investment advice from a financial advisor, that person should put the client's interests first and disclose any conflicts of interest that could potentially influence his or her advice. Sounds pretty reasonable, if you ask me. The irony is that about nine out of ten advisors are not required to act in the client's best interest. Furthermore, US law doesn't make it easy to differentiate the varying responsibilities a financial advisor has to you. Let's start with some definitions so we can begin to categorize these types of advisors.

Investment Advisor Defined

The Investment Advisers Act of 1940 defines a *registered investment advisor* (RIA) as "a person or firm that, for compensation, is engaged in the act of providing advice, making recommendations, issuing reports or furnishing analyses on securities, either directly or through publications." In short, advisors provide recommendations and are paid a fee as compensation for their expertise.

Investment advisors also follow the fiduciary standard. Like your doctor or CPA, an investment advisor has a fiduciary duty to you, which means that he or she has a fundamental obligation to always act in your best interest. Investment advisors must also disclose any and all conflicts of interest and are prohibited from making trades that will result in more revenue for them or their firm. You might be nodding your head and thinking that this is common sense. However, I assure you it's not so common!

Brokers Defined

The Securities Exchange Act of 1934 defines a *broker* as "any person engaged in the business of effecting transactions in securities for the account of others." The core job of a broker is to buy and sell investments. You'd think that would make it easy to differentiate between a broker and a fiduciary, but it's not quite that simple. In fact, recent legislation has made it even more complicated to figure out who you're working with. First, a little bit of history.

Historically, brokers have been held to what is known as the "suitability standard"; they were not legally required to act in your best interests, but rather to simply provide advice or transactions that were deemed "suitable." For example, they might have sold you a product or fund that was great for their own pocketbook when lower-cost or better-performing options were available. And this was entirely legal because it was considered a "suitable" sale. When was the last time you wanted anything that was merely "suitable"?![13]

---

13   Can you imagine going to a restaurant and choosing a "suitable" meal? How about choosing a "suitable" spouse? Would you rather have "suitable" investment advice, or advice in your best interests?

The SEC tried to improve the situation in 2019 by introducing Regulation Best Interest (or Reg BI for short). The idea was that brokers should be held to a higher standard when providing certain advice, so they are now required to act in their client's "best interest" in those circumstances. That sounds a lot like the definition of a fiduciary, so are brokers fiduciaries now? The answer is a definite no. SEC Chairman Jay Clayton explained the difference in a CNBC interview shortly after the new regulation was introduced:

> [Fiduciary duty is] a combination of care and loyalty. You owe somebody a duty of care, and you can't put your interests ahead of [the client's] interests. Best interest on the broker side has many of the same elements, but we want people to understand that the investment advisor space, and the broker-dealer space, are different. They're very different in the way people get paid. In the investment advisor space, it's more of a long-term relationship, where you get paid on a quarterly fee, yearly fee, and the advisor has a more portfolio lifetime relationship with you. Those are two very different relationships, and we want to be clear.

Here's the real kicker: Reg BI doesn't clearly define what "best interest" means! There's still uncertainty on how this will be measured and enforced, but one thing is clear: it's not the same legal standard of care as a fiduciary. The regulation expressly permits firms to "[offer] only proprietary products, placing material limitations on the menu of products, or incentivizing the sale of such products through its compensation practice." I don't know about you, but that doesn't fit my personal definition of "best interest."

So What's the Difference?

As confusing as the landscape might be, Americans have a keen BS meter. In a recent survey of American's perception of financial advisors, 60% of those surveyed believed that financial advisors act in their employer's best interests rather than the consumer's best interests.

So what's the difference between advisors who will work for you and those who work for their bosses? The bottom line is this: if your advisor is an independent investment advisor, then that person has a fiduciary duty to you and is subject to the highest legal standards of care. But if your advisor is a broker, they are not. For the average consumer, it's tricky to tell the difference. This is because most brokers operate under purposefully vague titles like "financial advisor." According to the *Wall Street Journal*, there are over 200 different designations for financial advisors, including "financial consultants," "wealth managers," "financial advisors," "investment consultants," and "wealth advisors." No wonder Americans are distrustful of financial advisors! You'll need to ask a few more questions and investigate accordingly.

Now you might be asking, Why do these mega-banks and brokers want to avoid the fiduciary standard? The reason is simple: selling proprietary products, and the various forms of compensation derived from these products, is a very lucrative practice. These firms would prefer to disclose these types of conflicts—typically in fine print on the back pages of long disclosure documents—rather than eliminate them. Many brokers work for companies that are publicly traded, and these practices help generate as much profit as they can for their shareholders.

At the end of the day, a broker not only has no fiduciary duty but instead is actually lobbying Congress to keep it that way. Keep that in mind when you're deciding who you want to trust with your finances.[14]

There are over 650,000 "financial advisors" in the United States. Most of them are brokers. That means most of the financial services industry

---

14   Imagine this: You pay a financial advisor and he shares his fee with his firm. That firm then spends some of that money lobbying Congress to allow its advisors to advise you without having to act in your best interests. That sums up the majority of the financial services industry.

isn't held to highest legal standard of care when managing your money. Scary, right? You can find out if your advisor is a broker by asking two key questions:

1. Are you a broker or investment advisor? Correct answer: investment advisor only.
2. Are you registered with the Securities and Exchange Commission or the Financial Industry Regulatory Authority (FINRA)? Correct answer: SEC only, not both (dually registered) and not just FINRA (just a broker).

Now that we have eliminated approximately 85% of financial advisors, let's narrow the field a bit further.[15]

Test #2: "Are You Really Independent, or Just Some of the Time?"
THE DUALLY-REGISTERED ADVISOR IS

THE ULTIMATE WOLF IN SHEEP'S CLOTHING.

So far, we have divided the financial advisory field into two main categories: independent investment advisors and brokers. However, we need to go one step further to make sure you are dealing with someone who must *always* act in your best interests, not just some of the time.

Unfortunately, US law allows financial advisors to be "dually registered," which means that they can be registered as both an independent advisor and a broker. I hope your jaw is hanging open as you read that

---

15   Note that I'm not saying that all brokers are bad. That is certainly not the case. There are ethical and unethical brokers just like there are ethical and unethical financial advisors. I am simply saying that you should, at a minimum, require that the person you hire to help you has a fiduciary obligation to act in your best interests at all times, and brokers don't meet that requirement.

sentence. How could someone be an independent advisor and be held to the highest legal standard of care, yet also be a broker who is not?

This is an extremely dangerous situation because this advisor can truthfully say he is an investment advisor and held to the fiduciary standard; however—and this is a huge *however*—that same person can switch from being an investment advisor, with a fiduciary duty to act in your best interests, to a broker, without the obligation to act that way *in the same conversation.* You read that right. By dually registering, an advisor can operate under the fiduciary standard in some situations and as a broker to avoid the standard in others. Good luck figuring out which is which. The dually registered advisor is the ultimate wolf in sheep's clothing. There are two ways to see if an "independent investment advisor" is also operating as a broker. First, ask directly. Second, look at her business card or website. If it says, "securities offered by *ABC* broker dealer," you are dealing with someone who is also a broker. If you are working with a dually registered advisor, do not be surprised if your investment portfolio ends up owning commissionable investments, variable annuities, or proprietary funds.

Which brings us to the third and final test.

Test # 3: "Are You Peddling Your Own Proprietary Products?"

Never ask a barber if you need a haircut.
WARREN BUFFETT

In my opinion, working with advisors who peddle their own product is the worst type of setup for an investor. The investor has gone through the effort to seek out an independent advisor and instead ended up with a salesperson in disguise. And make no mistake: when you hire a broker, you're hiring a salesperson. If you're going to pay an advisor your hard-earned money in exchange for advice, the least you should require that this person doesn't have a product to sell you and is held to the highest legal standard of care.

For example, you wouldn't walk to a Honda dealership and expect an impartial answer to the question, "What brand of car should I buy?" Without any market research or consumer feedback, the dealer will recommend that you buy a Honda. In the same way, you should never work with an advisor whose company, or affiliated company, has *proprietary funds* (funds that the company owns and that has a vested interest in pitching). If you do, don't be surprised when they end up in your portfolio.

If you are working with a broker or a dually-registered advisor, take a minute to look at your portfolio. Examine what you own. You will likely find that you own some of the funds owned by the affiliated company, sometimes under a separate brand name. Ask yourself this: "Are these the absolute best funds in the world for me?" The answer is probably no. What are the odds that your advisor just happens to work for the company that has the absolute best investment for any given allocation in your portfolio? It may happen at times, but it's unlikely. If an advisor works for a company that has its own funds or is affiliated with a company that has its own funds, move on with your search.

A Final Thought on Conflicts

I have often heard people say that although they work with an advisor who has a conflict, it doesn't matter because their particular advisor is trustworthy, or because they went to college together, or because their kids go to the same elementary school. To those of you who feel this sense of loyalty, keep in mind that your finances will outlive you. What sort of advice will your spouse or kids receive when you are gone? As an estate planning attorney, I have seen many instances of a surviving spouse being sold an expensive annuity by an advisor who pounced on an unsuspecting client who hadn't even had a chance to settle the estate! Also, you might be around a long time but might not be as sharp in your advanced age. When you and your family are facing difficult personal struggles, it is ideal to have a financial advisor who is required to be impartial and consistent. Warren Buffett is fond of saying he likes to buy a company that can be run by an idiot, because one day it will be. I recommend always using an independent advisor (who is not also a broker), because while the conflict of interest a broker presents may not be visible today, one day it likely will.

ADVISOR SELECTION CRITERION #2: CUSTOMIZATION

One of these things is not like the other.

BIG BIRD

One of the most important elements of proper portfolio design is customization, but the vast majority of portfolios sold are cookie-cutter models based largely on risk tolerance. These models are easily scalable and explain how mega-banks and brokers can manage trillions of dollars in assets. You are essentially getting one of their six "value meals." Tailoring a portfolio to an investor's specific situation is crucial to individual financial success, but it takes more work. However, it's worthwhile heavy lifting. Let's look at a few examples of how customization can benefit you.

Let's say you decide that you need to diversify your portfolio by moving a portion of your investments into new positions. In most instances, an advisor would sell all of your existing holdings and construct a new portfolio with the favored positions. The problem with this route is that it will likely have negative tax implications that cannot be overcome by the performance of the new positions. Said another way, by making the switch, you are costing yourself money that you are unlikely to recoup.

Let's take another example. Say that you determine that your portfolio should include a broad allocation to energy stocks. You find that the best way to accomplish this is to use an energy *exchange traded fund* (ETF) that owns thirty to fifty of the largest energy companies in the country. However, you already have a good chunk of your portfolio invested in Exxon Mobil and Chevron, both of which make up a large part of the index. Both holdings have grown by almost 100% since you originally purchased them. Rather than realizing a large capital gains tax by selling your Exxon and Chevron stock, it may be better to hold these positions and instead reduce the proportional amount of the energy ETF you are going to purchase. This kind of tailoring can make complete sense, but most prepackaged portfolios don't allow for such crucial tweaks.

The Difference Between a Money Manager and a Wealth Manager

A danger of working with a money manager, an advisor whose sole job is to manage your portfolio, is that this person is not equipped to consider you as an individual. Most people's experience of working with a financial advisor is being sold a group of funds and meeting once a year to see how they have done (and hear the pitch for a new investment or product). This one-size-fits-all approach of money managers is insufficient. For instance, at any given moment, a money manager may decide to allocate funds to real estate. That might be appropriate for their typical client, but it likely does not make sense for someone who has made a fortune owning real estate. The real estate client would already have funds allocated to that sector and would be at risk of overinvesting in one area and becoming vulnerable to a sudden market downturn.

These types of decisions can have a dramatic impact on your overall financial success. You should manage your finances in the same way a doctor tries to view your health: looking at everything holistically rather than as separate pieces. By seeing how the pieces fit together, your wealth manager should be able to make smart investments, taking into account your existing assets and future goals. And when you have a good wealth manager, your portfolio can end up more diversified than if you hire half a dozen of them. There is an enormous difference between managing money the same way across a number of clients and giving tailored financial advice.

One other benefit to customization? It helps you stick with your portfolio when the market's down or you're going through hard times. If you know your portfolio is tailored for your specific goals, you know why you own each of your holdings and *why* they are in each of your various accounts. This will make you far more likely to stick with the portfolio and refrain from making emotional choices when things get tough.

The Importance of a Financial Plan

An airplane is a finely tuned machine, made up of thousands of parts. It can function incredibly well, but but without a flight plan and continuous course corrections, the likelihood of getting to your destination is slim to none. Your portfolio is just one part of your financial plan. Think of your portfolio as the fuel for your plane's engine and your financial plan as the flight instruments that will keep you on course.

And just as the coordinates for Iceland are very different from those for Singapore, your financial plan should be tailored to you and where you want to go. A written and well-defined financial plan should guide all of your investment decisions (you'll learn how to build a financial plan in Chapter 5). If you're working with an advisor, that person, at a minimum, should capture information about your current assets, projected savings, and income sources and fully understand your financial goals before providing any guidance about investments. Everyone wants to jump right to the investments, but a well-defined plan is the key to keeping you on the path.

While the plan can get far more advanced than this, as it often does at Creative Planning, it is an essential prerequisite to a wealth manager's ability to give you competent advice. Whether it is basic or complex, if you are having your money managed without a financial plan, then you are working with a money manager, not a wealth manager, and likely not seeing anywhere near the benefits you can achieve with a more thorough approach to your financial well-being.

ADVISOR SELECTION CRITERION #3: CUSTODY

Brokerages and advisers should have independent custodians, and the government should have forced me to have an independent custodian. Client funds should be held by independent custodians. If they had, I would have been caught long ago. If I had had an inspection by the SEC, they would have looked at the custodian accounts and seen the funds on my books did not match the funds in the accounts, and I would have been caught.

BERNIE MADOFF

In 2008, the Bernie Madoff scandal received an enormous amount of press coverage. Madoff, considered one of the nation's top money managers, admitted that he was running the biggest Ponzi scheme in history: he paid for client withdrawals with money transferring in from new clients. The only reason Madoff was exposed is that he was faced with massive withdrawal requests from investors as the market plummeted; since he had spent or hidden most of his clients' money long ago, he didn't have any money to meet the new requests. With the stock market panic of 2008, new deposits couldn't keep up with the demand for withdrawals. With no new money left to hide behind, Madoff confessed to the greatest financial fraud in history.

What Bernie Madoff did was despicable. He not only stole money from the superwealthy and celebrities, but he bankrupted hardworking professionals and business owners and robbed hundreds of millions of dollars from charities and foundations. Many of Madoff's former clients were forced to sell their homes and belongings. Very high-profile foundations lost most of their money, and some were even forced to shut down. René-Thierry Magon de la Villehuchet, a wealthy businessman who referred clients to Madoff, committed suicide from the shame of association. I work with clients who were victims of this fraud, and it has been satisfying to see them recover the majority of their investments based on the work of the bankruptcy trustee overseeing the recovery efforts.

Media coverage reached a fever pitch largely because of the scale of the fraud but also because Madoff was not the only money manager stealing from clients. Now I can hear you thinking, "But that was more than ten years ago. There haven't been any of these news stories lately." You would be right, but Ponzi schemes come to light most frequently during market crashes, like the market plummet of 2008–2009. This is not because there are more crooks during those periods; rather, it is easier for them to get caught because they cannot meet the increased demand for withdrawals during a declining market. As Warren Buffett says, "It is when the tide rolls out that we see who has been swimming naked."

Some people in the media blamed the investors for not investigating their advisor. But how could an investor possibly have known what Bernie Madoff was doing? A background check would have shown a man who was a member of many exclusive clubs, served on the boards of charities and hospitals, and was actively involved in his religious community. He gave millions to various charities, and his clients included some of the world's most sophisticated investors. Madoff even served as the chairman of the NASDAQ. Yes, there were red flags. His funds were audited by a single accountant with two assistants. His investment returns, up about 10% every year, did not behave the way returns work in the real world. Nevertheless, it is misguided to fault the investors.

The real lesson we can learn from Bernie Madoff concerns custody. When an investor speaks with her advisor, one of the top questions she should ask is, "Who has custody of my money?" Madoff's clients wrote a check to Madoff Investments, and the money was deposited in the Madoff Investments account, which means that Madoff had custody of *all* his clients' assets. If he withdrew all the money from one investor's account and gave it to another investor making a withdrawal, investors had no way of knowing that the money had moved between accounts. Madoff's clients received doctored reports (which his own firm created) reflecting their returns, which rose every month and bore no semblance to what was actually in their accounts.

To avoid a financial nightmare like this one, the ideal way to work with an advisor is to have a separation of assets and advice. For example, use an advisor who opens an account for you at a national brokerage firm. You can then sign a limited power of attorney giving the advisor the right to place trades and only bill the account. The advisor should not have the authority to make any other withdrawals. Furthermore, if your advisor provides reports to you, you should also get an independent statement from the brokerage firm.

Literally thousands of investment managers across the country are advising clients in this manner. Because of this, you don't need to entrust your finances with anyone who insists on taking custody of your investable assets.[16] If you don't want someone to be able to steal your money, don't give it to them. It's that simple.

---

16   Certain types of investments require you to give up custody of your money, including some hedge funds, private equity funds, and real estate funds. If you are not in a position to perform tremendous due diligence on these funds, ask yourself if you really need this type of investment. For those who have significant assets, some of these alternatives can be very attractive. As you will learn in Chapter 10, I like many of these investments, am personally invested in them, and we use them where appropriate for Creative Planning's clients. However, when evaluating them for myself or clients, our due diligence meter is off the charts, especially when compared to publicly traded assets. It's fairly common for a client to bring me a "deal" and tell me that he is comfortable giving up custody because the person running the investment goes to the same place of worship, is from the same ethnic group, or the like. Well, that does not mean anything. In fact, most Ponzi schemes are affinity scams, where the promoter is preying on his own people, just like Madoff did.

ADVISOR SELECTION CRITERION #4:
COMPETENCE

Never ascribe to malice that which adequately

can be explained by incompetence.

NAPOLEON BONAPARTE

At this point, we have evaluated financial advisors on issues of possible conflicts of interest, level of customization, and custody of assets. We've eliminated many advisors based on these issues and can now move on to the thousands of independent advisors who check all the boxes we have discussed. They are true fiduciaries: they don't sell their own products and they don't demand to take custody of your assets—but they still need to be weeded out for competence. A financial advisor can have the best of intentions, but if that person isn't qualified, your chances of reaching your long-term financial goals are limited.

The financial advisory field is quite different than other professions like medicine, law, engineering, and education. Doctors go to medical school, and lawyers go to law school; engineers get a degree in engineering, and teachers pursue degrees in education. In comparison, the overwhelming majority of financial advisors—I would speculate well over 95%—have no college-level education in financial planning or investment management. Until recently, there wasn't even a college-level program offered. Some financial advisors have never even graduated from college and learn everything on the job. So how do you identify an advisor with competence and relevance?

One indication of advisor competency is to look for meaningful credentials. An advisor may have a veritable alphabet soup of impressive-looking designations after her name,[17] but most are likely meaningless. There are just a handful of designations that carry weight within the

---

17   The Financial Industry Regulatory Authority, the governing body of brokers, tracks and recognizes nearly 200 designations!

industry. Whenever financial planning is involved, you want to make sure you are working with a CERTIFIED FINANCIAL PLANNER™ (often listed as CFP®). If you need tax advice, you should be working with a Certified Public Accountant (CPA). For either of these designations, the advisor must satisfy specific education requirements, pass a comprehensive exam, and meet industry experience requirements. If estate planning or legal advice is involved, a law degree (JD), is a must.

At Creative Planning, we know that any one advisor is unlikely to check all these boxes, so we surround clients with a team of professionals who have the requisite credentials to be qualified to provide comprehensive advice. You should ensure your team has these credentials as well. There are also some specialty designations—like the Chartered Financial Analyst (CFA) or other designations related to insurance products—that you might encounter when looking at specialized investment strategies or insurance offerings, but you can pretty much ignore anything else.

As with any designation, a credential alone does not guarantee that you are getting the best possible advice, just like you can't identify the best possible doctor based on the fact he graduated from medical school. It does, however, indicate that he has demonstrated competency in his area of practice, which is the minimum you should demand of any advisor.

But Is the Advisor Right for You?

An independent advisor can have no conflicts, build custom portfolios, abstain from requesting custody of your assets, have the CERTIFIED FINANCIAL PLANNER™ designation, and still not be the right fit for you. First, be sure the advisor you choose works with people like you. For example, if you're scheduled to have heart surgery, you want to go to a doctor who successfully performs heart surgery all the time. If you are wrongfully accused of a crime,[18] you will look for a criminal defense

---

18   Or not wrongfully. I'm giving you the benefit of the doubt here!

attorney who has had prior success working with people in your situation. In the same way, when looking for a financial advisor, choose one who successfully works with people in your situation all the time. If you are just getting started, find an advisor who works primarily with clients at your stage of life. If you have a high net worth, choose an advisor who works primarily with high-net-worth households. You do not want your advisor learning at the expense of your financial security. When an issue comes up, you want your advisor to confidently say, "Been there, done that."

Second, make sure that what your advisor sells actually works. Most advisors are in the business of selling something, whether it is apparent to their clients or not. Even those who are truly independent often sell a strategy they know people want to buy. Some financial advisors sign on clients by telling them there is a way to participate in the upside of the market and, at the same time, get out before a downturn. A competent and ethical advisor knows that this cannot be systematically done and won't sell it. A competent but unethical advisor knows it can't be done, but will sell it anyway to make a quick buck.

I said early on that most advisors do more harm than good, then gave you a list of things to test for. You might be saying, "Geez! Is finding an advisor even worth it?" According to a recent study, an advisor following the principles set forth in this book can provide an added value of about 3% per year to their clients' assets. Researchers found that some years added negligible value, but others added value of well over 10%, most notably during periods of large market swings.[19]

If the principles of this book ring true to you, you should seek out a trusted advisor who is committed to partnering with you to plan for your financial future.

---

19   I personally think this study is wildly overrated, but I have no doubt that an advisor who meets the criteria set forth in this chapter will likely add meaningful value.

READY FOR A SECOND OPINION?

Creative Planning will provide you with a complimentary second opinion of your current investments and financial situation. We will help identify the major red flags in your accounts that discuss in this chapter such as . . .

- Unnecessary commissions or excessive fees
- Name-brand proprietary funds
- Conflicts of interest
- Opportunities for customization

Go to www.creativeplanning.com

Figure 4.1

WHAT TO AVOID	REASON
BROKERS	They are not held to the fiduciary standard and are not obligated to comply with the highest legal standard of care. You deserve better.
DUALLY REGISTERED ADVISORS	Dually-Registered Advisors: They are sometimes held to the fiduciary standard and sometimes not. You shouldn't work with someone that is only held to the highest legal standard of care "sometimes."
ANY ADVISOR, INDEPENDENT OR BROKER, THAT ASKS YOU TO CONVERT YOUR ENTIRE TAXABLE ACCOUNT TO CASH TO INVEST IN ONE OF THEIR MODELS.	This shows a blatant disregard for tax consequences that may be nearly impossible for even an excellent money manager to overcome.
A STOCK PICKER	There is nothing wrong with stock picking but it is not financial advice. The role of a financial advisor is to provide you with a personalized approach to money management, matching your investments to your goals. If someone is simply picking stocks, they are not really a financial advisor, but a money manager. If you believe stock picking works and that is all you are looking for, simply buy a low-cost mutual fund and move on.
ANY ADVISOR WITH A FEW MODELS FOR YOU TO CHOOSE FROM.	Watch out square peg, you are about to be shoved into a round hole. You want an advisor that can tailor a portfolio to your needs, not tailor your portfolio into their easy-to-manage model.
AN ADVISOR THAT MAKES COMMISSIONS SELLING INVESTMENTS.	In today's world, the best investment can be purchased without paying an advisor a commission. Avoid the conflict.
AN ADVISOR THAT MAKES INVESTMENT RECOMMENDATIONS WITHOUT FIRST DELIVERING A COMPREHENSIVE, WRITTEN FINANCIAL PLAN.	How can the advisor possibly know what is right for you if they don't know where things stand today and what you are trying to accomplish?

Figure 4.2

WHAT TO LOOK FOR

An advisor that works for an RIA and is not dually registered.
An advisor who works for an RIA that does not own any of its own products.
An advisor that takes the time to get to know you and your goals by first preparing a comprehensive, written financial plan, prior to making any investment recommendations.
An advisor whose firm has extensive experience working with people like you.
An advisor whose firm is capable of tailoring a portfolio to match your needs.
An advisor that will never automatically convert your taxable portfolio to cash prior to investing.
The financial world is changing and you no longer have to choose between a brokerage firm with breadth and depth or an RIA that does not have extensive experience. Lean on the collective due diligence of other investors and seek out a large RIA with extensive experience customizing portfolios for people like you.

Figure 4.3

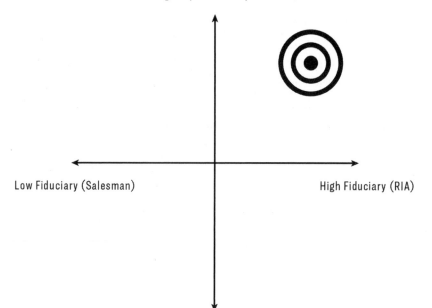

NOT ALL FIDUCIARIES
ARE CREATED EQUAL

CHAPTER FIVE

THE FOUR RULES OF INVESTING

A goal without a plan is just a wish.

ANTOINE DE SAINT-EXUPÉRY

We are told that we need to invest, but we rarely discuss why. And the why of investing is critically important. If we're saving for the future, what type of future do we want? During my long career in financial advising, I've had the opportunity to meet countless individuals and families. All too often, some became so focused on achieving the biggest returns possible that they lost focus on what's important, only to have their investments—and their relationships—collapse like a house of cards. I've seen families who didn't believe in purchasing insurance suffer unnecessary hardship when the primary income earner passed unexpectedly. I've seen individuals accumulate a tremendous fortune, only to lose nearly everything because their assets weren't properly diversified. I've seen individuals decide to deviate from their plan in a panic because they "trusted their gut," only to lose hundreds of thousands, or even millions, of dollars that they may never see again. In all cases, it only took one major shock to devastate their financial plan and, in many cases, negate a lifetime of work. Let's make sure that never happens to you.

I also have been able to work with an amazing team at Creative Planning to help thousands of families secure their financial future. We do this by putting together an investment plan tailored to their specific outcomes, taking the necessary steps to protect them from a catastrophic loss, and creating an appropriate estate plan to ensure their vision can continue long after they're gone. These families have peace of mind, knowing that they have the firm foundation necessary to protect them from life's inevitable surprises. They are disciplined as they follow their path, knowing that it will inevitably lead them where they want to go.

When it comes to crafting your investment plan, start by following the four rules of investing.

RULE #1: HAVE A CLEARLY DEFINED PLAN— FAILING TO PLAN IS PLANNING TO FAIL

Plan for what is difficult while it is easy, do what is great while it is small.

SUN TZU

Before you invest a single dollar, you must have a plan, just like before you a cook a meal, you need a recipe for all those ingredients sitting on the counter. A plan does not need to be a 150-page road map of how you will invest every minute for the rest of your life. A plan can be very straightforward but will serve as the north star for your journey.

For many people, having confidence that they can retire at a reasonable age is their primary goal, and that becomes the focal point of their investment strategy. However, for some investors who have already accumulated significant assets, retirement may be less of a concern, and their investment goals may be focused on realizing other objectives—perhaps funding a favorite charity or putting their grandchildren through college. Regardless of your specific goals, I have never run into an investor who doesn't want to be financially independent.

Financial independence is different from retirement; retirement means you are no longer working; financial independence means that as of today, you could quit your job, live the lifestyle you want, and never have to work for the rest of your life. There are plenty of people who are retired but not financially independent and may find themselves working again someday.

That said, you can be working and be financially independent. There are many people who have invested in such a way that they work because they want to, not because they have to. If you're retired and financially independent, it means your portfolio and income sources are stable and reliable enough to ensure you will never need to go back to work. What a feeling! Because the goal of being financially independent is almost universal, let's start with the path that leads to it, which has five basic steps: creating a net worth statement, developing a financial plan, running projections, and monitoring your progress.

Step 1: Create a Net Worth Statement

A net worth statement simply outlines your assets and your liabilities. Your *assets* are everything you own, valued at what you would receive if each was sold today. Your *liabilities* are everything you owe if you were to pay them off today. The difference between your assets and your liabilities is your *net worth*. Most people tend to look at what they own and not what they owe, but what you owe is arguably more important than what you own. For anyone with a mortgage, car payments, or significant credit card debt, this might be a face-the-music exercise.

When assembling your net worth statement, it's important to consider which of your assets are available to contribute to your goal of financial independence. Let's take two investors with the same goal: both want to accumulate sufficient assets by age 65 to generate $100,000 per year for the rest of their lives, adjusted for inflation. Both are 55 years old and have no outstanding debts. Frugal Frances has a net worth of $1 million: $200,000 is in her home and $800,000 is in IRAs and other investment accounts. Highroller Henry also has a net worth of $1 million: $600,000 is in his home, $200,000 is in his lake house, and $200,000 in IRAs and other investments. Assuming neither Frances nor Henry is willing to sell their homes to fund their financial independence goal, Frances is in much better shape with $800,000 of investments that, when invested wisely, bring money to her every day. Henry has only $200,000 in investments that are bringing money to him every day, but he has $800,000 of assets that actually pull money away from him every day (e.g., mortgage payment, property taxes, upkeep). The good news for Frances is that she will either reach her goal of financial independence more quickly than the ten years she estimated or be able to allocate a smaller percentage of her income each year to her investment plan.

Your net worth is an important number for financial planning purposes, but it doesn't tell the whole story. Always examine your *net worth statement* to determine which assets bring money to you and which pull money away from you. Your car or boat may show up on your net worth statement as an asset, but for financial independence purposes, it is most certainly a liability.

Step 2: Know Your Financial Goals, and Develop a Financial Plan

It sounds simple, but most people cannot clearly articulate their desired financial outcome. A financial goal must be both specific and realistic. An example of a vague (and therefore unrealistic) goal is, "I want to make a lot of money." Come on, people! We need to have a clearly defined purpose. A much more specific and achievable goal is, "I would like to retire at age 62 with a post-tax income of $100,000 per year adjusted for inflation, and I want to assume Social Security will not be there to help me." Now that is something we can work with!

Once you have your goals clearly in view, it's time to develop a financial plan that will get you there. Even if you are a high- or ultra-high-net-worth individual who may already be financially independent, creating a financial plan is still essential to realizing your vision. Your plan will help identify how much of your net worth must be allocated to meet your needs today versus how much can be comfortably earmarked for gifting to the next generation or the charities you support.

You should also explore asset protection techniques—like an umbrella policy or asset protection trust—because an unfortunate truth is that having money makes you a target for litigation. Finally, your advisor should determine any potential estate tax concerns and identify planning strategies that can maximize the transfer of wealth to your heirs while minimizing taxes.

A good financial plan evaluates more than just your progress toward financial independence. It should also evaluate how you would be affected by the unknowns—the things you can't control. For example, how would you and your family be affected by a long-term or permanent disability, the potential need for skilled nursing care later in life, or, for married couples, the untimely death of a spouse?

Step 3: Run a Projection

If I am going to drive from Kansas City to Florida, I had better make sure I have enough gas in the tank and supplies in the trunk. Similarly, you need to know if you're preparing effectively to reach your goals. The best way to do this is to run a projection (there are online tools to help you do this, or your advisor can run one for you). Be sure to exclude any assets that are not available to fund your financial independence goal. For example, if your net worth statement shows you have $800,000 today but you are planning to spend $150,000 on your kids' weddings and education, the projection should start with the $650,000 you have that is available to fund your goal ($800,000 minus the $150,000 you've earmarked for your kids). Then, include the money you are saving regularly, whether it's in your 401(k), an IRA, or a taxable account. These projections can get more sophisticated if you include Social Security, other income like pensions or rental income, potential inheritances, and other variables.

Because of the variety of scenarios that require evaluation during the planning process, many investors turn to a professional financial planner for assistance. Financial planners can use specialized software to quickly and thoroughly evaluate outcomes using different investment returns, retirement ages, and other variables to help you create the best financial plan for you. This person can also help you determine how much you will need to spend—and, consequently, how much you need to save—to be able to maintain your lifestyle in retirement. She can also recommend strategies that might help further optimize your plan, such as considering a Roth conversion or refinancing your mortgage.

Step 4: Determine If You Need to Adjust Your Goal

After running a projection, many people who are diligent in saving find they are much further along than they thought and are happy to see that their saving and investing are paying off. If you find that you are not on the path to financial independence, you may need to make adjustments to your goals, spending habits, or saving habits. For example, if your projection shows that to hit your goal, you need to have an investment rate of return of 20% per year, well, change the goal, because it very likely isn't going to work out. You can adjust your goal by pulling other levers, such as lowering your income need, saving more, pushing your retirement date out, or asking your kids to trim the budget for the fairytale wedding they want you to fund.

Let's go back to Henry and Frances for a bit. If Frances earns just a little over 7% on her money for the next ten years, she will have around $1.6 million in her various investment accounts by the time she's 65. If she becomes more conservative in retirement and lowers her expected return to 5%, she will earn $80,000 per year on her portfolio. Assuming she will also receive $20,000 per year from Social Security starting at age 66, Frances is on track to have $100,000 of income each year and will have reached her goal of being financially independent.

To increase the probability of maintaining her financial independence, Frances should save enough to build a more sizeable buffer. For example, if she saves an additional $1,000 each month, we can expect her portfolio to grow to around $1.8 million by age 65. The additional $200,000 she will have saved up by retirement will allow her to reduce her reliance on Social Security and the performance of the assets in her portfolio each year. These excess funds ($200,000) would be her retirement surplus.

Planning to have a surplus helps ensure that there are sufficient assets to meet your needs in the face of uncertainty. It allows a cushion for any unexpected expenses (like needing to put a new roof on the house), and it reduces your dependence on the markets to achieve your goals. If your current savings plan puts you just on the edge of financial independence, you will likely internalize the stress of every market movement; every good day will make you feel great about retirement, and every bad day will make you feel that you will have to live off ramen noodles and cat food in your golden years. Plan on accumulating a little more than you need for complete peace of mind.

Now let's revisit Highroller Henry. Henry needs to make some serious decisions. To achieve the approximately $1.6 million he would need to reach his goal of financial independence by age 65, he will need to save around $7,000 per month (remember, Frances had to save much less than $7,000 per month because a larger portion of her net worth was invested and growing). If this is feasible for Henry, great; he can save a higher amount each month than Frances and continue to spend weekends at the lake house. If it's not feasible, Henry will have to decide if he's willing to sell or downsize one or both of his homes, thereby pulling income toward, rather than away from, his goal of financial independence.

These sorts of decisions need to happen early on in your investing journey. You don't want to have regretful conversations with your spouse and loved ones about how you should have saved better. You should always have a clear understanding of where you are today financially: which assets are bringing you wealth, which assets are taking wealth away from you, and how much time you have to reach your financial goals. This enables you to determine if you should sell some of your assets today or as you approach retirement, or if you are able keep all of your non-income-producing assets (e.g., your vacation home or boat) and still achieve your retirement goals. You also need to determine if you're going to need to save more or less than you originally thought to attain your goals.

Step 5: Construct a Customized Portfolio

Once you understand your goals and how your financial habits may need to be adjusted to achieve them, you should construct a portfolio that has the highest probability of reaching your goals.

You may also have different plans with different levels of risk for different portfolios you own. For example, you may have separate investments set aside for education. This will have a different starting amount (what you have set aside for school) and a different goal (the amount of education you want to fund). You may have yet another goal for a second home, a wedding fund, or a trust set aside for kids or grandkids. If you have excess wealth, which means you have a larger pool of money than you need to achieve all of your goals, it is perfectly legitimate to allocate that portion of your portfolio to simply "beat the S&P 500" or anything else you may fancy. The key is to make sure that you have a solid portfolio in place to get you on track to financial independence. After that, the excess wealth can be invested in a variety of ways.

In each case, whether it is for retirement, education, excess wealth, or any other objective, first determine a specific goal. Everything else flows from that purpose.

Now What?

A doctor providing a prognosis for a long-term illness needs a lot of information before determining a course of treatment. The same is true with investing. Once you have a plan based on your goals and know how much you need to save, financial advisors can determine the best vehicles for wealth accumulation.

The first thing that most financial advisors (myself included) will recommend is that you contribute to an employer-sponsored retirement plan, like a 401(k) or 403(b) plan, to the extent that your contributions are matched by your employer. If your employer matches dollar-for-dollar for the first 3% of your contribution, it's hard to beat that immediate 100% rate of return. If this is the case, congratulations! This is a very generous benefit, and you are in the minority of the American workforce to have it. Never miss an opportunity to take an employer match.

After that, investors should try to max out contributions to a Roth IRA if they are eligible. Eligibility and limits are based on your adjusted gross income and marital status. These limits are subject to change each year, so you should check with an accountant to see if you are eligible to contribute, and if so, how much. Although you will not receive an income tax deduction for contributing to a Roth IRA, these accounts offer substantial advantages: investments in Roth IRAs grow tax free, and money can be withdrawn tax free in retirement.

After maximizing a Roth IRA, investors should go back to their employer-sponsored retirement plan and contribute up to the maximum annual limit. You receive an immediate income tax deduction equal to the value of your contributions, money in the plan grows tax free, and taxes are paid only when you withdraw the funds in retirement. Investors who are age 50 and older are also eligible to make larger "catch-up" contributions to both Roth IRAs and employer-sponsored plans, which can help accelerate progress to financial independence.

Investors who are self-employed or own their own business have other retirement savings vehicles available, such as an individual 401(k), SEP IRA, or SIMPLE IRA, that can take the place of an employer-sponsored plan. Each type of savings vehicle offers its own unique combination of advantages and disadvantages, so you should speak with a financial planner or investment advisor to determine which option is best for you.

After maxing out your employer-sponsored plan, savings decisions become more complex. Where you choose to place your money will be largely dependent on whether you're eligible for any other retirement plan options, as well as your tax bracket. The key is to save the amount of money needed to reach your financial independence goal in the most tax-efficient way possible.

How Do I Get There?

Knowing how much you need to invest to achieve your goals and having the resources to invest are often two different things. Some potential investors may have the cash on hand—in a savings account or other similar vehicle—but they are afraid to put it to work in the market in the event they have an urgent need for the funds. Others may have the desire to invest, but their cash flow is tied up servicing debt payments or committed to large expenses. For these people, finding the resources to implement their desired financial plan may seem impossible. Let's look at two of the most common factors that limit investing and the ways to remove these obstacles.

Emergency Cash Reserves

Having access to cash in the event of an urgent need is important regardless of whether you are a multimillionaire or a newly minted graduate. But there is a difference in having access to cash versus holding cash in an account (cash that is losing value each day to inflation). In today's low-interest-rate savings environment, having piles of cash in a savings account or money market account is about as useful to your financial independence goal as stuffing it under your mattress for twenty years. Any cash in excess of what you need in the near term, such as an anticipated purchase in the next year or two, should ideally be invested for long-term growth. A reasonable amount for emergencies—say, three to six months of expenses—should stay in the bank as well.

For your extended cash reserves—say, six to twelve months of expenses—there are plenty of options for accessing your funds while allowing them to work for you when you don't need them. For example, a line of credit on your home or highly liquid securities in your investment portfolio (like bond funds) can serve as sources of cash for a rainy day. But when it's sunny out, they can be in the market and growing.

Debt Payments

From student loans to a mortgage, the American dream for most people has been built on debt financing. When used responsibly, it can allow people to start their adult lives or be used as a resource to cover unexpected expenses. When used irresponsibly, it can become a crushing burden that gets in the way of achieving their dreams.

There's probably no more hotly debated topic in personal finance than the use of debt. There are "gurus" on both sides: ones who extol the virtues of the strategic use of debt and others who see it as a human scourge that should be avoided completely. Regardless of your own personal thoughts about debt, one thing is certain: the ability to use debt is always constrained by your capacity to handle the payments. I've known 80-year-old clients still happily paying their mortgage because they got a great low rate, and they have plenty of predictable and stable cash flows to make the payments. I've also seen other people struggle to implement any type of investment plan because there's not enough left at the end of the month after their portion of debts have been paid.

If debt is getting in the way of achieving your financial goals, it's important to reduce or eliminate any that will limit the effectiveness of your investment plan. Most consumer debts, like credit cards, charge annual interest rates that far exceed the expected return of your investments. Earning even high single-digit rates of return on your investments while paying double-digit interest rates on your debts is like trying to climb a mountain when you're weighed down with a 200-pound backpack.

So what can you do? The best course of action is to tackle the debts with the highest interest rate first; paying those down will reduce the impact of the high interest rate and keep the balance from spiraling out of control. At the same time, if your employer has a matching program for your retirement plan, contribute at least the minimum amount to the plan to get the full match (e.g., if the offer is 3%, contribute at least that much). As you begin to free up additional cash by paying off your debts, you can start to funnel money into a Roth IRA or other investment accounts, or increase your contributions to your employer-sponsored plan to accelerate your progress toward your goals.

Sometimes people have debts that aren't burdensome and wonder whether they should just pay everything off with money from their savings. The answer depends on what the alternative is. Those who are not comfortable investing the money, and the cash would just continue to sit in the bank, should pay off the debt. However, if they are open to investing the cash and can expect to earn a higher rate of return on the funds than they are paying on the loan, I recommend they invest the cash and continue to service the debt. They are more likely to end up with more money in the long term. In addition, if they decide they'd rather pay off their debts, they can withdraw the money from their investment account where it's been quietly growing.

As an example, someone who has a fixed-interest-rate mortgage at 2.5% (part of which may be tax deductible), is comfortable with debt, and is looking to have the highest net worth possible 20 years from now should likely invest her cash rather than apply it to the debt. However, someone

in the same situation but with a 7% interest rate should almost certainly
be paying off the debt.

> ### *Education*
> Education costs money, but then so does ignorance.
> CLAUS MOSER

Many investors consider paying for college education for their children to
be a primary financial goal. Unfortunately, many balk at the cost. It's true
that the cost of college has reached crisis proportions. Every now and then,
older clients will tell me, "Well, I worked my way through college." Today,
that option is rarely possible for college students. While wage inflation is
going up only a few points per year on average, the cost of college education has increased at more than double that rate. The math of working your
way through college no longer adds up.

Again, you need to begin with an understanding of where you're
starting from. For many, they're starting at zero: they have nothing set
aside for their children's education. Then we need our destination, which is
the specific school you want to pay for. Do you want to pay for four years
at a private college or six years at an in-state university? Do you want to
pay for all the education costs or just a portion?

Let's take Generous Ginny as an example. She wants to help pay for
her children's college education by covering 75% of the cost of an in-state
college for four years. With some quick research, we can determine the
total cost of tuition, fees, books, and room and board at the target school
in her state. We then adjust this figure to account for the average annual
increase in higher education expenses. Finally, we have the total amount
she needs by the time her children begin their respective college careers.

From there, we can calculate how much Ginny needs to set aside
each month to meet her education goal. This calculation assumes she'll
earn a reasonable rate of return on her investments each year and is based

on an allocation appropriate for how long she is able to save before each child begins college. For example, let's assume 75% of the total cost of attendance at her target school is $17,500 today and we assume costs will increase at 4% per year. Using those numbers, we can estimate that she will need to save $225,000 to send her 9-year-old daughter and 6-year-old son to college by their respective age 18. Assuming a 6% rate of return on the invested assets, she would need to save around $700 per month for her daughter and around $575 per month for her son to have enough saved by the time her children start school.

As with retirement savings, it's not enough just to know your current financial state, what you're trying to accomplish, and how much you need to set aside each month. When saving for education, you also need to know where the best places are to invest your money. For most parents, 529 college saving plans provide the perfect solution. By gifting money to a 529 plan, your contributions can grow tax free, and distributions for qualified higher-education expenses can be made tax free as well. Some states even allow a state income tax deduction for contributing to the plan. The only situation in which this type of plan wouldn't be ideal is if the family has a high net worth. For the ultra-affluent, it often makes sense to pay the university directly rather than fund a 529 plan.

With the rampant rise of costs for higher education, many families are looking for assistance anywhere they can get it. Need-based financial aid can be an important component in affording higher education, and how you save and pay for college can have a direct impact on your child's eligibility for aid.

The ins and outs of financial aid planning are outside the scope of this book, but there are a few general considerations to keep in mind when putting together your savings plan:

1. Parent-owned assets are treated more favorably than student-owned assets. When calculating aid eligibility, the balance in a

529 plan established by a parent is counted at a lower rate than balances in any accounts in the name of the student. Student-owned assets include custodial accounts established for their benefit (such as UTMA or UGMA accounts), so any funds earmarked for college should ideally be in a 529 plan or another account in the parent's name.

2. Distributions from 529 plans owned by other family members can reduce aid eligibility. For example, if you are using a 529 plan to save for college for someone who isn't your child—say, a grandchild or a niece—the college can treat withdrawals from that plan to pay for expenses as income to the student, which can reduce the amount of aid the student can receive the following year. Therefore, you should plan to support this student's junior- or senior-year expenses from these accounts so you don't reduce potential aid awards.

3. Income counts against aid more than assets do. Even if you structure your savings as strategically as possible, your income may preclude your child from receiving need-based financial aid. Be sure to investigate all sources of financial aid, including academic scholarships, work-study programs, and grants, but ensure your savings plan anticipates the possibility you might have to pay 100% of the costs.

RULE #2: BUILD A PORTFOLIO THAT ALIGNS WITH YOUR GOAL

If you don't know where you are going, you'll end up someplace else.

YOGI BERRA

Most of us have purchased a car at some point in our lives. Before we do, we have a sense of what we are trying to accomplish. During my college years, I needed a car that could get me from point A to point B, so I looked for cars that cost only a few thousand dollars and would work most of the time. When I got married, I needed a car that was more reliable, would almost certainly get me from point A to point B, and had amenities like a working air-conditioner. When I had children, safety became a priority, and I needed a car that was easy to get into and out of while holding squirming toddlers. As my kids got older, I found myself driving carpool to practices, and I needed a car that could handle rowdy teenagers and lots of sports equipment.

We all understand the effort and thought that goes into buying a new car. Interestingly, most investors give far less thought to their long-term investments. For example, it's not uncommon for the average investor to ask, "Is today a good time to buy stock in Apple?"

Sophisticated investors would look at this decision differently. They would determine the grand vision of what they are trying to accomplish, the specific financial goals they have, and then ask these questions: How much should I allocate to stocks? How much of my stock investment should be allocated to large company stocks? How many of these stocks should be US company stocks? Once those questions are answered, then they may ask, "Does Apple fit within my plan?" You may not consider yourself a sophisticated investor yet, but I assure you that after reading this book, you will have more knowledge than most professionals!

MOVING BEYOND GOALS

We've already discussed several specific goals people have for their investments, such as achieving financial independence or paying for their children's education. Some have a broader goal for their assets, such as providing a more comfortable lifestyle for their family in the future. Others have an even larger vision for their wealth, in which charitable causes or future generations of family members are the ultimate beneficiaries.

Accomplishing these goals may require different portfolios using different "ingredients," which will dictate what assets are most appropriate for balancing the desire for growth with the need for asset preservation.

This approach is radically different from the popular narrative that you should accumulate as much money as possible. Of course, most people want as much money as possible, but if that's your sole mission, it usually means taking on unwise investment risks. The objective for the assets in your portfolio should dictate the allocation, not the other way around. I hear what some of you are thinking: "I don't care about any of that other stuff. My goal is to make as much money as possible." Let me give you an example of why that might not be true.

Let's say that you have accumulated sufficient retirement assets that, coupled with your Social Security benefits, will enable you to retire in ten years and live on around $100,000 per year. If I ask you what your goal is for the next ten years and you tell me you want to create the biggest possible nest egg, we have an interesting dilemma. If this is truly your objective, the historical data and statistics strongly point toward having 10% or less of your portfolio in bonds, because most of the time, bonds are expected to earn significantly less than stocks over a ten-year time frame.

You might say, "That's fantastic! If that's what the statistics say, we'll invest everything in stocks."

However, the goal of retiring in ten years with $100,000 per year to spend requires a different portfolio from the goal of wealth maximization. If your goal is to have the highest probability of being able to successfully retire ten years from now, then a portfolio with anywhere from 20% to 30% in bonds would be appropriate. This is because while we expect a lower rate of return from bonds, the return is far more predictable. This reduces overall portfolio volatility, which in turn increases the chance of earning a specific target return. A high-stock portfolio has a higher probability of earning more than the target rate of return you need to retire, but it also increases the probability you'll substantially underperform your target rate of return as well. Presented with this set of facts, most investors go with the odds. Nothing is guaranteed, but they want the highest probability of achieving their retirement goal.

For the ultra-affluent, the same principle applies. There is a perception that the superwealthy have a secret money-making machine, take huge risks in the market, and are constantly doubling their wealth. This perception is largely divorced from reality; the wealthiest are far more focused on preserving their wealth than increasing it. Many of the ultra-affluent cite leaving generational wealth or a charitable legacy as primary goals, which can result in estate plans with many moving parts. They create foundations or trusts to act as framework for their financial planning and prioritize tax management so their wealth isn't frittered away. They understand that their objectives may require the construction of a portfolio where the primary goal is not wealth maximization but instead risk management or tax efficiency.

For example, let's say an ultra-affluent investor establishes a family foundation that requires 5% of the foundation's assets to be distributed to charities every year. A portfolio constructed for this foundation would not have the purpose of maximizing asset growth. In fact, almost all family foundations created by the ultra-affluent include a substantial allocation to bonds.

The main reason the ultra-affluent prioritize bonds in this way is that bonds provide security. With bonds in your portfolio, there's greater assurance that the annual distribution can be met without selling more volatile portfolio assets when they inevitably go down. If you look at any one of the recent major crises—9/11, the 2008–2009 stock market meltdown, or the coronavirus pandemic—in all cases, high-quality bonds increased in value, while stocks went down anywhere from 40% to 50%. During these rough patches, a foundation with an allocation to bonds could use a combination of the portfolio income and bonds to meet annual distribution needs rather than selling stocks during periods of market weakness, which would increase the probability that the foundation would lose all of its money and expire.

You will learn the specifics of how to construct and manage a portfolio in Chapter 10, but it doesn't matter if you're just starting out or have half a billion dollars: you must begin with a goal or vision in mind. Once you have an understanding of what you want to accomplish, the rest becomes easier.

RULE #3: REVISIT THE PLAN

You don't need a parachute to skydive. You just need one to skydive twice.

AUTHOR UNKNOWN

All of us have been in a race at some point in our lives. Whether it's a neighborhood dash down the block or a 400-meter Olympic event, all races have two things in common: a starting line and a finish line. And all serious athletes know exactly where they're starting from and where they need to end up.

Revisit your financial plan and projections once a year or whenever you undergo a significant life change (e.g., marriage, parenthood, significant change in income). During your review, you may notice that your net worth has changed because your portfolio performed better or worse than expected over the previous year. You may have received an unexpected bonus or an inheritance or had a liquidity event (like the sale of a property). The starting line has changed.

Perhaps your objectives are different now too. Maybe you want to retire sooner than you initially thought, or you now expect to work part-time in retirement. Perhaps the college your daughter wants to go to is twice as expensive as you initially thought. Maybe the baby you were going to have ended up being triplets. Maybe now you are married, or newly single, or healthier, or more ill, than expected. The finish line may have moved.

All sorts of things can change in your personal life that should result in changes to your portfolio. Note that the emphasis on changes to the portfolio is based on personal changes rather than changes in various markets.

Let's say a 60-year-old investor has a goal of living on $100,000 per year at age 62. Her projections assumed a portfolio rate of return of 6%, and she was right on track for her goal. However, at her annual review, the portfolio's performance shows a return far better than projected due to a strong bull market. The investor is also growing wary of portfolio volatility as she approaches retirement. Lucky for her, she no longer needs a 6% rate of return to accomplish her goals. The portfolio projections show a 5% rate of return is all she needs. Given these circumstances, the investor may choose to pull back her exposure to stocks and increase her exposure to high-quality bonds. She would be doing this knowing she's decreasing her expected long-term rate of return, but increasing the probability of getting a 5% rate of return with reduced volatility.

THE ULTIMATE RULE: DON'T MESS IT UP!
Seen on CNBC:

Host: So is this a buying opportunity?

Guest: I wouldn't be a buyer of this market today (S&P at 2,710), but I would be a huge buyer at S&P 2,680.

This interaction illustrates precisely the wrong way to look at your portfolio. Why would an investor allocate to stocks at S&P 2,680, but not at S&P 2,710? Once you have your portfolio in place, stay disciplined. Follow the pattern of investment decisions outlined in this chapter or work with an advisor who understands, accepts, and invests with these principles. Ignore the noise, never panic, don't deviate during a crisis, and, most important, stay focused on your goals.

If all of these factors have you wanting a second opinion on your current portfolio design, we will provide a complimentary look under the hood. Visit www.creativeplanning.com.

CHAPTER SIX

MANAGING RISK

> Everyone's got a plan until they get punched in the mouth.
> MIKE TYSON

Risk management is a part of your daily life: locking your doors when you leave the house, putting on a seatbelt before you shift into gear, and looking both ways before you cross the street. When it comes to investing, *risk management* is the concept of making sure that you've managed your exposure to financial loss. For investors who have already set up a disciplined savings plan or accumulated substantial assets, the greatest threat to their financial independence is a catastrophic loss from something happening *outside* the markets and *outside* their control, like a house fire or a death in the family. Improving your investment return incrementally doesn't matter if you lose everything to an unfortunate incident.

Many of us spend more time deciding what kind of pizza we should order for the family ("Will Suzie eat the pepperoni this time?") than we do on the type of insurance we should have to protect them.[20] While risk management is a part of wealth management, you may be asking yourself what place it has in a book about making you a sophisticated investor. The bottom line is that it's critically important to protect yourself

---

20 Some of us spend even more time on what type of pizza crust we should order. To be fair, this is also a decision worthy of careful consideration.

from as much financial risk as possible. If you don't have insurance, you are *self-insuring*, meaning that for any risks (and life has plenty), you will bear the full economic burden of a poor outcome. Often investors abandon their investment plans in shaky markets because they fear the potential financial impact of their personal risk exposures if their portfolio value drops. For example, an investor may exit stocks during a bear market for fear that if he passes away suddenly, his family wouldn't have enough money.

Sophisticated investors never allow themselves to be put in that position. With a good plan, all of your risks are under control regardless of the markets, allowing you to stick with your strategy (and sleep at night too).

Let's make sure you're protected, shall we?

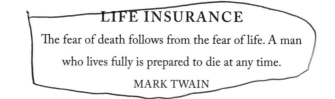

LIFE INSURANCE

The fear of death follows from the fear of life. A man who lives fully is prepared to die at any time.

MARK TWAIN

It has been said that life insurance is sold, not bought. And very rarely do couples wake up in the morning, turn to each other, and say "Honey, let's go shopping for insurance!" But for many people, life insurance plays a critical role in both risk management and wealth management.

The basic concept of life insurance is simple: in the event of your death, an insurance company will pay a *death benefit* to your beneficiary. In exchange for this, you pay the insurance company a certain amount of money. Pretty simple, right? Of course, it has become much more complicated than that in recent years. The insurance industry has created all sorts of insurance products—and investment products masquerading as insurance—that have made this a much more difficult and complex decision.

One of the challenges of buying insurance is the structure of the insurance industry. As a rule, insurance agents operate on commission: they receive a portion of the premium payment from the policies they sell. While there is nothing inherently wrong with people receiving commissions for selling insurance products, it does create a possible conflict of interest. Given the choice, will the agent recommend the product best suited for the individual (i.e., the lowest cost to meet the need) or the one that is best for the agent (i.e., pays the highest commission)? As a consumer, one way to protect yourself is to know what you need and why you need it before you go shopping for a policy.

At Creative Planning, we recognize that risk management is a critical part of helping clients with their overall security, and because of that, we have affiliates that help with coverage such as life insurance. In a typical year, over 95% of the policies our clients obtain are term insurance policies, which are the least profitable products in the industry but ideally suited to the needs of most people.

Term Insurance

Term insurance is the most appropriate type of life insurance for nearly all Americans; however, insurance agents don't often recommend it because it results in the lowest commission for them. With a term insurance policy, you're insuring your life for a specific period of time. Let's say that your financial plan makes it clear that as long as you keep saving for the next 15 years, your family will have all they need to meet their needs for the rest of their lives. One potential pitfall for this plan is that if you die tomorrow, your family loses both you *and* your cash flow.[21] Instead of the family needing the money you saved in 15 years, they're going to need it right now. This means (1) the money doesn't have time to grow and (2) no more

---

21 To call this a "pitfall" is a bit of an understatement.

income will be added to that investment.[22] To compound the problem, withdrawals will not only start 15 years earlier than planned, but also last 15 years longer than anticipated. This sort of thing can derail both your investment plan and your family's future.

Early in my career, I recommended term insurance to a physician. He waved off my suggestion because he had read an article that said that all insurance is bad. Unfortunately, he passed away unexpectedly within a year, leaving his family in financial turmoil. His wife and daughter suffered unnecessary financial hardship for many years, on top of the emotional loss of losing a husband and father. I still work with the family today, and it saddens me to know that their suffering could have been lessened by a term insurance policy costing only a few hundred dollars a year.

All responsible human beings should ensure they have enough assets in place to protect their family in the event of their death. If you don't have a sizeable nest egg and cannot self-insure for this risk, term insurance is an easy solution. It's comparatively inexpensive because the odds are high that you'll live past the term. If you buy a 15-year term insurance policy, insurance companies fully expect you to live past the 15 years, which significantly reduces the likelihood that they will have to pay the death benefit. Many insurance agents use this statistic to dissuade investors from purchasing term insurance, because you are unlikely to get a return on your investment. This argument misses the point; it's like arguing you should feel disappointed that you've had homeowners' insurance for years and your home didn't burn down once! This is exactly what insurance is for: insuring against an improbable occurrence by transferring a small portion of your wealth in exchange for protection from economic catastrophe.

Determining how much life insurance you need should be an integral part of creating your financial plan. There are many methodologies used to

---

22   Even if you are like Patrick Swayze in Ghost and you return to help make pottery, let's assume you won't be making a significant impact on the family's income.

estimate how much life insurance a person needs. Unfortunately, most of them make zero sense.[23] For example, one popular rule of thumb is that you should purchase life insurance equivalent to five times your income. If you make $100,000 per year and have $5 million saved, you likely don't need a $500,000 insurance policy because your family will get by just fine with your existing assets. However, if you just graduated from medical school with $250,000 of debt, purchased a $700,000 home, and have three little kids, then five times your income is likely nowhere near enough to support your family.

As we learned when building portfolios, the best method is to customize your insurance to fit your specific situation. First, add up the costs of your unfunded goals should you die today, such as supplemental income to provide for your family, a college education fund, or paying off outstanding debts (including a mortgage and any car payments). Once you determine the amount of insurance you need, the term (i.e., the length of the policy) can be set by calculating how long it will take you to become financially independent from an insurance perspective.[24] For example, if you need $500,000 of term insurance today, when will the need go away? You can calculate the answer by determining when your need for insurance will expire based on how long it will take you to accumulate amount of the assets you need to match the policy amount. If, based on your savings rate, you will have saved another $500,000 in 15 years, you only need a 15-year policy.

One last note on term insurance: many people forget to think about the potential need for life insurance on a nonworking spouse. Even though there would be no income to replace at their passing, nonworking spouses

---

23   At this point, you shouldn't be shocked.

24   This may be a different time from when you are financially independent from a retirement perspective. For example, once your children are through college or your mortgage is paid off, you no longer need to carry insurance to cover those liabilities, but you may need to keep saving for retirement.

typically handle many household responsibilities (e.g., childcare, transportation, housekeeping) that the surviving spouse would likely have to pay to have covered. This is an important consideration.

Survivorship Life: Maximizing the Value of your Estate

For affluent individuals with large estates, life insurance is often incorporated as part of their comprehensive estate plan. The insurance industry has a product called *survivorship life* (or a *second-to-die policy*), which is a single policy covering the lives of two spouses or domestic partners. The policy pays out only after both insured individuals have passed. Because two lives are insured, the death benefit is greater than a policy would be on only one individual. For those with taxable estates, this type of policy can provide liquidity to pay for any number of expenses, potentially preventing a business or farm from being sold to pay estate taxes. Coupled with an irrevocable trust (more on this later), the death benefit can pass to the heirs completely tax free.

The focus of a survivorship life insurance policy is slightly different from that of a term life insurance policy. Rather than planning for premature death, a survivorship life insurance policy is primarily used for estate tax planning. After all, both insured individuals must pass before the policy pays out. Consequently, the goal of the policy is to maximize the value that a couple can gift each year tax free to pay for the policy premiums. The death benefit of the policy becomes the maximum amount that the annual premium gifts will support. We revisit this in greater detail in the next chapter.

Insurance as an "Investment"

The rule of thumb here is to be sure that the type of insurance policy you're considering meets your specific needs. Survivor needs are almost always best served by a term insurance policy. Survivorship life and other highly specialized products, like universal life or premium-financed insurance, can be used to provide estate liquidity for the affluent, but typically insurance should *never* be purchased as an investment in and of itself. Because of this, variable life insurance and variable annuities don't really have a place in a sophisticated investor's portfolio. These types of products combine investing with insurance and drive up the costs of both.[25] Instead, sophisticated investors will invest their money efficiently and purchase term insurance separately to cover survivor's needs.[26]

> ## DISABILITY
> Time and health are two precious assets we
> don't appreciate until they are depleted.
> DENIS WAITLEY

What do you think is your greatest asset? You may think it's your home, or possibly your retirement account. For most people, though, our greatest asset is our ability to earn a wage. Think about the goals you have for yourself and your family. All of those goals, whether saving for your first home, your child's education, or charitable contributions that will outlast you, are likely dependent on one thing: your ability to earn.

My dad is a physician and has worked incredibly hard his entire career. At one time—with a mortgage, three kids on their way to college, and wanting to enjoy travel and retirement at some point—his goals were to pay off his home, make sure his kids got a good education, and become financially independent. Other than dying prematurely, the only thing that could have derailed that plan was a disability that prevented him

---

25 Someone gets rich with these kinds of policies. It's just that it's the insurance agent, not you!

26 No matter what the insurance agent tells you. And yes, I know, he's really, really nice.

from working. If he had become disabled without any insurance in place, none of his goals would have been achievable. This is why those who are earning the money necessary to fund their goals should insure their ability to earn.

Early in my career, I worked with a pain management physician who had lost part of his thumb to a blender. This was a much bigger deal than it may sound, because he used his thumb every day to give patients injections. He couldn't work anymore, but his disability coverage kicked in and ensured that his family's needs were met. These scenarios are more common than you may think, and I've personally worked with clients who were impacted by traumatic injuries or debilitating diseases like multiple sclerosis, Lyme disease, and ALS. In many cases, disability coverage is what saved the financial security of these families.

Disability insurance breaks down into two main types: short-term disability and long-term disability. Short-term disabilities are classified as disabilities that prevent you from earning income for 90 days or less. Since the time away from work is comparatively minimal and the financial impact is usually not disruptive to your long-term finances, purchasing this type of insurance is often unnecessary. Long-term disabilities are those that prevent you from earning income longer than 90 days, up to the rest of your life. The risk of this type of disability to your financial independence is important to consider.

Like life insurance, the purpose of paying for disability insurance is to transfer a little bit of your wealth to an insurance company in exchange for a stream of income to help meet your family's needs should you become permanently disabled. We all feel bulletproof until we aren't, so I encourage you not to shrug off this section. If you've already accumulated enough wealth to pay off your home, be financially independent, ensure your kids go to college, and so on, there is no need to obtain this coverage or to keep an existing policy in place. But if there's a chance that a disability could have a negative impact on the financial future of your family, it's worth looking into a long-term disability policy, taking into account your health now, your income, and other relevant factors when making your decision.

Employers typically offer both short- and long-term disability coverages for their employees, so it's a good idea to start there to see what is available (or what you may already have). If your employer doesn't offer this benefit or doesn't offer enough coverage, you may be able to obtain private disability insurance. It's best to speak with a financial planner to see if disability insurance is appropriate for your situation and what type of policy would be most beneficial.

LONG-TERM CARE

Forty percent of individuals who reach age 65
will enter a nursing home during their lifetimes.

MORNINGSTAR

Paying for long-term care is a primary concern for many Americans, and rightfully so. The cost of a nursing home varies across the country, from around $95,000 per year in Arizona to over $155,000 per year in New York City. Given that just 44% of the population over age 50 has more than $100,000 in liquid assets, it shouldn't be much of a surprise that most people who enter nursing homes are broke within a few years. However, if we look deeper at the statistics, they show that 68% of people who enter a nursing home die within a year of admission. What should you make of this?

Well, if you're fortunate enough to have a multimillion-dollar portfolio, a properly structured investment allocation would spin off the money needed to cover the cost of long-term care. For someone in that situation, entering a skilled nursing facility would usually result in a decrease in their spending. Perhaps in the golden days of their retirement, these high-net-worth individuals were traveling the world and spending $200,000 year, but nursing homes in most parts of the country cost half of that. Because needing long-term care eliminates many other expenses, high-net-worth individuals don't need to carry insurance to protect against long-term-care expenses.

Everyone else, however, has quite a quandary. For those with a few hundred thousand dollars in assets, it is nearly impossible to afford adequate long-term care insurance. For those with a solid income and over $500,000 in assets, you may find yourself sandwiched between needing some insurance coverage and not wanting to spend so much on it that you derail your retirement savings plan.

Ultimately long-term care is the largest contingent risk for many people, and determining the appropriate course of action requires the assistance of a financial planner who can provide options to adequately address your personal risk without spending so much on coverage that you can't retire.

HEALTH INSURANCE

Doctors today have access to tools and treatment options that were unimaginable just a generation ago. Every day, researchers are finding ways to manage and treat diseases that even a decade before were deemed completely hopeless. The unfortunate by-product of this innovation is cost. Without health insurance, expenditures for all but the most routine office visits can quickly balloon beyond the means of most families. Health insurance is a must for all individuals.

If it is offered, the best option is a group insurance policy through your employer. Group policies tend to be the most cost-effective way to get coverage for several reasons. First, many employers subsidize the cost of coverage for their employees, so you don't have to pay the full cost of your policy. Second, the prices of these policies are based on the average characteristics of the group, so the cost of coverage tends to be lower than what an individual could get on the open market.

If your employer offers a flexible spending account (FSA) or health savings account (HSA), you should take advantage of these tools to help with the cost of medical expenses. With these accounts, you allocate a portion of your paycheck to be deposited into the account each month. You can then use these funds to pay for medical expenses as they are incurred, including copays, prescription costs, and other expenses not covered by your insurance policy.

With an FSA or HSA, the accounts are funded with pretax dollars from your paycheck, much like your 401(k). This has two benefits: you don't pay tax on the money going into your FSA or HSA, which can reduce your tax liability, and the withdrawals to pay for medical expenses aren't taxed either, saving you money on your medical expenses. You're saving money on both ends! For example, if you deposit $1,200 into your FSA account, all of it can be used to pay for a medical bill. If you didn't have an FSA and you were in the 25% tax bracket, you'd have to earn $1,600 pretax dollars to have the $1,200 needed to pay that same bill. One thing to keep in mind is that with an FSA, the money is "use it or lose it." Any funds left in the account at the end of the year expire, so you want to budget your savings accordingly.

If your employer offers a high-deductible health plan, it may offer an HSA as well. An HSA has the same basic features as an FSA, but the funds do not go away at the end of the year. Instead, they can be invested and grow over time. After you retire, you can use the funds to pay for medical expenses tax free. HSA plans are unique with this triple tax advantage:[27] your contributions reduce your taxable income, they grow tax-free, and distributions aren't subject to tax in retirement. Not too shabby! For this reason, the best way to use an HSA is to make the maximum contribution each year but not dip into it for any medical expenses.[28] Instead,

27   "Triple tax advantage" sounds like a really cool figure skating move rather than a really cool financial planning benefit.

28   It's crazy how Congress passes tax laws that encourage unexpected behavior.

you should pay out of pocket to preserve the assets in the plan for future expenses in retirement. If your cash flow won't allow that, you're probably better off using an FSA instead.

For those who can't get coverage through their employer, individual policies are available. When shopping for health insurance, people tend to be cost-conscious, but it's important to keep in mind a couple of factors when evaluating your options. The first is that risk dictates the cost of policies. To an insurance company, risk is measured by who has more money on the line when a claim is made. Insurance costs you more money when the insurance company takes on more of the risk. To lower the cost of insurance, you have to take on more of the risk. As the saying goes, you get what you pay for.

The second consideration is what *you* need from the policy. Do you have frequent doctors' appointments or take several medications? If so, the out-of-pocket costs associated with each plan will be important to you. Do you need to see specific doctors or specialists? If you do, you'll need to verify that your preferred hospitals or physicians accept that insurance to ensure you get the care you need.

For retirees, health insurance is often an expense they fail to consider when planning for retirement, particularly if they retire before becoming eligible for Medicare at age 65. For most early retirees, the best course of action is to remain on your previous employer's plan for up to 18 months after you retire. Depending on how early you retire, you may also need to obtain private health insurance to cover the gap between when the 18-month continuation period ends and Medicare starts.

Once you are on Medicare, certain copays and other expenses typically covered by traditional health insurance are now out-of-pocket expenses. For this reason, it's a good idea to enroll in a Medicare supplement plan that fills in the gaps. These types of plans can offer comprehensive coverage at a very reasonable cost, and they allow you to better control and plan for your health care expenditures in retirement.

Figure 6.1

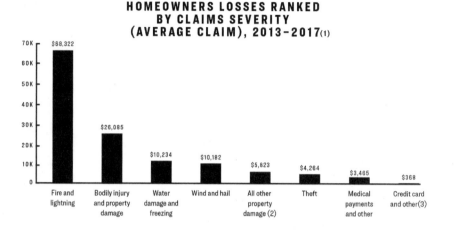

HOMEOWNERS LOSSES RANKED BY CLAIMS SEVERITY (AVERAGE CLAIM), 2013-2017(1)

(1) For homeowners' multiple peril policies (HO-2, HO-3, HO-5, and HE-7 for North Carolina). Excludes tenants and condominium owners policies. Accident Accident-year incurred losses, excluding loss adjustment expenses, (i.e., indemnity costs per accident year incurred claims). Excludes Alaska, Texas, and Puerto Rico.

(2) Includes vandalism and malicious mischief.

(3) Includes coverage for unauthorized use of various cards, forgery, counterfeit money and losses not other-wise classified.

"About 1 in 17 insured homes has a claim each year."

*INSURANCE INFORMATION INSTITUTE CALCULATIONS,

based on ISO®, a Verisk Analytics® business, data for

homeowners insurance claims from 2013–2017.

Homeowner's insurance protects you by covering damage to your home, but only within the limits of your policy. Sadly, most people don't know the limits of their policy until they make a claim. There are only a few of us who could afford to rebuild our dream home if it were destroyed by a fire, tornado, earthquake, or other natural disaster, but most would still elect to carry homeowner's insurance. The odds that we would experience the total destruction of our home is rare, but it does happen. Happily, because this is a rare occurrence, homeowner's insurance is inexpensive to purchase relative to the value of the property that is protected.

As with all other insurance, the first step is to determine the amount of protection you need, which in the insurance world is referred to as *dwelling coverage*. This requires you to evaluate the replacement value of your home, which is different from its market value. Your dwelling coverage should reflect what it would cost to rebuild your home from the ground up, using the same or similar materials. In some areas of the country, the cost of materials has continued to increase even though property values have remained level, so it's important to understand what current building costs are and ensure your dwelling coverage is set appropriately. Your insurance agent will have access to average costs in your area and is your best source of information for this calculation. In the case of high-value homes, an appraisal of the property may be required to determine the cost to rebuild.

It's important to note that your insurance company will fully cover damages to your home only if the amount of your dwelling coverage is at least 80% of the replacement value of your home. For example, let's say that one of the water pipes in your home bursts, causing $50,000 worth of damage. If the amount of dwelling coverage listed on your policy is $350,000 but your insurance carrier estimates the actual replacement value of your property is $500,000, even though the amount of dwelling coverage on your policy more than covers the $50,000 of damage, the insurance company will send you a check for only $43,750 (minus any deductible).[29] This is an eye-popping moment for many in this situation.

Many people are surprised to discover that their policies do not provide as much coverage as they think because of internal caps on how

---

29   The insurance company uses a ratio of the amount of coverage you actually have (in this example, 70% of the replacement value) compared to the amount of coverage that you should have (80% of the replacement value of your home). $350,000/$400,000 = 87.5%, so the company will cover 87.5% of the $50,000 claim, or $43,750.

certain types of damage are covered by the policy or payout limitations for valuable articles. For this reason, it often makes sense for high-net-worth individuals to work with specialty insurers that have products designed to protect high-value homes, rental properties, or other valuable or unique property (e.g., yachts, collectors' vehicles). Most policies also limit coverage on jewelry, furs, antiques, and other high-value items. If you are concerned about protecting the value of these items against loss, it's important that you speak with your insurance agent about adding coverage to your existing policy or, possibly, a separate valuable-articles policy.

Reducing Your Premium Today

Another important component of your homeowner's policy is your *deductible*, which is the dollar amount of any claim you are required to pay before your policy kicks in. I discussed self-insuring previously, which is simply the idea that you carry some—or all—of a risk yourself. With a homeowner's policy, one way you can self-insure is through your deductible.

Statistically, it makes the most financial sense to have a deductible in the range of about 1% of your home's replacement value (assuming your cash flow would allow you to make that payment and the premium savings are meaningful). As you carry more risk by having a higher deductible, your premium should decrease by enough to justify the money you would have to pay in the event of a claim.

The impact of changing deductibles can vary widely based on a number of factors, such as your personal claim history, the claim history in your area, the insurance company, and the age of your home. Because it is impossible to say for certain what the right deductible is for every person, a good rule of thumb is to look at a five-year break-even period, meaning you should save enough in annual premiums over five years to make up for the increased deductible. If you had a $1,000 deductible and you raise it to $2,500, you should only do so if your premium will go down by at least $300 per year, because you now have $1,500 more at risk.

Another aspect of your policy you should evaluate is your liability coverage. If you have an umbrella policy, and you probably should (more on that soon), the liability coverage on your home and auto policies should coordinate with the requirements of your umbrella policy. If you do not have an umbrella policy, the amount of liability coverage you need should be evaluated with your agent based on your specific situation.

Finally, depending on the part of the country in which your home is located, there are other coverage considerations, such as flood, earthquake, hurricane, or wind and hail coverages, which are best discussed with your agent to ensure you have the appropriate coverage.

AUTO INSURANCE

If I had asked people what they wanted,

they would have said faster horses.

HENRY FORD

If you own a car, you're legally required to purchase auto insurance to drive it on major roads. This ensures that if you cause an accident, you have sufficient resources to cover the resulting costs for which you are liable. Many people choose to purchase comprehensive or collision coverage, which provides additional protection for damage to your vehicle. Before you buy these additional coverages, take a minute to evaluate the associated deductibles. If your cash flow allows for it, a higher deductible could save you money in the long run. But if the car is driven by your teenage son, a lower deductible may be more appropriate to guard against the high likelihood that he'll get in an accident. In either case, just as with your homeowner's deductible, the decision to move to a higher deductible should always be evaluated based on the amount of premium savings realized.

As your car ages, it may also be appropriate to drop any comprehensive or collision coverages from the policy, also known as carrying *liability-only* coverage. We've all had a car worth about $1,000 at one point in our lives,[30] and there's no reason to insure it to the max.

As with your home, your liability coverage should match up with the requirements of your umbrella coverage. If you do not have an umbrella policy, your liability coverage depends on your personal situation and your agent's recommendation. When determining your liability coverage, it's important not to rely on the statutory minimum requirements imposed by most states. With the increasing costs of vehicles and medical care, it's easy to get into a situation where multiple vehicles are damaged (or multiple drivers are injured), which could push you to the limit of your insurance coverage and force you to pay the excess costs out of pocket.

Of special note are adult children who drive vehicles that you own and are covered under your insurance policy. When adults, who do not otherwise have a marriage-like relationship, co-mingle their assets, they can also co-mingle their liabilities. If an adult child causes an accident while driving a car you own and becomes subject to a lawsuit because of the accident, you may find your assets are at risk because you're the owner of the vehicle. Doesn't sound fair, does it? If you are in a position where you no longer provide any financial support for your children other than the insurance and vehicle he or she is driving, the safest way to avoid this potential risk is to transfer the ownership of the car to your child.[31] It will likely increase the premium for the car, but in most cases, paying the increased premium is well worth the reduced liability exposure. However, each situation is different and needs to be evaluated with your insurance agent.

30   I've had three!
31   Or tell them to take Uber.

UMBRELLA POLICY

*So many things happen for every event, and if you try to manipulate it, it
means you are struggling against the whole universe, and that's just silly.*

DEEPAK CHOPRA

An umbrella policy is just that: insurance that covers umbrellas. If you
own a high-quality umbrella, perhaps one with a picture of Paris on it or a
fun polka dot design, you should consider getting it insured. Just kidding.
Writing about insurance is making me delirious. Nonetheless, we are
almost done with risk management. Stay with me![32]

An umbrella policy is an excess-liability policy that covers you above
and beyond the liability limits of your home and auto policies. It's often
overlooked, yet can be the catch-all that keeps you protected from a number
of specific and highly risky situations. It covers all sorts of things that can
happen any time and for any reason, often unfolding in ways we couldn't
imagine. If you hit a pedestrian crossing the street or little Johnny's parents
sue you for an injury he incurred while jumping on your trampoline, these
are the times where an umbrella policy can cover your assets. We live in
an increasingly litigious society.[33] You can do everything in your power to
secure your financial independence, but none of that matters if you lose a
large and costly lawsuit. For this reason, it makes sense for many people
to purchase an umbrella policy. When you make this purchase, you are
getting the ability to access the team of attorneys who work for the insurance company in the hope that this team will settle any liability issues that
may come up.

While the odds of a liability issue arising that would require the
coverage of an umbrella policy are very low, it does happen, and in many

---

32   Look, let's just be candid with one another: risk management isn't the most fun part of personal
finance. I'm doing my best here!

33   I can practically hear you thinking, "No kidding, Captain Obvious!"

cases, it is the only event that can permanently derail someone who is already financially independent. Thankfully, umbrella policy premiums reflect these low odds and are inexpensive relative to the protection they provide. A good starting point for an umbrella policy is $1 million of coverage, but $2 million to $5 million (and in some cases, higher) may be appropriate, depending on your net worth. It is important to note that your umbrella policy coverage does not need to match your net worth dollar-for-dollar; the policy should be a carrot for settlement, not an entrée. Rather, you just need a high level of confidence that any suit brought against you would be settled under the policy limits. Your agent can provide guidance on the amount of protection appropriate for your situation relative to the cost of the coverage. Once you have a policy in place, you need to examine any homeowner's and auto policies to ensure that your liability coverages under those policies match with the requirements of your umbrella policy. Because an umbrella policy is an extended liability policy, any gaps in the coverage required by the umbrella policy and the actual coverage provided by your home or auto policy come out of your pocket. These policies must be evaluated in advance; otherwise, while you are busy paying attention to other things, like living your life and managing your portfolio, you could lose everything because of a small gap in coverage.[34]

---

34   Phew! We made it. Give yourself a pat on the back. You are seriously committed to doing all you can to improve your financial life. Or you really love insurance. I'm guessing it's the former. Nice job getting through the chapter. It gets much easier from here.

CHAPTER SEVEN

ESTATE PLANNING: YOUR FINANCIAL ENDGAME

> Someone is sitting in the shade today because someone planted a tree a long time ago.
>
> WARREN BUFFETT

If you've done everything laid out in the previous chapters, congratulations! You've made tremendous progress in addressing the key components of your financial plan. It's now time to look beyond how your plan will benefit you and to focus on who will benefit from your assets after you're gone because there's one constant in this world: no matter how successful your plan is, there will be a time when you're no longer around to enjoy it. And if you don't plan accordingly, the government will be waiting with outstretched hands.

Whether you want to simplify things for your family in the event of your death or you want to leave a legacy that benefits future generations, proper estate planning ensures that your wishes are met with the minimal amount of administrative costs and taxes. Planning for what happens after death doesn't make your death any more likely to happen. It does, however, help ensure the fulfillment of your goals and vision beyond your life span.

GETTING STARTED WITH THE BASICS

Procrastination is like a credit card: it's a lot of fun until you get the bill.

CHRISTOPHER PARKER

When I bring up estate planning, the first question I often get asked is, "When should I think about estate planning?" The answer is simple: if you don't have any documents in place, the time is *right now*. In the event of your death without the proper documents, you potentially yield important decisions (like who will receive your property and who will raise your children) to the probate courts. Do you want a stranger deciding how your family divides up your assets and who gets custody of your kids? I didn't think so. And even if you have documents completed, any significant changes to your personal or financial situation merit a review of your estate plan—for example:

- A new child
- Moving to another state
- A significant change in your net worth (e.g., receiving an inheritance, winning the lottery)
- Acquiring or selling a business
- Marriage or divorce (for you or one of your beneficiaries)
- A desire to change beneficiaries or how your assets will be distributed
- A death in the family
- Any changes in the estate or gift tax laws

Since "right now" isn't the answer most people are looking for, next come the excuses:

- *"I don't really have that much, so it's not important."* Even if your affairs are simple and clear-cut, you still need an estate plan. If it's not important, why do you work? Why do you invest? Why do you budget? You know it's important. You just don't want to deal with it.

- *"I have a lot, so it's going to be a hassle."* If you think it's going to be a hassle to set up the documents now, imagine what it will be like for your loved ones if you become incapacitated or die. If you have significant assets, you should begin your estate planning immediately.
- *"My personal situation is complicated."* If you think your situation is complicated and will involve tough decisions (e.g., problem children, children from multiple marriages, fourteen former spouses), imagine what it will be like to have your estate go through probate. The probate court will make all of those tough decisions for you without the benefit of your input.

The reality is that for a majority of individuals, only a few critical documents need to be in place to create a solid estate plan. It's not that complicated, so take an afternoon and put your affairs in order. Your family (and your financial advisor) will thank you.

There are four main issues you are addressing with your estate plan: incapacity planning, planning the distribution of assets at your passing, avoiding probate, and minimizing or eliminating estate taxes. That's it! For the ultra-affluent, asset protection may come into play as well. But for most people, only the four issues apply. Let's look at these in order.

ISSUE #1: INCAPACITY PLANNING

Let's imagine a client walked into my office and told me: "If I'm incapacitated, I really don't care who makes health care decisions for me, and I don't care who handles my financial affairs. If a choice has to be made, I think the government will make wise and sound decisions, so I'm happy to leave it up to them." This may seem like a ridiculous statement, but if you haven't done any incapacity planning, that's exactly what you're saying!

Incapacity is a legal term that means you are no longer capable of managing your own affairs.[35] It can be brought on by a medical issue at any age, such as being in a coma. Or it could be brought on by the natural aging process, when an individual has lost the mental acuity to make informed decisions about her own well-being. Regardless of the reason, in the event that you can no longer make financial and medical decisions for yourself, you either need a legal document granting another person the authority to make these decisions on your behalf, known as a *power of attorney*, or the probate court needs to appoint someone.

ISSUE #2: DISTRIBUTION OF ASSETS

The best things in life are free.

But you can keep 'em for the birds and bees.

Now give me money (that's what I want).

BERRY GORDY AND JANIE BRADFORD,

"Money (That's What I Want)"

When most people think of estate planning, they usually focus on the most obvious piece of the puzzle: specifying who will inherit their assets after they're gone. Just as with health care and financial decisions, if you don't formally express your wishes in advance, the probate court will make these decisions for you.

In the event there is not a clear allocation of assets, the door is open for financial turmoil and family conflict. Stories of heirs fighting with each

---

35   Note there is a difference between legal incapacity and simply bumbling your way through some things. I have tried to explain this to my wife who claims I am incapacitated every time I am responsible for traffic directions, our kids' carpool, or managing our social calendar.

other over their inheritances, siblings fighting about who gets Grandma's antique engagement ring, and relatives coming out of the woodwork to claim a piece of even a modest estate are far more common than we'd like to believe. In the event of a death, tensions are high and the one person who could set things straight is no longer there. That's why it's essential that you make your wishes clear and save your family the distress of figuring it out on their own. Think your kids love each other? They certainly might, but the real story unfolds long after you are gone, when every asset you have ever worked for is liquidated and divided among them. While most estates are distributed amicably, it's not uncommon for one of them to show up at the table singing the lyrics that opened this section.

If you die without an estate plan, you die *intestate*, and the intestacy rules of the state you live in will dictate who will handle your affairs and receive your assets. In other words, if you don't draft a plan, the state has one for you! Every state has its own line of succession rules that determine who is entitled to receive your property and in what proportion. The court will also appoint a guardian for any minor children. Often the time delay, administration, and costs associated with dying intestate reduce the amount of money the beneficiaries will ultimately receive (and they may not even be the same beneficiaries you had in mind!).

Wills

If you want to know the true character of a man,
share an inheritance with him.
BENJAMIN FRANKLIN

The most common document at the centerpiece of an estate plan is a will. You have four major decisions to make when drafting your will:

- *Choose your beneficiaries.* Your will is your chance to determine whom you want to inherit your property. Expressing your wishes in writing is not only important legally, but it helps eliminate disagreements among your family members about how property should be divided after you're gone.

- *Choose an executor.* An executor is the person you name in your will to pay your taxes and debts, collect and manage your property, and distribute your assets in accordance with your will. The executor will file your will with the court, manage your assets during the probate process, handle the day-to-day details of your estate (e.g., credit cards, car leases, mortgage), and set up an estate bank account, as well as many other duties. Many people choose a family member, a close friend, trust company, or a lawyer. Choose carefully!

- *Choose a guardian.* If you have minor children, you can specify a *guardian* in your will, which is the person (or people) you want to raise your children in the event of your death. You want to select a guardian who is interested in the job (and, you hope, shares your values and beliefs).[36] The guardian should also be old enough to handle the responsibility of child rearing but young enough to be around to raise your children. If your will does not name a guardian, anyone interested in taking care of your children can ask a judge for guardianship. The judge will then decide who will get to raise your children, using his or her judgment alone to decide what's in the "best interest of the child."

Outright Distributions Versus Testamentary Trusts

When determining how your assets will be distributed, you have the option to give the money or property directly to the beneficiary (called an *outright* distribution), or you can specify that the assets be held in a *trust* for the

36   Duh!

beneficiary. A trust is simply a legal arrangement to hold assets. A *testamentary trust* is a trust that is created and funded at death. Testamentary trusts can serve many functions, but the primary purpose is to specify how your money should be used for the benefit of your children or other beneficiaries after you die.

Let's say a married couple has $400,000 of assets that will be split equally between their two children, who are currently aged 19 and 20. If both parents pass today, each child will get $200,000 worth of assets with no restrictions—which begs the question: What would you have done with $200,000 at age 19 or 20? Instead, these parents include a provision in their will for a testamentary trust that would allow their children to receive distributions from both the principal amount of assets used to fund the trust and any income these assets generate for their health and education until they are 30 years old, at which point, the balance of the trust would be distributed to them.[37] The will would also name a *testamentary trustee*, which is the person or company you select to hold the money, invest it, and distribute it in accordance with the terms of your testamentary trust.

ISSUE #3: AVOIDING PROBATE

This is a court of law, young man, not a court of justice.

OLIVER WENDELL HOLMES JR.

If an estate has a certain amount of property, it will be subject to *probate* whether a will exists or not. The terms *probate* and *probate court* have come up several times already, but what is probate exactly? *Probate* is the process by which a court establishes the validity of a will (if there is one) and recognizes the executor specified in the document (if there is no will, the court will appoint an *administrator*). Probate also requires certain documents and

---

37   I am convinced 30 is the new 21.

reports to be filed in accordance with the law, facilitates the payment of taxes and debts, and distributes what is left under court supervision.[38] The main point of probate is to give your creditors time to seek payment of the money you owe them and give your executor time to collect any money owed to you. Probate also establishes titles to real estate if necessary.

You might say, "So my estate has to go through probate. What's so bad about that?" I'm glad you asked! There are a few aspects of probate that many people may wish to avoid:

- *Control of assets.* During the probate process, beneficiaries cannot sell your assets, and the executor can sell assets only with the permission of the court.
- *It's a lengthy process.* The probate process lasts approximately six months at a minimum but typically lasts at least a year. It can take even longer if matters become complicated by a will contest (where the validity of the will is challenged), business problems, or anything else unusual. The timing also varies greatly by state.
- *It can get expensive.* Again, this varies by state, but it's possible for costs to stretch into the tens or even *hundreds* of thousands of dollars for some estates undergoing probate.
- *It's subject to public record.* Do you ever wonder how the details of a celebrity's estate make it to the press? The answer is simple: anything in probate is a public record. Anyone can gain access to the court records detailing your personal financial affairs, plan of distribution, and list of assets. For many people, the thought of their most personal financial information being made public is dismaying. You may think that no one will be interested in your affairs, but some people actually "work" probate records,

---

38   What could possibly go wrong?

looking for people who are going to inherit substantial sums of money and they might be very interested in your beneficiaries. The court will also require a certain number of publications to broadcast your death in order to give your creditors a chance to make a claim against your estate.[39]

What's more, if you own property in multiple states, a separate probate proceeding, called *ancillary probate*, is usually necessary in *each* of those states. For example, if at your passing, you lived in New York City but you maintained a condo in Florida, your estate will need to go through separate probate proceedings in both New York and Florida.

Having a will can speed up the probate process, but it cannot eliminate it; in fact, having a will pretty much *guarantees* probate. Assuming you are not excited by the prospect of the probate process, here are some techniques you can use to avoid it:

- *Certain assets can bypass probate.* Any assets with a named beneficiary aren't subject to probate, such as life insurance policies and retirement accounts. It's important to note that if a beneficiary is not named on these assets or the primary beneficiary has passed away and no contingent beneficiary is named, the proceeds will be paid to your estate and subject to probate.
- *Some states allow additional assets to bypass probate.* This point varies widely. If you have a small estate, you may be able to avoid probate if the types of assets you own happen to be exempt in your state.
- *Joint ownership.* Assets owned in joint tenancy avoid probate at the first owner's death. However, relying on this method as

---

39   So other than the loss of control, length of time, high costs, and public nature, it's really not so bad.

a probate-avoidance technique poses several drawbacks. Joint ownership only *delays* probate until the surviving owner passes, and it does not eliminate probate if both owners pass simultaneously. There are also potential liability and tax issues introduced when retitling individual property to joint ownership.
- *Establish a revocable living trust.* A properly funded, revocable living trust *avoids probate of all assets.*

Revocable Living Trusts

I had an inheritance from my father, It was the moon and the sun. And though I roam all over the world, The spending of it's never done.

ERNEST HEMINGWAY, For Whom the Bell Tolls

Nearly a decade ago, I worked with an amazing couple in the Upper Midwest who had made their fortune in real estate. Their estate plan used wills instead of trusts because their attorney had advised them that probate was "no big deal" and trusts weren't necessary. Sadly, the husband passed away more than four years ago; today, his wife is *still* waiting to sell his assets as she waits for them to be processed in probate court. Probate is a messy process, even for smaller estates, and it's a completely optional process that can be easily avoided.

Many people understand the importance of a will; however, fewer people are as familiar with trusts and how they work. A common perception is that trusts are the exclusive domain of high-net-worth individuals. This couldn't be further from the truth. A revocable living trust can be the centerpiece of any estate plan, no matter the net worth of the individual, *and* help you avoid probate.

Simply put, a revocable living trust is a legal arrangement to hold assets. Because this trust is put in place during your lifetime, it is a *living* trust, and because the trust is written to allow you to terminate the arrangement at any time, it's *revocable.* So although the name looks intimidating, a revocable living trust is just "a legal arrangement created to hold your assets, which you can end at any point during your life."

What makes a revocable living trust (let's just call it a living trust) attractive is that any assets it owns are not subject to the probate process. During your lifetime, you can manage all of the assets owned by the living trust as if they weren't even in there—spend money out of living trust bank accounts and deduct the mortgage interest on your living trust–owned home on your tax return—because *you* are named both the grantor and trustee. If you become incapacitated, a *successor trustee* whom you name takes over the administration of the trust until you recover or is tasked with distributing the assets according to the terms of the living trust if you pass away.

A living trust works in the same way as a will: you can name your beneficiaries, create provisions for testamentary trusts, and earmark charitable contributions. I can hear you asking, "If a living trust is so great, why doesn't everyone have one? What's the catch?"

My response is simple: living trusts *are* great, if you ask me, and anyone with a good amount of assets subject to probate *should* have one. If you don't have any significant property that would be subject to probate—perhaps you rent your apartment, lease your car, and all of your other assets have named beneficiaries—there may not be much of an advantage in having a living trust; however, for many, the ease of estate planning with a living trust makes it an attractive option.

There are two main considerations when using a living trust versus creating a will: cost and paperwork. Drafting a living trust is more expensive than just drafting a will. The second is the paperwork involved with changing the ownership and beneficiaries of your assets. The terms of a living trust affect only the assets it controls, so in order for your living trust to control your house, your bank accounts, and your investment accounts, you have to change the ownership from your name to the name of your living trust. Retitling these assets is called *funding* the trust.

What happens if something doesn't get titled into the name of your living trust during your lifetime? To accompany your trust, you'll also need a *pour-over will*, a simple document that ensures any property outside your trust gets moved in at the time of your death. This really is more of a safety net to secure your assets; just like any other will, a pour-over will must be probated, so getting your assets retitled to your living trust is critical. There's not much point in going through the time and expense of creating a trust if the whole estate must be probated because the trust was never properly funded.

Two final thoughts on probate. I frequently hear, "Why should I care about probate? I'll be dead." First, a living trust helps you if you are incapacitated, since your successor trustee can manage your assets until you recover. Second, in the event of your death, your estate is no longer about you; it's about the survivors. Adding the complexity of court proceedings when your family is grieving your loss adds unnecessary stress at the worst possible time. Assets and accounts can be frozen until released by the courts, making it difficult to pay final expenses and run the household.

Another comment I hear frequently is, "I don't need a living trust. Probate is simple in my state." Some states have taken tremendous strides to simplify their probate proceedings, but you know what is even simpler? Not going through probate! I've personally worked with many clients who were assured by their attorneys that probate would be simple and easy, only to spend *years* resolving the estate. By the time you add up the time spent in court and potential headaches, a living trust can seem like a bargain.

Financial Affairs

If you become incapacitated, there is not only the medical aspect of your care to be concerned with, but also the administration of your affairs—for example, paying bills, signing legal documents, and interacting with other entities on your behalf (e.g., the phone company or your insurance provider). No one has the authorization to act on your behalf without a valid power of attorney document. If you become incapacitated without this document in place, your spouse, relatives, or friends may have to go before a judge to get the authority to handle your financial affairs.

If this is the case, a probate court public hearing will be required. Like any other court proceeding, it can take a significant amount of time, involve lawyers, and incur considerable expense. If the court does appoint an agent to handle your financial affairs, your right to handle these responsibilities will be taken away from you and given to someone you did not choose. Even after the court appoints an agent (which the court calls a *conservator*), there are other hassles to deal with. Your conservator will probably be required to post a bond, which serves as insurance in case the conservator steals or mishandles your property, and he or she will still need to get court approval for certain transactions. Sounds like fun right? Absolutely not. And there is simple way to sidestep that nonsense.

A *durable power of attorney for finances* is a document in which you designate someone to make financial decisions for you. A *durable* power of attorney differs from a regular power of attorney in that it remains valid even if you become incapacitated and cannot make decisions for yourself, which is usually the time when it is most needed. Many people give their financial agent broad power over their finances; however, you can give your agent as much power or as little power as you wish. For example, some people limit the ability of their financial agent to give themselves or others money and property.

Health Care

A few years ago, a client of mine called me in hysterics. I could barely understand what she was saying as she sobbed and relayed her story. Her daughter had been involved in a serious car accident while driving back from college and had been airlifted to a local hospital. Because her daughter was 19, my client no longer had an automatic legal right to make health care decisions on her daughter's behalf. Her daughter went on to make a full recovery, but my client was shaken by her own powerlessness in the situation. Ever since then, I have advised my clients to have a health care power of attorney in place not only for themselves but for their adult children as well.

Approximately 75% of Americans die in a hospital or other health care facility. If you do not complete the appropriate documents, your care will be left to the discretion of the providers treating you. In many of these cases, the physician is charged with preserving your life by whatever means possible. This may or may not be consistent with your belief system and personal wishes regarding end-of-life care. When a question arises about a serious procedure or life-prolonging technique, the doctor may not ask your close relatives for consent. And even if a doctor does consult a partner or relative, problems can arise if there are disagreements regarding the proper course of treatment. In some situations, these disagreements can wind up in probate court,[40] where a judge will be called on to decide who will choose the course of your treatment (the court calls this person your *guardian*). This can be costly, time-consuming, and emotionally painful for all involved.

Completing a few basic health care documents will allow you to exercise control over your health care options and help ensure that your wishes are carried out. A *durable power of attorney for health care*, also known as a *health care proxy*, gives another person the authority to make health care decisions for you if you are unable to do so. The person you name as your health care agent should be someone you trust to carry out your wishes. And keep in mind that every health care decision is not a life-or-death experience worthy of a *Grey's Anatomy* episode. A health care power of attorney can cover decisions like moving you from the care of one doctor

---

40   Yep, here we are in probate again. It's worse than the DMV.

to another or from one health care facility to another. The person you name as your agent can be a spouse, relative, or friend. It is important to recognize that the agent you select may have to deal with family members, physicians, and others who may be driven by their own beliefs and interests rather than yours. If you feel this may be the case, be certain that your agent will be capable of carrying out your wishes in the face of confrontation. It is also helpful to select a health care agent who lives nearby, if possible, as well as a backup agent in the event your first choice is unavailable or unwilling to act.

A living will (also known as a *declaration*, a *directive to physicians*, or a *health care directive*) sets out your wishes as to which procedures you would like provided or withheld in the event you are unable to communicate such wishes yourself. Once the doctor receives the living will, he or she must follow its instructions or transfer you to the care of another doctor who will. Unlike a health care power of attorney, in which you give someone else the power to make decisions for you, a living will allows you to make the decisions yourself. A living will covers matters such as organ donation, pain management, and the use of CPR (when patients don't want to be resuscitated, this is called a DNR—*do not resuscitate*). Make sure you get this done for you and your spouse (if you are married), and check to make sure your parents and adult children have them in place as well.

ISSUE #4: MINIMIZING OR ELIMINATING ESTATE TAXES

I want to leave my children enough that they feel they can
do *anything*, but not so much that they do *nothing*.
WARREN BUFFETT

For most people, estate tax planning is not and never will be a concern. The reason is that as of 2020, the IRS will allow you to give away $11.58

million over your lifetime (or at your death) without paying any taxes; this is referred to as your *lifetime exemption*. If you give away more than that amount when you're alive, you pay a *gift tax*, and if you give away more than that after you're dead, you pay an *estate tax*. Both gift and estate taxes are assessed at the same rate: 40%.

But wait, there's more. The IRS also allows you to give away $15,000 per year to whomever you choose without counting against this lifetime limit; this is referred to as your *annual exclusion*. This means that you could give away $15,000 per person to all of your friends and family every year and still give away $11.58 million when you die, paying no gift or estate taxes on any of it. That can add up to quite a sum.

Married couples can give each other an unlimited amount during their lives or at death, so estate tax is paid only at the death of the surviving spouse (and only if there is a taxable estate). Married couples also get to combine their lifetime exemption amounts, so estate taxes are only due if the combined net worth exceeds $23.16 million.

It should be noted that when we are talking about the estate tax exemption, we are talking about federal taxes. Some states impose their own taxes on property transfers at death, in addition to any estate taxes owed. This can capture many in the middle class, especially since life insurance is counted in these calculations.

Estate and gift tax laws are highly contentious and hotly debated in modern politics. Consequently, it's possible that the laws could change in such a way that your estate may become subject to taxes.[41] It's important to periodically review your estate plan with an attorney to make sure you understand how any new laws will apply to you and your estate.

The most straightforward way to reduce potential estate taxes is to spend your money.[42] The estate tax is based on how much is left in

41   They might have changed six times already by the time you read this.
42   I bet you weren't expecting that strategy, were you?

your estate when you die, so if you spend enough to reduce your total assets below the lifetime exemption amount (again, right now it's about $11 million), you could potentially avoid any estate taxes. Plus, if you use your resources to travel with family, spend time with friends, attend concerts, or otherwise pursue your passions, you're bound to get more enjoyment out of your money than your executor will get by writing a check to the IRS.

For many individuals with taxable estates, spending enough money to avoid taxes is not a reasonable solution to the problem and more sophisticated planning is required. Ultimately, estate tax planning comes down to strategies for making the most of three options: maximizing the value of your annual gifts, lifetime exclusion, and charitable giving. Many of these strategies can be used while you're alive, at your passing, or in some combination.

First, there are many ways to give gifts during your lifetime to reduce potential estate taxes:

- *Give up to $15,000 per year directly to your intended beneficiary* Married couples can split their gifts, so a spouse can give an additional $15,000 per year to the same person. If the beneficiary is married, you and your spouse can each give the beneficiaries spouse $15,000 per year as well. That means one married couple can give another married couple $60,000 per year with no gift tax consequences and without reducing your lifetime exemption.

- *Pay for college education expenses.* You can use your annual gift of $15,000 to fund a 529 college savings plan for a beneficiary. You may even qualify for a state income tax deduction for the gift as well. If the student is already attending college, tuition payments can be made directly to the school without counting against your annual gift limit for that beneficiary.

- *Pay for medical expenses.* You can pay for the medical expenses of friends or family members without counting against your annual gifting limit as long as the payments are made directly to the care provider.
- *Charitable giving.* Any money you give to charitable organizations does not count towards the gift tax or estate tax calculation.

Gifting directly to a beneficiary is straightforward (and generous!), but the downside is that you have no control over how the funds will be used. Just like the testamentary trust example, many individuals would like to place limitations on how their gifts are used. This is most effectively done using an *irrevocable trust*. Like a testamentary trust, an irrevocable trust allows you to decide how beneficiaries can use the funds, such as providing for their health, education, maintenance and support; however, unlike the revocable living trust, an irrevocable trust *cannot* be revoked, altered, or amended. Once the trust is established and funded, it's out of your control. In fact, you will name a trustee to make all decisions regarding how the funds are managed and distributed. So what's the benefit of an irrevocable trust? It's considered to be a separate legal entity, so the assets it contains are not subject to estate taxes when you pass away (you just have to set up and fund the trust more than three years before your death). Also, if the trust is established properly, the assets inside can be protected from creditors, divorce, legal judgments, and other risks.

Here are some ways to use an irrevocable trust:

- *Receiving annual gifts.* Rather than giving your annual gifts to your beneficiaries outright, it may make more sense to gift them to an irrevocable trust instead, particularly if a beneficiary is young or has difficulty managing money.

- *Holding life insurance.* Sheltering life insurance in irrevocable trusts is so common that this type of trust has its own acronym: the ILIT, which stands for *irrevocable life insurance trust.* Many people know that the proceeds from life insurance policies are not subject to income tax; however, it's not as widely known that the proceeds are subject to estate tax. To prevent a life insurance policy from being subject to estate tax, an existing policy can be transferred to an irrevocable trust, or, better yet, a new, permanent policy can be created within the trust. The trust is then funded with the cash needed to pay the premium payments for the life insurance policy, and when the insured individual(s) pass away, the death benefit is paid to the trust beneficiaries *without* being subject to estate tax or income tax. This is advantageous for high-net-worth individuals, not only because this arrangement provides a significant source of funds that are not subject to tax, but the annual premium payments to the trust to pay for the policy reduce the taxable estate as well. Let's say a 55-year-old married couple has an estate valued at $25 million, and they have three children. They want to use the full, annual gift exclusion for their children to pay the premium on a joint life insurance policy inside an irrevocable trust. Their annual premium will be $90,000 per year ($15,000 gift × 2 spouses × 3 children = $90,000), and based on their underwriting results, if they make this premium payment for the rest of their lives, they can get a permanent life insurance policy with a death benefit of approximately $13 million. If they both pass at age 85, they will have reduced their taxable estate by $2.7 million ($90,000 × 30 years = $2.7 million) by paying the premiums, and their children will share the $13 million proceeds from the insurance policy tax free. These funds are frequently used to provide the cash necessary to pay final expenses and settle large estates.

- *Use your lifetime exemption.* For ultra-high-net-worth clients, giving away their full lifetime exemption ($11.58 million if single or $23.16 million if married) to a beneficiary through an irrevocable trust helps protect that considerable gift and may save them a substantial amount of money. But why would anyone want to give away that much money today? Let's say that you have assets currently valued at $10 million, and you expect those assets to increase significantly in value over your lifetime and be subject to estate tax in the future. By giving the assets to the trust today, you pay no taxes on the transfer because it's less than your lifetime exemption amount. Fast-forward twenty years to your passing: the assets inside the trust are now valued at $20 million and pass to your beneficiaries tax free. If the $20 million had been passed directly to your beneficiaries at your death instead, it's likely that all or a significant portion of the inheritance would have been subject to estate tax.

Irrevocable trusts can be created ahead of time, like the ones described, or can be created at your passing. Remember our friend the testamentary trust? That's just an irrevocable trust created at death.[43] For example, in blended families where there are children from previous marriages, it's not uncommon for an irrevocable trust to be created at death that provides income to the surviving spouse but leaves the trust principal to the children of the deceased spouse.

Irrevocable trusts can also be used in more sophisticated planning strategies such as asset protection, providing financial support for family members with special needs, Medicaid planning, charitable gift planning, business sale planning, and much more. A financial planner or estate

---

43   You won't be around to make any changes to it, so that's about as irrevocable as it gets.

planning attorney can help you identify which strategies are most appropriate for you and your situation.

Charitable Planning

You make a living by what you get. You make a life by what you give.
WINSTON CHURCHILL

Americans are among the most generous people in the world, and for many investors, charitable planning has become a primary goal in their financial planning. Giving money away should be simple (and it often is), but for high-net-worth individuals wanting to leave a charitable legacy, there may more sophisticated options worth exploring.

Many high-net-worth individuals use their money to benefit society through routine annual gifting. However, many would like to continue their philanthropic impact after they've passed, creating a legacy of charitable giving carried on by future generations. With proper planning, these goals can be realized; the appropriate legal structures to receive the gifts can be created, these structures can be funded and managed, and administrators can be chosen to carry on the legacy after the investor is gone.

Let's look at some ways you can maximize your charitable giving and financial legacy:

- *Leave the right assets to charity.* Many times, individuals name their children as the beneficiary of their IRA or retirement account, and they specify a bequest of cash or other property to a charity. This isn't always the best solution. For example, if you leave a traditional IRA valued at $100,000 to your children and a piece of land valued at $100,000 to a charity, your children will have to pay taxes on the distributions from the IRA. If instead you leave the IRA to a charity and the land to your children, the charity can cash out the IRA with no tax consequences, and your children can sell the property at your death without paying taxes.[44]

- *Work with a donor-advised fund.* A *donor-advised fund* is a public charity that maintains an account funded by a charitable individual (that's you) and assists in distributing those assets to support the charities and causes most meaningful to that individual. The account can be funded during life or at death and is relatively inexpensive to manage. You simply fund your account, get an immediate income tax deduction, and direct when and where you want the money to go. This can be a great way for individuals with moderate, or even considerable, means to fund a charitable legacy.

- *Establish a private foundation.* For ultra-high-net-worth individuals, creating a private foundation can be a great way create a multigenerational charitable legacy. A *private foundation* is an independent charitable entity run by a staff who direct the operations of the foundation and the distribution of assets to support the charitable mission. There are more rules and regulations regarding the use and distribution of funds from a private foundation, which, along the salaries of the staff, can make it more expensive to operate, but family members can be paid a salary for their work with the foundation. A foundation can be funded with assets either during the individual's life or at their passing, and it can be administered by the individual and/or their descendants.

- Bonus tip for you high-net-worth individuals out there: if you plan to leave a substantial amount to charity on your passing, you should revisit your thinking. If instead you make that gift to a charity while you're living, even if it's to your own

---

44   A simple yet elegant solution if I do say so myself.

foundation or donor-advised fund, you will not only avoid the estate tax but also receive a significant income tax deduction as well.[45]

Developing a vision for the type of charitable legacy you wish to leave is essential in determining which tools and techniques are most appropriate for your portfolio. For example, let's say that your goal is to create a foundation capable of distributing $50,000 to charities starting this year and continuing indefinitely (adjusting for inflation each year). In order to accomplish this, you would need to endow your foundation with approximately $1 million today. Additionally, the foundation's portfolio would need to be structured to allow most of the annual distributions to be paid for by income and asset appreciation, preserving the principal for future generations. As with any other goal, you can design a portfolio to create a savings plan only after you've developed a framework for what you're trying to accomplish.

So far, we've discussed retirement planning, education planning, and charitable planning, but you may have noticed that we haven't yet picked any investments. However, we've covered the most important decisions—determining what you'd like to accomplish, developing a framework for saving, and identifying the best vehicles available to provide the highest probability of success—and laid the foundation for what's to come. Once your planning is complete, you can begin to construct portfolios designed to accomplish each goal.

If you want to become wealthy, start *acting* like the wealthy.[46] Begin with a clearly articulated vision, and then point your efforts purposefully in that direction.

---

45   This concludes our public service announcement for the 1%.

46   Note this does not mean talking with a snobbish voice or pouring champagne on the ground for fun.

GET IT DONE!

Just do it!

NIKE[47]

Whether your net worth is $100,000 or $100 million, you need an estate plan, and not just you. Your adult kids need an estate plan, your parents need an estate plan, and your neighbor down the street should probably have one too. This is the easiest part of pursuing financial freedom, and it takes just an hour or two with an estate planning attorney. Yet this is the planning aspect people are least likely to execute on. Why is that? There are three reasons people avoid estate planning: they don't like confronting their mortality, they don't want to make tough decisions,[48] and they think it's going to take a lot of time.

When it comes to an estate plan, having something in place is always better than nothing. Your documents can always be revised to adjust to changing circumstances, but having something in place will give you and your family peace of mind. It will allow you to rest easy, knowing that you've avoided undue stress, unnecessary taxes, and the specter of probate. And if you're fortunate enough to have a high net worth, and your goals include generational wealth or a charitable legacy, proper estate planning can help ensure that more of your hard-earned money goes to benefit the people and causes you care about rather than to the government. Even though it's hard to consider what things will be like when you're gone, it's worth the modest time and effort. Just do it!

---

47   Nike did not pay anything for this reference. Note to Nike's lawyers: we will accept swag bags. We know you do it with rappers already. This is sort of the same thing.

48   It only seems overwhelming, much like the menu at the Cheesecake Factory: it appears as if the options are endless, but after just a moment of reflection, the selections seem obvious, if only by process of elimination. You somehow get through it.

YOU DID IT!

Yes! You have an estate plan in place. Let's recap what other plans need to be in place before we start investing (or you have already begun investing, this will inform which additional investments we should choose):

- Net worth statement
- Retirement projections
- Other projections such as education
- Insurance projections
- Risk management plan, including life, disability, long-term care, health, home, auto and umbrella insurance (always getting exactly what your plan requires and nothing more)
- Estate plan, including necessary documents like trusts, wills, financial powers of attorney, health care powers of attorney, and charitable planning documents

These elements comprise the basics of financial planning and *must* be addressed to ensure your financial well-being. Think of these items as all the equipment you need to begin the climb; without them, you risk not making the summit. The plans set out in this chapter will allow you to chart your course and protect you and your family in case of an unforeseen danger.

At Creative Planning, we evaluate all of these considerations before selecting a single investment for our clients. We can't design the proper portfolio for you unless we understand where you are and where you want to go. It also doesn't matter how great an investor you become if you lose everything due to a disability, a death in the family, or some other event that wasn't accounted for in your overall plan. Is your advisor doing this for you? If not, you can move one item to the top of your planning list: find a new wealth manager.

PART III

THE TRAILHEAD

CHAPTER EIGHT

HOW MARKETS WORK

Risk comes from not knowing what you are doing.

WARREN BUFFETT

Since this is ostensibly a book about investing, let's start this chapter with a hot tip for a proven winner. This investment has earned about 10% per year over the last 88 years and has a consistent, upward trajectory. Check it out in Figure 8.1!

Figure 8.1

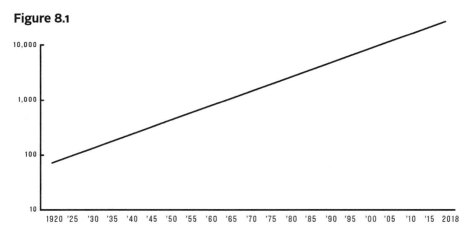

If you are like most other Americans, this sort of consistently lucrative return seems like a dream. Now what if I told you that this return was real? Well, it is real, and, even more intriguing, it's readily available to you.

What is this incredible, magical investment? It's something you've definitely heard of: the stock market.

THE MARKET TIMING PARADOX

There are a number of major studies comparing the performance of the average individual investor to that of the major indexes, like the S&P 500 or the Dow. These studies all show the individual investor lagging behind the index, with some suggesting the performance gap can be as much as several percentage points each year. So what keeps investors from earning the full market return?

One reason is that investors try to time the market. *Market timing* is the idea that there are times to be in the market and times to be out of it. On the surface, it sounds appealing. Why would you want to participate in the stock market when it's down? But as you will see, it's impossible to predict these ups and downs with any level of consistency. And as with many other things, consistency is the key to seeing the full returns.[49]

Let's get one thing straight right out of the box. Market timing doesn't work. It just doesn't. And don't tell me you don't market-time either. Have you ever said or thought anything like this:

> "I have cash on the sidelines, and I am just waiting for things to settle down."

> "I have a company bonus in my account, but I'll wait for a pullback."

> "I'll invest after [insert a lame excuse here—some options: the election, the new year, the market corrects, the debt crisis passes, Congress works out the budget, Brexit's figured out, etc.]."

---

49   Not to mention the tax and transaction costs. And sleepless nights.

All of that is market timing.

Why would anyone want to get in the way of an investment that has perpetually produced such fantastic returns? Market timing may seem like rational thinking, but it actually betrays an emotional outlook. Let me explain. The stock market doesn't go up in a completely straight line. Drawn as the returns actually happened, the graph looks like the one shown in Figure 8.2. With the benefit of hindsight, we can see that while the market dipped many times over the course of 88 years, it has been on a consistently upward trend. For those who live through those market dips, it can seem like the end of the world. Imagine the emotional turmoil of the Great Depression or the inertia and futility of inflation in the 1970s. In recent memory, the feeling of powerlessness seen during the panic of 2008 and the following recession is still very much with us. With investing, even a few weeks can seem like a lifetime, especially when the market is moving against you. And with the rise of the 24-hour news cycle and advances in smartphone technology, it's never been easier to obsess over micromovements in the market. Living through moments like these often causes people to think they should avoid downward trends in the market,

Figure 8.2

DOW JONES INDUSTRIAL AVERAGE, NONLINEAR RETURN

when downs are completely normal. This causes people to sell stocks and lose out on the benefits of long-term investing.

The first step to making informed decisions about your investments is to rid yourself of any misconceptions about the stock market. Recognizing what's normal in the market is likely to dramatically improve your investment performance. Side effects of this new awareness may include reduced stress levels, increased probability you will achieve your investment goals, and improved quality of life.

To be clear, there are many types of "markets." The previous graphs represent the Dow Jones Industrial Average, an index of 30 large US companies that allow us to review a 100-year history of finance. Today the more common index is the S&P 500, which is an index of 500 large US companies like Microsoft, Google, Procter & Gamble, and McDonald's. While there are thousands of stocks, the 500 of the largest companies make up about 80% of the entire US market capitalization, or the total value of the market.[50] This is because companies like McDonald's, in the S&P 500, are 50 to 100 times larger than companies like the Cheesecake Factory.[51]

Just so no one thinks I am being selective with my love of the most widely recognized stock market index, the premise of upward growth holds true for small US stocks, international stocks, and emerging markets stocks. The point is that all broad markets do the same thing: go up. A lot.

All of this looks pretty good, right? But to get these returns, you need to avoid making the first big mistake: market timing. This isn't as easy as it sounds because a lot of people might encourage you to make this mistake.

---

50   *Capitalization* is a fancy word for the total value. A company's share price, multiplied by the number of shares in existence is their market capitalization.

51   Clearly, market capitalization is not a reflection on whose desserts are better. More on that later. This is also my second Cheesecake Factory reference in this book so clearly I am due for a visit.

Figure 8.3

MARKET TIMER CAMPS

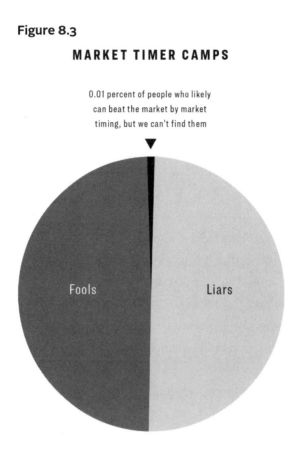

0.01 percent of people who likely
can beat the market by market
timing, but we can't find them

Fools   Liars

Among them are talking heads on TV, your friend at work, your brother-in-law who "jumped out right before the last crash,"[52] and the majority of the financial services industry.

This group of market timers can be divided into two camps, as illustrated in Figure 8.3:

This chart isn't scientific. I don't really know what percentage of market timers are foolish and what percentage are dishonest. I do believe though, that all market timers fall into one of these two camps, and both are dangerous. Let's take a look at both groups.

---

52   Lots of people also claim to have seen Big Foot and the Loch Ness Monster.

The Fools

What to do when the market goes down? Read the opinions
of the investment gurus who are quoted in the WSJ. And, as
you read, laugh. We all know that the pundits can't predict
short-term market movements. Yet there they are, desperately
trying to sound intelligent when they really haven't got a clue.

JONATHAN CLEMENTS

There are perfectly honest investors and advisors who really believe they
can time the market. They believe they know something no one else knows,
or they see something that no one else sees. They will often tell you they've
been right before, and maybe they were—once. These folks are like your
friend who tells you, "I killed it, baby!" when he returns from gambling
in Vegas but conveniently leaves out the five times he lost. These advisors
forget their bad decisions and remember their good ones. They may be well
intentioned, but ultimately they cause harm to their portfolios—and to the
portfolios of anyone who trusts them.

The Liars

There are three kinds of people who make market predictions. Those who
don't know, those who don't know what they don't know, and those who
know darn well they don't know but get big bucks for pretending to know.

BURTON MALKIEL[53]

Other financial advisors know that the market can't be timed, but their
living depends on convincing you that they can "get you out" with their
"downside protection." This is the easiest sale in the financial advisory

---

53   Burton Malkiel wrote a revolutionary book on this subject, *A Random Walk Down Wall Street*.
He is an advocate of using indexes at the core of a portfolio and active management in certain spaces
"around the edges," a philosophy I agree with.

world. Who doesn't love the idea of participating in the stock market's upward movements and avoiding all pullbacks? Sophisticated investors know that this isn't possible, but there will always be people who want to hear this. As long as those people exist, there will be tens of thousands of professionals at the ready to sell them snake oil.

I have also found that many financial advisors have been exposed to all the information they need to change their point of view away from market timing, but a big paycheck makes it hard to accept the facts. Much like a cult member finding definitive proof the cult's founder is a fraud, the financial advisor can find the reality too much to accept and simply remain delusional and ignorant. As Descartes said, "Man is incapable of understanding any argument that interferes with his revenue."[54]

WHY IS IT SO HARD TO BEAT THE MARKET?

In an efficient market, at any point in time, the actual price of a security will be a good estimate of its intrinsic value.

EUGENE FAMA

There are many reasons market timing doesn't work, and there are as many reasons investment managers will try to tell you that it does. Let's start by looking at the big picture, then work our way through the investment gurus and their actual results.

Efficient Markets

The *efficient market hypothesis*, developed by Nobel laureate Eugene Fama, argues that it's tough to beat the market because markets are efficient at incorporating all relevant information. Since a bunch of smart people (and

---

54   Also a very smart guy, but reading his books will teach you nothing about investing.

not-so-smart people) all know the same thing about any given stock or bond, it is impossible to have a sustainable edge that will allow you beat the market return.

What this means in practice is that because there are so many market participants—individuals, institutions, high-speed computers—all actively buying and selling the same securities all the time, new information is "priced in" almost instantaneously. Whenever something good or bad happens that changes the expected earning potential of a company or the market as a whole, the subsequent flurry of trading activity causes the price of the stock to move quickly up or down until it reaches a point where the stock price reflects the economic value of the new information. By the time the average investor gets around to placing a trade, any edge this person thought he or she had is long gone.

Where there appear to be patterns that the market can be beat, it is almost always due to an investor taking on additional risk. For example, there is evidence that small company stocks perform better than large company stocks over long periods of time, but this is very likely because they are riskier (more volatile).

The Masses Get It Wrong, Over and Over Again

We do not have an opinion about where the stock market, interest rates, or business activity will be a year from now. We've long felt the only value of stock forecasts is to make fortune tellers look good. We believe that short-term market forecasts are poison and should be kept locked up in a safe place, away from children and also from grown-ups who behave in the market like children.

WARREN BUFFETT

The average investor routinely and spectacularly mistimes the market. At the bottom of the 2001 bear market, investors moved a then-record amount of their money from stocks to cash. They then reentered the market when it recovered. At the bottom of the 2008–2009 crisis, investors broke the previous record for stock market withdrawals, moving their money to cash in new record numbers. This is herd mentality at its finest. Today the market is up several-fold from those low levels. Investors mistimed the market perfectly, breaking records both ways, both times at exactly the wrong time.

The Media Get It Wrong, Over and Over Again

He who predicts the future lies, even if he tells the truth.

ARABIAN PROVERB

Typical investors get their financial information from the media. It's important to note that the total value of this media-provided information regarding market direction calls is zero. Actually, it is less than zero because if you follow the guidance of the media on market calls, you are likely going to create a negative, rather than a neutral, result.

Prognosticators in the media are eager to give you big, bold market calls. I have been on several national business channels, including CNBC and FOX Business. Prior to the show, the producer often asks me for my thoughts on "where the market is going" and is disappointed when I answer that over the short run, "I don't know." One national cable network even branded me "The Time Machine" advisor because I kept prefacing my advice by saying I had no idea what would happen in the short run but was very confident about the long run.[55]

Financial advisors find it lucrative to push the idea of market timing, and news outlets don't challenge them because they gain more viewers when their guests make wild market predictions.

Let's take a quick look at just exactly how unwise it is to follow the lead of pundits in the media!

---

55   The graphics were quite amusing with my head sticking outside of a time machine that looked mainly like an old-school phone booth. My brother-in-law will never let me forget it.

Economists Get It Wrong, Over and Over Again

Forecasts may tell you a great deal about the forecaster,

but they tell you nothing about the future.

WARREN BUFFETT

Economists have shown no ability to predict the direction of the economy. There are simply too many variables, many known and some unknown, for anyone to do so with any sort of accuracy. History provides us with two great anecdotes to this point.

On October 15, 1929, Irving Fisher, whom Milton Friedman declared the "greatest economist the United States has ever produced," asserted that "stock prices have reached what looks like a permanently high plateau." The following week, the market crashed, taking us into the Great Depression and beginning a free fall that would cause the Dow to lose 88% of its value. It would be nearly 80 years before another stock market would fall as quickly or steeply. And of course, in *that* case, there was another high-profile economist making a bold prediction just prior to the turmoil. On January 10, 2008, Ben Bernanke stated, "The Federal Reserve is currently not forecasting a recession."[56] The economy didn't listen, and a few months later, it slid into the worst recession since the Great Depression, taking the stock market down more than 50% along the way.

"Okay," I hear you thinking, "So those two guys weren't very good at predicting the market, but that doesn't mean there aren't others who get it right!" Well, thanks for bringing that point up. Let's take a look at the entire field of economic forecasters who make strong predictions to see how those prediction tend to shake out.

---

56   Now ponder this for a moment. The Federal Reserve is arguably run by the best economic team on Earth. If they can't predict what is going to happen and they control interest rates, which drive at least part of what happens, how are you, your friend, or your financial advisor going to predict what happens?

Figure 8.4

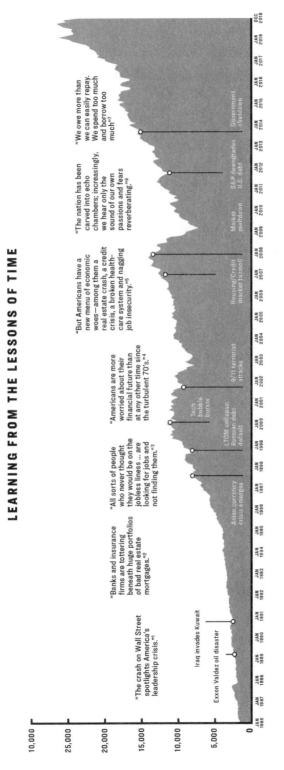

LEARNING FROM THE LESSONS OF TIME

"The crash on Wall Street spotlights America's leadership crisis."[1]

"Banks and insurance firms are tottering beneath huge portfolios of bad real estate mortgages."[2]

"All sorts of people who never thought they would be on the jobless lines ... are looking for jobs and not finding them."[3]

"Americans are more worried about their financial future than at any other time since the turbulent 70's."[4]

"But Americans have a new menu of economic woes—among them a real estate crash, a credit crisis, a broken health-care system and nagging job insecurity."[5]

"The nation has been carved into echo chambers; increasingly, we hear only the sound of our own passions and fears reverberating."[6]

"We owe more than we can easily repay. We spend too much and borrow too much."[7]

Exxon Valdez oil disaster

Iraq invades Kuwait

Asian currency crisis emerges

LTCM collapse, Russian debt default

Tech bubble bursts

9/11 terrorist attacks

Housing/Credit market turmoil

Market meltdown

S&P downgrades U.S. debt

Government shutdown

JAN 1986 JAN 1987 JAN 1988 JAN 1989 JAN 1990 JAN 1991 JAN 1992 JAN 1993 JAN 1994 JAN 1995 JAN 1996 JAN 1997 JAN 1998 JAN 1999 JAN 2000 JAN 2001 JAN 2002 JAN 2003 JAN 2004 JAN 2005 JAN 2006 JAN 2007 JAN 2008 JAN 2009 JAN 2010 JAN 2011 JAN 2012 JAN 2013 JAN 2014 JAN 2015 JAN 2016 JAN 2017 JAN 2018 DEC 2018

0 5,000 10,000 15,000 20,000 25,000 10,000

Fortunately, I didn't need to spend time researching to figure this out. Economists Jerker Denrell and Christina Fang compiled all the predictions in the *Wall Street Journal's* Survey of Economic Forecasts spanning July 2002 to 2005. They then narrowed their search to isolate the group of economists who had proven to be the most successful at predicting unlikely outcomes. To do this, they defined an "extreme" prediction as one in which the economist's outlook was either 20% higher or 20% lower than the average prediction.

Denrell and Fang then looked at the other predictions of this group and found that these economists, the ones with the best success rate at predicting "extreme" events, actually had a worse record overall. In other words, an economist who makes a crazy prediction is likely to hit a home run every now and then, but even more likely to strike out far more than normal. Is this the type of person you want to get investment advice from? Here's the deal: *The more certain a forecaster is of his or her prediction, the less likely this person is to be right and the more likely the prediction is a derivative of showmanship.* When it comes to investing, the bolder the prediction is, the less valid the source. If you care about your financial well-being, the data strongly suggest you would be far better off ignoring them. Joe Stiglitz, a Nobel Prize-winning economist,[57] has said that economists get it right "about 3 or 4 times out of 10". With those odds, I'll pass. You should too.[58]

---

57   Here we go again with the Nobel Prize winners.

58   Or anytime you hear a bold stock market or economic prediction, just add the words, "or not" to the end of it!

Investment Managers Get It Wrong, Over and Over Again

Sure it would be great to get out of the stock market at the high
and back in at the low, but in 55 years in the business, I not
only have never met anybody that knew how to do it, I've never
met anybody who had met anybody that knew how to do it.

JOHN BOGLE

There are thousands of financial advisors claiming to have "market indicators" that help them time the market. But as Don Phillips, the managing director of Morningstar, said, "I can't point to any mutual fund anywhere in the world that's produced a superior long-term record using market timing as its main investment criterion". I find this to be a compelling statement. If you're betting your life's work on market timing, and the guy who runs the firm that is best known for measuring the performance of funds has never seen it work well, perhaps it's advice worth listening to!

The bottom line is this: there is no evidence that investment managers can time the market effectively and repeatedly. The odds of getting it right over time are extremely low, and only fools would play such a game with their life's savings. Even bigger fools would pay someone else to gamble with their money this way. If you saw a gambler with a huge stack of chips on a winning streak, would you assume that this person will always keep winning? Like Vegas, the odds are so stacked against the market timer that any long-term outcome other than failure, whether it be modest or catastrophic, is rarely avoidable.[59] A word of advice: if you are meeting with a financial advisor who says she can move your money to cash before a downturn, look elsewhere.

---

59   Rule #1 of investing: Avoid colossal failure. Colossal failure is bad.

Newsletters Get It Wrong, Over and Over Again

The only way to make money with a newsletter is by selling one.

MALCOLM FORBES

Tens of thousands of Americans subscribe to market timing newsletters. These Americans are paying a fee and spending a lot of time reading these updates, only to increase their chances of underperforming the market.

In 1994, John Graham and Campbell Harvey, analyzing data provided by Mark Hulbert,[60] conducted what many consider to be the most comprehensive study on the ability of newsletters to predict the market. They looked at over 15,000 market timing predictions from 237 newsletters over 13 years. The conclusion was overwhelming: 75% of the newsletters produced *negative* abnormal returns. Following the advice of most of these letters created negative performance! The once-famous *Granville Market Letter* produced an average negative annual return of -5.4%. The *Elliot Wave Theorist* letter, a favorite of doomsday fanatics, produced a negative annual return of -14.8%.[61] During the same time frame, the S&P 500 earned 15.9% per year, outperforming a full three-quarters of the newsletters.

You might ask, "What about the 25% that did match or beat the market?" The study actually overstates the performance of these newsletters because getting in and out of the market is expensive. Had the study accounted for fees, transaction costs, and taxes, the underperformance would have been even worse! Finally, the authors took their study further, checking to see if winners keep on winning. The conclusion is clear: "Winners rarely win again." The authors are harsh and definitive in the conclusion of their study: "There is no evidence that the letters can time the market."

---

60   Mark Hulbert runs a service that tracks newsletter predictions and performance.

61   Isn't it interesting how the doomsday fanatics end up losing their money despite their desperate attempts to save it?

Mark Hulbert's own research shows that the few newsletters that do outperform the market in any given year are not the same in future years. And further data show that not a single market timing newsletter has beaten the market over the long run!

WHAT SMART INVESTORS HAVE TO SAY ON MARKET TIMING

The market timing Hall of Fame is an empty room.

JANE BRYANT QUINN

Of the great investors of all time, none advocate market timing. J. P. Morgan, who dominated finance in the nineteenth century, was asked by a young investor what the market would do. Morgan replied, "It will fluctuate, young man. It will fluctuate." Benjamin Graham, the father of modern investing, advocated against market timing, saying in 1976, "If I have learned anything over these 60 years on Wall Street, it is that people do not succeed in forecasting what is going to happen in the stock market." John Bogle, the founder of Vanguard, the largest fund company in the world, said repeatedly that he found market timing impossible and futile. Warren Buffett, who is peerless in modern-day investing, has mocked market timing repeatedly, citing it as the stupidest thing investors can do. He has many thoughts on the subject including, "Forecasters exist to make fortune-tellers look good," and more to the point, "I have *never* met a man that can time the market."

So what is an investor to do? After all, economists, prognosticators, advisors, and newsletters garner media attention because everyone wants an edge to help them get ahead. If you can't rely on any of these gurus to help you, how can you protect yourself? The answer is by having a solid plan for your investments, which makes you prepared for market volatility before it even happens. I keep an umbrella in my car because I know at some point it will be raining, and I'll need it. When investing in the markets and constructing a portfolio, we need to expect a little rain from time to time as well; in the case of the markets, this means everything from corrections (a "summer shower") to bear markets (a "torrential downpour").

MARKET CORRECTIONS

You get recessions, you have stock market declines. If you don't understand that's going to happen, then you're not ready. You won't do well in markets.

PETER LYNCH

It has been said that only two things are guaranteed in this world: death and taxes. I'd argue they missed one: *stock market corrections*. How can I make such a bold prediction? I can make it because stock market corrections happen all the time. Predicting one is like predicting it will rain again in Seattle.

What exactly is a *correction*? A correction is a market drop of 10% or more. If the market drops by 20%, a correction becomes a *bear market*. How often does a correction occur? Since 1900, corrections have happened approximately every year on average, so it's important that you understand them and feel comfortable riding them out. If you are 50 years old, you can look forward to experiencing about another 35 or more!

Some might say, "Why not get out of the market once it drops 10%, but before it turns into a bear market?" The reason is that most corrections never achieve bear market status. Historically, corrections average a drop of 13.5%, most last less than two months, and the average length clocks in at just 54 days. Fewer than one out of five corrections actually turns into a bear market. Said another way, the market shrugs off a correction 80% of the time.

With this in mind, selling your positions and going to cash when a correction occurs doesn't make sense. Most of the time, you would be moving to cash right before the bottom. You could do incredible damage to your portfolio if you sold out during even just a few corrections. We know that corrections happen all the time, we know that most corrections do not turn into bear markets, and we also know that the markets have recovered from every single correction in history. It seems totally absurd to panic and go to cash.

As with market timing, some financial advisors try to predict market corrections. Sometimes there's a reason the markets correct, and sometimes there's not; it is, however, enjoyable to watch market pundits make fools of themselves trying to *predict* a correction. Figure 8.5 illustrates both how stubborn the market can be and how professionals fail to predict market corrections.

Figure 8.5

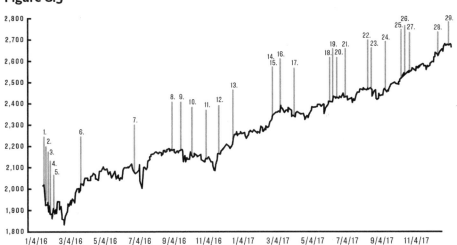

Each of the following numbers corresponds to the date of the prediction in the graph:

1. "George Soros: It's the 2008 Crisis All Over Again," Matt Clinch, CNBC, January 7, 2016
2. "Is 2016 the Year When the World Tumbles Back into Economic Crisis?" Larry Elliott, *Guardian*, January 9, 2016

3. "Sell Everything Ahead of Stock Market Crash, Say RBS Economists," Nick Fletcher, *Guardian*, January 12, 2016

4. "Here Comes the Biggest Stock Market Crash in a Generation," Chris Matthews, *Fortune*, January 13, 2016

5. "These Are Classic Signs of a Bear Market," Amanda Diaz, *CNBC*, January 20, 2016

6. "The First Big Crash Is Likely Just Ahead," Harry Dent, *Economy & Markets*, March 14, 2016

7. "Clear Evidence That a New Global Financial Crisis Has Already Begun," Michael T. Snyder, *Seeking Alpha*, June 17, 2016

8. "Citigroup: A Trump Victory in November Could Cause a Global Recession," Luke Kawa, *Bloomberg*, August 25, 2016

9. "Stocks Are Inching Closer to the Second Correction of 2016," Michael A. Gayed, *MarketWatch*, September 7, 2016 (15)

10. "Reasons for a 2016 Stock Market Crash," *Money Morning*, September 26, 2016

11. "Economists: A Trump Win Would Tank the Markets," Ben White, *Politico*, October 21, 2016

12. "We Are Very Probably Looking at a Global Recession with No End in Sight," Paul Krugman, *New York Times*, November 8, 2016

13. "Economist Harry Dent Predicts 'Once in a Lifetime' Market Crash, Says Dow Could Plunge 17,000 points," Stephanie Landsman, *CNBC.com*, December 10, 2016

14. "Now Might Be the Time to Sell Your Stocks," Laurence Kotlikoff, *Seattle Times*, February 12, 2017

15. "4 Steps to Protect Your Portfolio from the Looming Market Correction," John Persinos, *Street*, February 18, 2017

16. "The US Stock Market Correction Could Trigger Recession," Alessandro Bruno, *Lombardi Letter*, March 1, 2017

17. "Three Key Indicators Are Saying That a Stock Market Crash in 2017 Is a Real Possibility," Michael Lombardi, *Lombardi Letter*, March 28, 2017

18. "Critical Warning from Rogue Economist Harry Dent: 'This Is Just the Beginning of a Nightmare Scenario as Dow Crashes to 6,000,'" Laura Clinton, *Economy & Markets*, May 30, 2017

19. "Why a Market Crash in 2017 Is More Likely Than You Think," *Money Morning*, June 2, 2017

20. "The Worst Crash in Our Lifetime Is Coming," Jim Rogers, interview with Henry Blodget, *Business Insider*, June 9, 2017

21. "It's Going to End 'Extremely Badly,' with Stocks Set to Plummet 40% or More, Warns Marc 'Dr. Doom' Faber," Stephanie Landsman, *CNBC*, June 24, 2017

22. "Three Reasons a Stock-Market Correction Is Coming in Late Summer or Early Fall," Howard Gold, *MarketWatch*, August 4, 2017

23. "The Stock Market Is Due for a Significant Correction," Mark Zandi, *Fortune*, August 10, 2017

24. "Brace Yourself for a Market Correction in Two Months," Silvia Amaro, *CNBC*, September 5, 2017

25. "4 Reasons We Could Have Another October Stock Market Crash," David Yoe Williams, *Street*, October 2, 2017

26. "Stock Market Crash WARNING: Black Monday Is Coming Again," Lana Clements, *Express*, October 7, 2017

27. "Morgan Stanley: A Stock Market Correction Is Looking 'More Likely,'" Joe Ciolli, *Business Insider*, October 17, 2017

28. "Chance of US stock market correction now at 70 percent: Vanguard Group," Eric Rosenbaum, *CNBC*, November 29, 2017

29. "Stock Market Correction Is Imminent," Atlas Investor, *Seeking Alpha*, December 19, 2017

The takeaway? Corrections happen all the time, most do not turn into bear markets, and the markets have recovered from every single correction in history. So don't panic, and don't cash out.

Figure 8.6

S&P 500 INTRA-YEAR DECLINES VS. CALENDAR YEAR RETURNS
DESPITE AVERAGE INTRA-YEAR DROPS OF 13.9%,
ANNUAL RETURNS POSITIVE IN 29 OF 39 YEARS

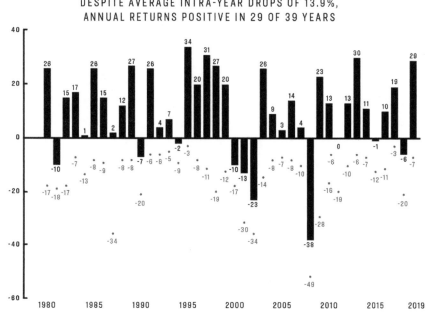

BEAR MARKETS

*If you have trouble imagining a 20% loss in
the stock market, you shouldn't be in stocks.*

JOHN BOGLE

Bear markets don't happen nearly as often as corrections, but they also happen all the time. A bear market is defined as a market drop of 20% or more, and they typically occur every three to five years. All told, there have been 35 bear markets since 1900, with only 15 since 1946.[62] The four

---

62   Those who clamor for the "good old days" of market stability don't know their history. These are the same people who would love to go back to the good old days without heating, air conditioning, indoor plumbing, phones, the Internet, and advanced health care!

most recent bear markets have reflected a number of crises, including a terrorist event, an economic meltdown, a European debt crisis, the obligatory oil crisis that happens every decade or so[63], and a global pandemic. The average decline in a bear market is 33%, and more than a third of bear markets drop over 40%. On average, a bear market lasts close to a year, with nearly all of them lasting between 8 and 24 months. Bear markets are frequent, and equally as frequently, they go away!

IT'S EXACTLY THE SAME, BUT DIFFERENT

The four most dangerous words in investing are "This time it's different."

JOHN TEMPLETON

If we know that every bear market eventually becomes a bull market, then why do people panic and go to cash? The answer is that while bear markets tend to be caused by an event that creates an immediate and dramatic shock to the fundamentals of the market, the events that create these shocks tend not to be the same.

What makes a free market economy work is the ability of *suppliers* to freely move their goods and services to meet the *demand* of those who need them. When these two forces are in balance, the market is said to be in *equilibrium*.[64] These same forces help determine the price of stocks and pretty much anything else that is bought and sold around the globe.

In a bear market, these normal market forces experience a significant disruption. For example, after 9/11 the markets plummeted into well below today's levels because of a disruption in demand. Before the drop ended, the S&P 500 had cratered 44%, with the NASDAQ down 78%. In the

---

63   So everyone can complain about oil prices being too low for a while and then go back to complaining that they are too high

64   Here ends the world's shortest economics lecture.

Figure 8.7

BEAR MARKETS: HOW OFTEN, HOW LONG, AND HOW SEVERE?

YEAR(S)	NUMBER OF DAYS IN LENGTH	% DECLINE IN S&P 500
1946–1947	353	-23.2%
1956–1957	564	-19.4%
1961–1962	195	-27.1%
1966	240	-25.2%
1968–1970	543	-35.9%
1973–1974	694	-45.1%
1976–1978	525	-26.6%
1981–1982	472	-24.1%
1987	101	-33.5%
1990	87	-21.2%
1998	45	-19.3%
2000–2001	546	-36.8%
2002	200	-32.0%
2007–2009	515	-57.6%

days, weeks and months following the terrorist event, factories, businesses and services remained open and operating all over the world. The issue certainly wasn't a lack of supply. The problem was that everyone stayed cooped up in their homes, reluctant to go about doing things that make an economy go, like buying things. Americans wondered if there would be other terrorist events to follow, if the government could put measures in place to prevent them from happening, and how long it would take to feel generally safe. Over time, people did start to return to normalcy, demand resumed, and the markets fully recovered, moving on to new highs.

The 2008 and 2009 financial crisis was the opposite. We all know the story: the big banks were reckless with their own money and their investors' money and before it was over, the financial system became paralyzed because of a lack of supply. The lending world had frozen. No one could get or maintain a loan to do nearly anything. Without a supply of funds, businesses began to fail, contracting the supply of all sorts of things. At the same time, Americans felt less wealthy, and were consumed with a healthy dose of fear. That combination resulted in Americans not wanting to buy anything until they felt secure. When the market bottomed on March 9th, 2009, it was down 53% from its high. In this case, the crisis was eventually resolved by the federal government backing up banks (taking care of the supply side) and giving consumers tax breaks, lowering the cost of borrowing and providing many other financial incentives to consumers. That combination, along with other measures, finally stabilized the system and incentivized individuals to spend money (taking care of the demand side). Over time, people did start to return to normalcy and the markets fully recovered, moving on to new highs.

In early January 2020, the world learned of a novel coronavirus, soon to be known as COVID-19, presenting itself as form of pneumonia that was not only highly contagious, but it had the ability to quickly turn deadly. Within months, the disease had spread across the globe, with over 23 million confirmed cases and 800,000 deaths worldwide.

Stock markets around the globe dropped by over 30% in less than a month as each day brought news of more infections, deaths, business closures and quarantines.

In this case, the market was reacting to shocks in both supply *and* demand. Even before quarantines were ordered, people began staying at home and avoiding large public gatherings—like movie theaters, shopping malls, or sporting events—to reduce the risk of infection. Demand for goods and services had been interrupted. At the same time, factories and stores began shuttering to help control the spread of disease. Travel restrictions shut down flights, cruises, hotels and theme parks. The supply of goods and services had been interrupted. As the weeks continued, uncertainty around how long these disruptions would last, and how long the recovery would take, fueled additional drops.

At the same time, we began to witness something else. The government began to implement drastic and novel approaches to supporting the economy. Individuals began practicing social distancing while working to keep essential services operating. Doctors and researchers began developing and improving treatment options, and gradually, the outlook began to improve. Slowly but surely, a "bridge" was being built between the previous bull market and future prosperity.

But those who know their market history understand this cycle. We've experienced this with other bear markets throughout history. Those of us who lived through any of the major market downturns vividly recall the initial widespread fear and uncertainty that ultimately gave way to a full recovery and even greater highs.

Because each major drop that causes a bear market is motivated by a different story, investors panic, believing that "this time is different." Although the story behind each bear market may be different—be it a computer-driven crash, a tech bubble, a terrorist event and war, a liquidity crisis, or a global disease outbreak—the result is always the same: the economy finds a way to forge ahead.

The next time we encounter a bear market, remind yourself of everything we've endured in the past 80 years: World War II (1940s), the Vietnam War (1960s/70s), hyperinflation (1970s/1980s), the commodity crisis (1970s/1980s), the real estate and banking collapse (1980s), the emerging markets crisis (1980s), the "flash crash" (1987), the Asian contagion crisis (1990s), the tech bubble bursting (2000), the 9/11 attacks and subsequent wars in Afghanistan and Iraq (2001), and the liquidity crisis (2008).[65] If the economy has survived all of this, it can get through the next bear market too. And those are just the big examples. Countless mini-crises pop up from time to time, inciting prognosticators to predict a bear market, whether it is a credit downgrade of the United States, a budget debate, an election, or whatever happens to be on the news cycle of the day. In December 2018, US stocks dropped 19.8% from their high, almost touching bear market territory, over concerns about a breakdown in tariff talks with China and rising interest rates.

Although a bear market is inevitable, it's not predictable. As with market corrections, no one is able to consistently and repeatedly predict the timing of a bear market.

It's important to note that in order to take advantage of bear markets, you need to know when to get out, when to get back in, and then do it repeatedly. Good luck finding the guy who has done that. He doesn't exist. He's an urban legend.[66] You want to believe that he exists, and for a while you believe he does exist. Then there comes a point where you know enough to know that he doesn't exist, but you can't admit it yourself. And then finally, maybe you will accept it. It doesn't help that there are a lot of people running around pretending to be the guy you want so badly to believe in.

---

65 Note that the United States and its economy have also survived parachute pants, knee-high socks (twice), neon baseball caps, and the Kardashians. Literally nothing can derail our progress.

66 He lives in La-La Land with the Tooth Fairy and the Easter Bunny. The only difference is that we eventually are mature enough to realize the latter two aren't real.

Figure 8.8

FROM BEAR TO BULL

YEAR(S)	NEXT 12 MONTHS (S&P 500)
June 13, 1949	42.07%
October 22, 1957	31.02%
June 26, 1962	32.66%
May 26, 1970	43.73%
October 3, 1974	37.96%
August 12, 1982	59.40%
December 4, 1987	22.40%
September 21, 2001	-12.50%
July 23, 2002	17.94%
March 9, 2009	69.49%

I hear you saying, "But what about [insert name of economist/trader/ crackpot] who was on TV the other day talking about how they predicted the crash?" The thing with many of these people is that they are always predicting something bad will happen, and eventually they're right, just like a broken clock is right twice per day. Unfortunately, you've got a better chance of getting the correct time from a broken clock than you do getting correct market timing advice from an investment guru on TV.

WHEN BEAR MARKETS TURN, THEY MAKE
PEOPLE ON THE SIDELINES LOOK SILLY

The idea that a bell rings to signal when investors should

get into or out of the stock market is simply not credible.

I do not know of anybody who has done it successfully

and consistently. I don't even know anybody who knows

anybody who has done it successfully and consistently.

JOHN BOGLE

I hope by now you agree that it's not possible to repeatedly and successfully get in and out of the stock market. However, you might be thinking,
"I'll at least go to cash until things settle down, and then I'll jump back
in, only missing a small part of the recovery." I'm afraid this won't work
either! No one gets an email one morning saying that the bull market is
starting. Instead, markets tend to have a few false starts and then they
turn like a rocket, recovering swiftly and decisively (and leaving the
market-timing folks behind in a cloud of dust). Figure 8.8 illustrates this
point clearly.

VOLATILITY HAPPENS

Our stay-put behavior reflects our view that the stock market serves as a

relocation center at which money is moved from the active to the patient.

WARREN BUFFETT

Sometimes a year goes by without the market experiencing a correction,
much less turning into a bear market. Sometimes the market posts a solid
return at the end of the year, and looking back, everything seemed easy.
However, this is very rarely the case. Since 1980, the market has had an
average intra-year decline of 13.9%, but still ended with a positive return
in 29 of the previous 39 years. That's a wide range! Markets move around

a lot, so you had better get used to it. Better yet, accept it, embrace it, and love it![67]

As we've established, bear markets are very common as well. If you are 55 years old, you've got about seven or more bear markets on the horizon. Are you going to panic every time? Are you going to try to time your way in and out of each one? No you're not, because you know better! Just as markets always recover from corrections, bear markets always become bull markets. So why do so many investors panic? Because for most people, investment decisions aren't based on rational thought; they're based on emotion.

CONSUMER CONFIDENCE

Consumer confidence surveys found to be "useless."

DEAN CROUSHORE, University of Richmond

During bear markets, commentators tend to talk about *consumer confidence*, since much of the economy is driven by consumption. Consumers who don't feel confident about the economy likely won't spend money. If they don't spend money, then companies can't make money. And if companies don't make money, the markets won't be able to recover. This line of thinking makes sense, were it not for one important fact: the market isn't looking at today. The market *always* looks to tomorrow. From a market perspective, where the economy is today and how consumers feel today are far less important than what the future may hold. Bull markets tend to emerge right when investors feel the *worst* about the future. Figure 8.9 summarizes how the stock market performed the 12 months after consumer confidence was measured at less than 60%.

67   You know you have arrived as a sophisticated investor when you relish corrections and bear markets as opportunities gift-wrapped by the gods and delivered to your doorstep.

Figure 8.9

WHO NEEDS CONFIDENCE?

CONSUMER CONFIDENCE <60%	NEXT 12 MONTHS (S&P 500)
1974	+37%
1980	+32%
1990	+30%
2008	+60%
2011	+15%

BE SURE YOU CAN LIVE
WITH YOUR ALLOCATION

Know thyself.

SOCRATES

I have three kids, and whenever we go to the amusement park, I watch them examine the various roller coasters. Some of the coasters are too boring for the little ones, and some get the older one excited. When the oldest was younger, I would get a "maybe not this time" sort of glance when we looked at the upside-down roller coasters. It's always a process to decide what sort of ride they can handle.

In the past, I used to go on whatever roller coaster they wanted. In recent years, I have often found that to be a regretful decision, particularly during the slow climb up some ridiculously high hill and the subsequent nausea-inducing drop. Even then, though, I realize that trying to get off the roller coaster in the middle of the ride is not a good idea. In fact, the odds are very good I'll come out the other end in one piece if I just hold on and follow through to the end.

The markets are the same.

The bond market is like the kiddie coaster at Legoland—almost anyone can handle it. The stock market is like a big-time roller coaster at Six Flags: it's exciting and has many twists and turns. The real estate market is like Space Mountain at Disney World: fast and in the dark. The commodity market is more like the Detonator: a ride that lifts and drops you unpredictably. All of these rides have differing levels of speed and volatility. Some people find the volatile ones thrilling; others find them nauseating. But in all cases, the rides generally reach a peaceful conclusion, even to the passengers who are wondering what exactly they just got themselves into.

The best time to evaluate your preferred roller coaster is when you're standing on the ground (i.e., when the market is relatively stable). It is much easier to make that decision then rather than once the ride starts up again, and one day it will definitely start again.

This is easier said than done. Americans are great at forgetting things—a useful coping mechanism that allows us to move on. After going on a roller coaster with my son, I tell myself I won't do it again. But the next time I am at the amusement park with him, I agree to the stomach-dropping ride, not totally remembering how bad it actually felt the last time. Now, I no longer forget, and we make sure to take a friend of his along.

Smart investors customize their roller coaster, taking parts of various markets to build a portfolio that meets their short-, intermediate-, and long-term needs. A portfolio can twist and turn, taking on the volatility necessary to meet the investor's specific goals, but should be structured within the parameters that the investor is prepared to handle. For many, the best portfolio is one that accomplishes the intended goals with the least amount of volatility. If the volatility is outside your limit of tolerance, you may need to adjust your goal or your savings plan.

UNDERESTIMATING THE
RISK OF MARKET TIMING

I never try to make money on the stock market. I buy on the assumption they could close the market the next day and not reopen it for five years.

WARREN BUFFETT

By now, we have established that market timing is ineffective. You might be saying, "What's the big deal? I can miss out on some gains in exchange for having my cash safely in hand." This is always the main objection to remaining invested through market downturns. The answer is simple: the risk of being out of the market is *far* greater than the risk of being in. Imagine you received a large sum of money (like a bonus or inheritance) and are deciding between investing now or waiting for a random, unquantifiable event that will make you feel more confident about putting your money in the market. If you invest now, there are three possible outcomes: the market will go up (always a good thing), it will go sideways (nothing wrong with getting those dividend checks), or it will go down (hey, it happens, but it doesn't last forever). If the market goes down, there are two things to remember: (1) you're still receiving dividend income and (2) the market will go back up. You lose nothing by keeping your money invested, as any downside in the market is temporary and immaterial to a long-term investor. What happens if you keep your money in cash? We have the same three options, with different results:

1. It could go up. (Look at all that money you didn't make!)
2. It can go sideways. (How's that 0.06% interest on your savings account treating you?)

3. It can go down. (If you were scared to invest before, are you really going to interpret a dropping market as a signal to buy? Let's be honest: we both know the answer is no!)

Here's the part that most people overlook: if you are in cash when the market moves up, you may have *permanently* lost the opportunity to realize those gains. Yes, it may still go back down again in the future, but will it go all the way back to its previous low? Maybe. But maybe not. If it doesn't drop back down to that level, investors sitting in cash will never be able to recover the missed return again. Ask all those folks who went with the herd and cashed in during 2008, only to see the market skyrocket in the years following. Sitting on the sidelines typically means *permanently* missing the upside. Alternatively, for the individual investing today, the worst thing that can happen is *temporarily* experiencing the downside. Major difference.

MAYBE I'M PERFECT[68]

Only liars manage to be "out" during bad
times and "in" during good times.
BERNARD BARUCH

Despite all evidence to the contrary, some people believe that they're "Mr. Perfect." That they can find a way to time the market perfectly, and that all the data I just described don't apply to them. To test those who say they can invest perfectly under these conditions, the Schwab Center for Financial Research evaluated the five decisions available to an investor who has $2,000 in cash to invest every year for 20 years:

---

68   You shouldn't believe *everything* your mother tells you.

1. Leave all the money in cash.
2. Fully invest immediately each time.
3. *Dollar-cost-average*[69] the cash into the market over the course of the year in equal monthly installments.
4. Unintentionally invest all of the money on the *worst* possible day every year (buying in on the day of the market's yearly high).
5. Be lucky enough to invest all of the money on the *best* possible day each year. (This is you, Mr. Perfect, waiting until the market is at the *exact* lowest point of the year to invest all your cash.)

The results are surprising, to say the least. The investor who *perfectly* timed the market ended up with $87,004, while the person who invested everything immediately came in a close second with $81,650. If you agree that you are not going to be able to invest all your money on the absolute best day possible every single year for the next 20 years, investing the cash right away seems like a reasonable compromise. The difference of $6,000

Figure 8.10

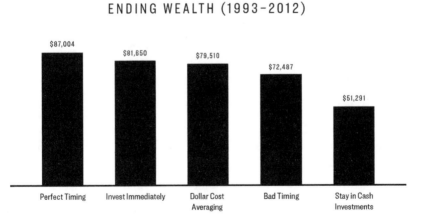

EVEN MARKET TIMING TRUMPS INERTIA
ENDING WEALTH (1993–2012)

69 *Dollar cost average* simply means putting the money into the market over time in equal increments.

between perfect timing and immediate investing is almost negligible. And notice that those who invest on the worst day of the year still make $22,000 more than those who remain in cash. Once again, being in the market is better than being out!

LEARNING TO FLY

I'm learning to fly, but I ain't got wings.

TOM PETTY

There comes a time when the baby birds need to leave the nest, take that jump, and fly off. Many investors have tried that before, only to land flat on their faces. Back in the nest, they struggle looking for a time to take the jump again.

If we look back in history, there is no example of the stock market taking a dollar from anyone. Someone who had no concept of investing and simply bought into the S&P 500 saw huge profits over the past 10, 20, or 30 years. Truckloads of money have been lost, however, by investors who made mistakes with their portfolio or by using advisors who made market timing or security selection mistakes. And even more has been theoretically lost by those who stayed in cash and didn't invest at all. An investor who bought into the market at any time in history rather than staying in cash would likely have more money today. Let's take a look at the so-called unluckiest investors:

Those who invested right before the 1987 crash:	S&P 500 at 334
Those who invested right before the early 1990s recession:	S&P 500 at 363
Those who invested the day before 9/11:	S&P 500 at 1,096
Those who invested the day of the 2007 stock market high:	S&P 500 at 1,526

Figure 8.11

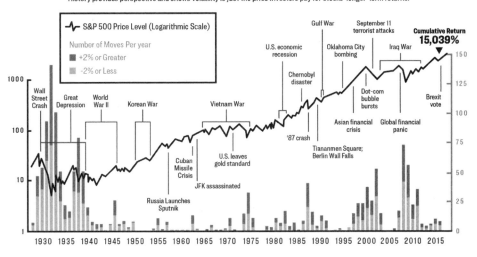

MARKET VOLATILITY IN PERSPECTIVE

Short-term market volatility can be trying for even the most disciplined investors.
History provides perspective and shows volatility is just the price investors pay for stocks' longer-term returns.

While these individuals may have invested at "unlucky" times, they still did much better than the bird that stayed in the nest, waiting for the "right" time to take the jump. As of the writing of this book, the S&P 500 was at 2,830, but that does not include dividends, which averaged over 2% and are equivalent to over 460 additional points since 2007. Even the investors who went in at the worst possible times are far ahead of the "investor" sitting in cash, waiting for things to "settle down."

Many are scared off by headlines that say, "The market is at an all-time high." Well, that is often true, *but it happens all the time.* If that sounds too scary a time to enter the market, the odds are high you will never be comfortable.

The reply to this argument, of course, is that it's always better to enter after a market corrects or crashes; however, no one knows when that will happen or, more important, how high the market will go before that happens. If the Dow goes from 25,000, to 26,000, then drops back to 25,000, what have you accomplished by sitting in cash other than missing out on dividends? Also, I have yet to find the investor who is nervous at Dow 25,000 but feels superfantastic about investing at Dow 23,000. If you are nervous when things are too good, you aren't going to feel better about investing when things don't look so hot. Whatever crisis du jour is happening, rest assured the market will likely find a way to survive and move on; it always has. Figure 8.11 sums it up nicely.

The market is going to do what the market is going to do. Understanding that corrections and bear markets are frequent and normal and that no investment manager, economist, or any other prognosticator can likely time it right is a major step toward truly understanding how markets work. For disciplined investors, the time to invest is always today, and that is only because yesterday is no longer an option. You are ready to fly with the markets now that you have knowledge to serve as your wings.

CHAPTER NINE

IT'S ALL IN YOUR HEAD

The most important quality for an investor
is temperament, not intellect.

WARREN BUFFETT

Humans aren't really wired to be great investors; it's just not the way we are built. We tend to be wary of change but *also* impulsive, and we often make decisions based on emotions or "intuition" rather than facts. All of us come with built-in and nurtured biases that can lead us down the wrong path. Before you know it, your well-planned journey has taken you right off a cliff! To stay on track, you will need to be aware of these biases and guard against them.

Most people who get excited about investing dive into research, read market timing or stock picking letters, use online services, and constantly watch financial news. The idea is that the more information they have, the more knowledgeable they will be and the less likely they will be to make a mistake. As you already know, it doesn't really work this way. If you have a reasonable level of intelligence and you understand the basic principles of this book, you will likely outperform the great majority of investors. The key is not to mess things up.

Unfortunately, there are plenty of ways to do just that. So far, we have examined strategies that are likely to do far more harm than good, like working with a broker or trying to time the market, but there is nothing

I have seen cause more financial destruction than the emotionally driven mistakes investors make. The key is to recognize your behavioral impulses so that you can knowingly protect yourself from making these mistakes. Let's dive in.

FEAR, GREED AND HERDING

Be fearful when others are greedy and greedy when others are fearful.

WARREN BUFFETT

In a 2014 interview, former Federal Reserve chairman Alan Greenspan reflected on all he had learned. Interestingly, rather than economic or historical analysis, he shared his observations of human behavior:

> If you can grit your teeth through and just disregard short-term declines in the market or even long-term declines in the market, you will come out well. I mean you just stick all your money in stocks and go home and don't look at your portfolio you'll do far better than if you try to trade it. The reason that's the case is this asymmetry between fear and euphoria.[70] The most successful stock market players, the best investors, are those who recognize that the asymmetric bias in fear vs. euphoria is a tradable concept and can't fail for precisely this reason. So there are stabilities here which are very important, but along with them are more junk statistics, more junk analysis, and more stock market letters than should be allowed to be written. It's just sort of ridiculous.

Over his career, Greenspan learned that almost everything is noise and that the best investors are never scared into selling, embracing the

---

70   Mr. Fancy Pants using the word euphoria in place of *greed*. Same idea.

Figure 9.1

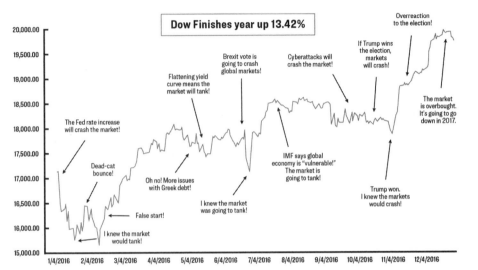

DOW JONES INDUSTRIAL AVERAGE
JANUARY 1, 2016–DECEMBER 31, 2016

Dow Finishes year up 13.42%

Overreaction to the election!

If Trump wins the election, markets will crash!

Brexit vote is going to crash global markets!

Cyberattacks will crash the market!

Flattening yield curve means the market will tank!

The market is overbought. It's going to go down in 2017.

The Fed rate increase will crash the market!

Dead-cat bounce!

Oh no! More issues with Greek debt!

IMF says global economy is "vulnerable!" The market is going to tank!

Trump won. I knew the markets would crash!

False start!

I knew the market was going to tank!

I knew the market would tank!

20,000.00 · 19,500.00 · 19,000.00 · 18,500.00 · 18,000.00 · 17,500.00 · 17,000.00 · 16,500.00 · 16,000.00 · 15,000.00

1/4/2016 2/4/2016 3/4/2016 4/4/2016 5/4/2016 6/4/2016 7/4/2016 8/4/2016 9/4/2016 10/4/2016 11/4/2016 12/4/2016

opportunity to buy when others are fearful. Greenspan is basically endorsing only one tradable concept: control your fear and greed. Control your emotions, avoid the herd, and things are very likely to work out. That's some pretty interesting insight from the person considered to be the most powerful person on earth for much of his tenure.

Figure 9.1 shows a typical year in the market, along with some of the color commentary that accompanies each market movement. Does any of this sound familiar? These types of comments reflect the fear and greed that fuel many of the worst market decisions. Fear and greed are two of the most powerful forces (and ugliest qualities) in our lives. They affect the way we live our daily lives, and they can have disastrous consequences for investors. While the legendary names in investing know how to control these emotions, novice investors can fall prey to these feelings, as financial and popular media feed the frenzy with the help of market "gurus" and pundits. Fear and greed combined with our instinctive herd mentality is a recipe for disaster.

As humans, we were born with the instinct to move in herds, follow the crowd, and seek the safety of consensus. When markets are declining and every voice in our ear, from the media to our friends, is yelling, "Abandon ship," our instinct to follow the herd (combined with the irresistible force of *fear*) leads us to do the same. When markets are gaining and the voices in our head are telling us, "Go all in," our herding instinct (combined with the equally irresistible force of *greed*) encourages us to join the group.

While our instinct to follow the group may have served us well when our ancestors were hunting mastodons, it's a killer for portfolios today. Fear drives investors to leave underperforming markets, and greed drives them to buy into markets that are outperforming, thus herding themselves in the *wrong* direction at the *wrong* time. This happens in nearly every bull market *and* every bear market, as shown in Figure 9.2.

Despite the markets' persistent upward growth, investors consistently do irreparable damage to their portfolios by allowing themselves to fall

Figure 9.2

INVESTOR CASH FLOWS

	Date	Equity Weighting	Investor cash flows over the prior two years (in millions)		Stock market performance (cumulative)	
			Stock Funds	Bond Funds	Prior 2 years	Subsequent 2 years
Early in '90s bull market	1/31/1993	34%	—	—	—	—
Bull market peak	3/31/2000	62%	$393,225	$5,100	41%	-23%
Bear market bottom	2/28/2003	40%	$71,815	$221,475	-29%	53%
Bull market peak	10/31/2007	62%	$424,193	$173,907	34%	-29%
Bear market bottom	2/28/2009	37%	-49,942	-83,921	-51%	94%

prey to fear and greed. Investors in bear markets often become net sellers (selling more stocks than buying); had they done nothing, they would have gone on to realize significant gains. Sophisticated investors instead recognize a bear market as an opportunity to buy more, often referred to as *opportunistic rebalancing*. Significant market drops provide an opportunity for investors to purchase more of the assets they want in their portfolio at a substantial discount, so they sell off a portion of their bonds during downturns to buy stocks. This is a strategy that adds tremendous value to their portfolio during the inevitable recovery. This approach always pays off; the only question is how long it takes. Throughout his storied career, Warren Buffett has maintained his investment positions during times of investor panic while he simultaneously and aggressively adds to his substantial portfolio. His comment that sophisticated investors should "be fearful when others are greedy, and greedy when others are fearful" is sage advice for those looking to avoid the pitfalls of fear, greed, and herding.[71]

Dr. Frank Murtha, cofounder of the behavioral economics firm MarketPsych, said, "Investing is stressful, and that stress causes us to make emotional, usually fear-based, decisions during difficult market periods." He further states that fear-based decisions impede reaching financial goals because they are centered on emotional rather than financial needs, specifically the desire to "feel in control again." Removing emotion from your financial decisions is essential to being successful in the market. Not only does that help you avoid rash decisions made in panic, but it allows you to take advantage of the opportunities that market volatility provides. Rather than being a destructive force, volatility should be a tool for future growth.

---

71   I have found it is better to follow his investment advice rather than his diet advice. Warren famously eats McDonald's for breakfast every day, followed by several Cherry Cokes, and goes downhill from there.

Confirmation Bias

Confirmation bias is our most treasured enemy. Our opinions,
our acumen—all of it, are the result of years of selectively
choosing to pay attention to that information only which
confirms what our limited minds already accept as truth.

INA CATRINESCU

After a few meetings with clients in New York, I offered to take my local team to dinner. They highly recommended a local steak house. I explained that being from Kansas City, I was game to go anywhere, but I already had steaks and barbecue covered. They in turn *insisted* that New York simply had the best steaks. We debated a bit, and then, to no one's surprise, we ended up at the steak house. The waiter brought out a cart with all the cuts of beef beautifully displayed. He took his time going through each cut, eventually working his way to the strip steak.

The waiter explained that this steak was their very finest, and he recommended it above all other steaks. Then he ended with a flourish, declaring, "In fact, it just came in from Kansas City today!" Now, of course, I heard exactly what I wanted to hear: that Kansas City has the best steaks. My colleagues argued it was also proof that New York has the best of everything, all the time! This, my friends, is confirmation bias at work.[72]

Confirmation bias is the tendency for people to seek out and value information that confirms their preconceptions and beliefs and to avoid, undervalue, or disregard information that is inconsistent with their beliefs. Take politics, for example. A conservative individual may read the *Wall Street Journal*, the *Weekly Standard*, or the *National Review*; view the Drudge Report online; listen to Rush Limbaugh, Sean Hannity, or Glenn Beck on the radio; and watch FOX News. In contrast, a liberal individual may read the *New York Times*; view the *Huffington Post* and Salon.com online; listen

---

72   I must admit, it was a fantastic Kansas City strip steak.

to NPR; and watch John Oliver, Bill Maher, or MSNBC. Both individuals are looking for sources of information that likely confirm their ideas, while avoiding those that may conflict with their ideas. How often do you seek out new channels, websites, or political commentators who espouse views opposite to your own? If you are like most other people, you probably spend the bulk of your time validating what you already believe to be true.

Everybody thinks they are right about everything—from fiscal policy to the proper way to hang a roll of toilet paper[73]—and constantly seek validation of those beliefs. Our brains have a hard time believing new ideas that don't fit with what we already know (or what we think we know), a phenomenon psychologists call *cognitive dissonance*. Instead, it's much easier for us to accept additional information that already aligns with the facts as we perceive them. Perhaps not surprisingly, highly intelligent people do the exact opposite: they seek out opposing views, challenge their own ideas, and occasionally even alter their own convictions. Sophisticated investors do the same.

There is plenty of evidence that confirmation bias plays a major role in most investors' decisions. For example, an investor who likes a particular investment is likely to seek out information (from places like online message boards) that validates her choice of the investment. Even an accomplished investor like Warren Buffett says he finds himself becoming a victim of confirmation bias; he addresses this by actively seeking out investors with strong opinions counter to his own.

If you are attracted to a particular investment, I recommend that you challenge it rigorously. How could this investment go wrong? If this investment were to lose money, how would it happen? And what risks does this investment present? By forcing yourself to acknowledge the potential flaws in a particular strategy, you open yourself up to exploring ideas and beliefs contrary to your own. And that makes you a better investor.

---

73 The "experts" say over is the correct way. For those of you who are obsessive-compulsive like me, feel free to put the book down and immediately "correct" any toilet paper in your home that is noncompliant.

THE OVERCONFIDENCE EFFECT

The problem with the world is that
intelligent people are full of doubt, while
the stupid people are full of confidence.

CHARLES BUKOWSKI

Recently members of a firm that runs an alternative investment fund came to our offices to present their investment ideas. They spoke with great confidence, using words like *certainty* and *riskless*. I was immediately concerned. A good financial advisor knows that there are a lot of unknowns, and that nearly nothing in the investment world is "certain" or "riskless." This firm's representatives convinced us that either they didn't really understand the market, thus leading to their overconfidence, or they did understand it yet were willing to mask the risks. Either way, our interest quickly diminished. The overconfidence they projected was enough for my team to thank them for their time and dismiss their entire offer from consideration.

The *overconfidence effect* states that an individual's *subjective* confidence in his judgment is reliably greater than his *objective* accuracy, especially when confidence is relatively high. Simply put, people tend to think they are better and smarter than they really are. This is different from trusting in your abilities, which is a reasonable measure of confidence; it's believing that your abilities make you better than everyone else.

In his book, *The Psychology of Judgment and Decision Making*, Scott Plous wrote that "overconfidence has been called the most 'pervasive and potentially catastrophic' of all the cognitive biases to which human beings fall victim. It has been blamed for lawsuits, strikes, wars, and stock market bubbles and crashes." That's not an exaggeration. Countless studies speak to the enormous impact of the overconfidence effect: 93% of student drivers believe they are above-average drivers, 94% of college professors think they are above-average teachers, and good luck finding someone who doesn't think he or she is an above-average lover.[74] A study relating to the character of students has always been a favorite of mine: 79% said their character was above average, in spite of the fact that 27% admitted to stealing from a store in the past and a whopping 60% revealed they had cheated on an exam in the previous year![75]

The overconfidence effect has also been examined in the investment world, with revealing results. Finance professors Brad Barber and Terrance Odean compared the investment performance of men to that of women. After examining the trading patterns of 35,000 households during a five-year period, they found that the men's overconfidence in their abilities resulted in 45% more trading activity than their female counterparts. Not only did this excess trading cause the men to underperform the women, with their average annual return 2.65% lower, but they also paid more in transaction fees and taxes. Being overconfident is expensive.

What about the professionals? After all, they have access to more information about companies, sophisticated analysis software, and specialized training. If you can't trust your own abilities, you can at least trust theirs. Right? Research has shown that when investment analysts are 80% confident a stock will go up, they're correct only 40% of the time. In 2006, James Montier asked 300 professional fund managers to rate their performance; 74% of the managers believed their job performance was above average. Andrew Zacharakis and Dean Shepherd discovered that when venture capitalists were asked about their belief in their portfolio companies' chances of success, a whopping 96% of the venture capitalists exhibited overconfidence! This brings us to an important study in overconfidence. In *Psychology of Intelligence Analysis*, Richards Heuer researched the behavioral

---

74   Who would want to claim otherwise!

75   Research shows that when someone says they are 99% confident, they are really 80% confident. I can never get this out of my mind because so many people use the saying, and I simply can't take it seriously anymore!

biases of CIA analysts. A key finding of his research was that once an analyst had the *minimum* amount of information to make an informed judgment, additional information did not increase the *accuracy* of the judgment, just the *confidence* in the judgment to the point of overconfidence.

This underscores what lies at the root of the overconfidence bias problem: we humans misinterpret additional *information* as added *intelligence*. Instead of the additional information granting us more insight, it often serves to reinforce our beliefs and strengthen our convictions. In investing, this is often to our detriment. The more that investors research and gather information, the more they are compelled to trade, and the more they trade, the more they underperform. Ultimately the overconfident investor creates unnecessary effort and stress, as well as wasting precious time and money.

If you think you're too smart to be taken in by this effect,[76] I should note one more tidbit from Plous's research: "Discrepancies between accuracy and confidence are not related to a decision maker's intelligence." Not only that, but there is significant evidence that greater intelligence leads to greater overconfidence. Perhaps ignorance really is bliss!

ANCHORING

The anchoring heuristic appears to be prevalent
throughout human decision processes.
TODD MCELROY AND KEITH DOWD

In the 1970s, psychologists Daniel Kahneman and Amos Tversky identified the "anchoring" effect, research that opened the floodgates on a human bias that has an impact on all sorts of decision making. *Anchoring* is a term psychologists use to explain the way the brain takes mental shortcuts to arrive at conclusions. In short, we have a tendency to overrely on the first piece of

---

76   How ironically overconfident of you!

information that enters our brain. This piece of information is the "anchor." Once the anchor has been set, all of our future decisions revolve around this anchor, contaminating rational thinking. If you are ever uncertain of a correct answer, you are likely to fall victim to the anchoring bias and make a guess based on the most recent information you've heard. For example, if asked whether the population of Zimbabwe is greater or less than 20 million, you will give an answer. If then you were asked what you think the actual population is, you will likely give an answer somewhat close to 20 million.[77]

Both novice and experienced negotiators understand anchoring. The first price thrown out in a negotiation often becomes the anchor for all future discussions. Marketers also have seized on the anchoring effect to influence consumers' spending habits. In a fascinating experiment,[78] Brian Wansink, Robert Kent, and Stephen Hoch set up a display of Campbell's soup, advertising that it was on sale for 79 cents and there was no limit to the number of cans shoppers could buy. They then set up a different display with the same sale but a sign that read, "Limit of 12 per Person." The shoppers who purchased the soup without a limit bought an average of 3.3 cans. The shoppers who purchased the soup with a "limit" of 12 cans purchased 7 cans. The shoppers became anchored to the number 12, assigning meaning to it (for example, "Wow! This must be a really good deal and the grocery store doesn't want me to buy a lot or they'll lose money"). There are many, many more studies on the anchoring effect. It is real, it is vivid, and many of us have been unknowing victims of it for years!

Where am I going with this? In investing, the anchoring effect is often the purchase price of your stock. If you purchase a stock for $50 but it's later priced at $30, you may hold onto it until it gets back to $50 (or even buy more because you think it is worth the $50 you originally paid). If instead the stock goes from $50 to $70, you may sell the stock, thinking

---

77 As of 2019, the population of Zimbabwe was 14.65 million people. You were so close!

78 I have been told I am easily fascinated.

it is overvalued because the price is now higher than the original $50 you paid for it. In these situations, your decision making is clouded by your anchor. Many investors fall victim to anchoring by buying a stock that has come far off its highs ("It's a bargain now!") or not purchasing a stock that has run on to new highs ("It's too overpriced now!"). The reality is that the stock is often priced pretty darn close to where it should be, with an equal number of buyers on one side and sellers on the other. The only reason the investor thinks it is a "great bargain" or "overpriced" is the direction it has moved from its past anchor price. With an awareness of the anchoring effect, you can avoid holding losers too long and selling winners too early. And maybe you can save some money at the grocery store too.

ILLUSION OF CONTROL

Figure 9.3

People like to feel that they are in control or, at the very least, responsible for the outcome of their actions. If you are a nervous passenger in cars, you know exactly what I'm talking about. You don't mind being in the car as long as you're the one with your hands on the wheel and your feet on the pedals. Driving the car makes you *feel* that you're in control of the situation.

Illusion of control is defined as our tendency to overestimate our ability to control events, even taking responsibility for outcomes we cannot possibly influence. Think of the route you take to work or some other frequent destination. You probably think you can control how fast you get there by timing your departure and devising the best route. In fact, the speed limit, the amount of traffic, timing of the lights, random traffic accidents, geese crossing the road, and the presence of construction crews are not only determining factors in how long the trip will take, but they're completely beyond your influence. Put succinctly, sometimes we can exert influence over a situation, but don't mistake influence for control.

This effect is observed in other areas of life as well.[79] Psychologist Ellen Langer, who named this effect, conducted an experiment involving a lottery. Participants were allowed to choose their own numbers, or they were given tickets with random numbers. They were then given the opportunity to trade in their ticket for one with better odds of a payout. Langer found that those who had chosen their own numbers were more reluctant to give them up. Although these lotteries were completely random, the participants acted as if their choice of numbers was material to the outcome.

Many people behave in this manner with their investments. Investors often have a difficult time letting go of the positions they picked or those that they are familiar with, even if a more broadly diversified portfolio gives them a higher probability of achieving their goals. Sophisticated investors know that their actions are largely not responsible for their portfolio's performance; instead, the markets are.

LOSS AVERSION AND THE
ENDOWMENT EFFECT

Let's try this on.

EVERY JEWELRY STORE CLERK EVER

Daniel Kahneman and Amos Tversky are known for their research on *loss aversion*, the bias humans have to *avoid* a loss rather than *make* a gain.

---

79   An entire book can be written on parenting being the ultimate illusion of control.

In other words, we fear losing more than we enjoy winning. Extensive research on this bias shows that we experience about twice as much pain from a loss than the pleasure we experience from a win.

In one of their studies, they split people into two groups: one group had pens with $3.98 price stickers and the other group did not have pens. They then asked the no-pen group how much they would pay to purchase a pen and the pen group how much money they would sell their pens for. The no-pen group valued the pens at a much lower amount than the pen group did. Why is this? The answer is simple: the pen group didn't want to feel as though they had lost by selling it for less than $3.98, and the no-pen group didn't want to feel that they lost by paying more than $3.98.

Have you been to a jewelry store lately? The salespeople always offer to put the jewelry in your hands or ask if you want to try it on. They are trying to employ loss aversion to convince you to buy their product. In this form of loss aversion, known as the *endowment effect* or *status quo effect*, once you have a pen, jewelry, or any other item in your hands, it feels like it's yours and you don't want to lose it.[80]

Loss aversion causes more damage among investors than perhaps any other group. It is the reason investors sit in cash, despite knowing full well that they are losing the purchasing power of their money. The average money market yield has been well below inflation for decades, yet investors are willing to lose a little bit of money each day to avoid the perceived larger losses that come with real investments. With a plan like this, the purchasing power of your money can be cut in half in just 24 years!

Loss aversion is the reason you won't give away the jeans that haven't fit since 1994, the sweater you haven't worn since 2003, and all of the stuff that's just sitting, unused, in your garage. Loss aversion is the reason that you hang on to a stock long after it has dropped. You don't want

---

80   "Let's see if this necklace fits you." "I bet this blouse would look lovely on you. Let's try it on." "How about we take the car for a test drive?"

to acknowledge the loss, which would require you to admit you made a mistake. Far better to just wait until it (maybe) recovers, right? When I speak with clients who have an investment they won't sell until it recovers, I ask them a simple question: "If you had cash instead of this stock, knowing what you are trying to accomplish, would you buy the same stock today?" The answer is almost always no, and when it is, we know the investor is hanging on because of loss aversion. Understanding the impact of loss aversion on our decision making can help us become better investors.[81]

MENTAL ACCOUNTING

Since the conscious mind can handle only a few thoughts at any given time, it's constantly trying to "chunk" stuff together to make the complexity of life a little more manageable. Instead of counting every dollar we spend, we parcel our dollars into particular purchases. We rely on misleading shortcuts because we lack the computational power to think any other way.

JONAH LEHRER

Richard Thaler is known for his work in the field of behavioral economics and for identifying and defining *mental accounting*, the process of dividing one's current and future assets into separate, nontransferable portions.

In a study highlighting the impact of mental accounting, participants were asked to imagine the following scenario: You've decided to see a movie and paid the admission price of $10 per ticket. As you enter the theater, you discover that you have lost the ticket! Unfortunately, the ticket cannot be recovered. Would you pay $10 for another ticket? Only 46% of the participants said they would purchase another ticket. The participants were then asked to imagine a different scenario: You've decided to see a movie where admission is $10 per ticket. As you enter the theater, you

---

81   And make us less likely to clutter our way onto the next episode of *Hoarders*!

discover that you have lost a $10 bill. Would you still pay $10 for a ticket to the movie? Although the economic impact was precisely the same as with the first question, 88% of the participants said yes: they would buy a ticket!

Under both scenarios, participants were asked to spend $10 on a ticket, despite essentially losing $10 earlier. The difference in the responses is attributable to the powerful effect of mental accounting. Once participants had a ticket, they assigned it to the "entertainment" column of their mental account. They had already lost their budget for the movie, so they weren't going to go over budget and buy another ticket. Those in the latter group lost $10; however, they had not yet assigned the $10 to the ticket and were therefore willing to purchase a ticket despite their earlier loss. The study shows that we don't view every dollar the same, even though it would make good financial sense if we did.

Psychologist Hal Arkes's research shows us that mental accounting is the reason tax refunds and lottery winnings are often blown quickly. Mental accounting puts those funds in the "free money" column. Sociologist Viviana Zelizer, referencing a study on the Oslo prostitution market, notes that the principle even applies to how those in world's oldest profession spend their income. Prostitutes, it turns out, use their welfare checks and health benefits to pay rent and other bills, and use the money they acquire selling sex to purchase drugs and alcohol. It seems that mental accounting is ingrained in the human condition.

Mental accounting affects the way we make decisions in everyday life, but it shouldn't affect sophisticated investors. Investors who look at each individual investment separately create separate mental accounts for each holding. If you hold separate investment accounts, keep in mind that you should not judge them individually but rather ask if they contribute appropriately to your long-term objective. By looking at the big picture, you can far more easily judge if you are on track for your long-term goals. Looking at each holding or subaccount piecemeal can trigger mental accounting and result in poor decision making. One way to dampen the impact of mental accounting while investing is to aggregate as many of your investments as possible into one account. This makes it far easier to make judicious decisions with the whole picture in mind.

RECENCY BIAS

Investors project out into the future what they have most
recently been seeing. That is their unshakable habit.

WARREN BUFFETT

Recency bias is the tendency to project recent experiences or observations into the future. This allows us to make predictions about the future based on events in the recent past.[82]

Despite the many amazing capabilities of the human mind, we rely on identifying patterns to help simplify our decision-making process. Sometimes the patterns we observe can be helpful. If you see a patrol car in the same spot several days in a row, you're going to make a point of watching your speedometer in that area. However, when it comes to investing, recency bias can be costly and dangerous.

Studies show that brokers tend to promote the hot stocks that have outperformed the market in the previous year, only to have those recommendations underperform in the following year. Investors tend to gravitate toward investments that have risen over many consecutive months, expecting the trend to continue, only to arrive just as the party is ending, missing out on all the gains and participating in all the losses instead. After the tech bubble and 9/11 spurred consecutive bear markets, many investors anticipated another bear market and missed out on the subsequent

---

82   Recency bias is also the reason my 17-year-old son isn't allowed to stay out past midnight at his next school dance. It's also the reason he wants to stay out past midnight at his next school dance.

recovery. After the 2008–2009 financial crisis, many investors viewed every market pullback as an indicator of a pending market crash.

If only the market really worked like this. Instead, in any given year, there is a very good chance that the market will end the year in positive territory, regardless of where it finished the year before. Furthermore, the odds are good there will be a correction, regardless of what happened in the weeks, months, or year prior. An investor can expect about two bear markets in any given decade, regardless of what happened the decade prior. Just as getting heads three times in a row when flipping a coin does not change the odds of getting tails on the next flip, the recent past is not a reliable indicator of what to expect in the markets.

One way to counter the effects of recency bias is to impose a disciplined system for managing your money. For example, if your portfolio consists of 60% stocks and 40% bonds, you might allow yourself to rebalance back to the original ratio only when your allocation drifts by more than 5%. By adopting a systematic approach to your investment decisions, you help prevent recent market events from influencing your actions.

Recency bias can have positive and negative implications in real life, but unchecked, it often causes far more harm than good when it comes to investing.

MYOPIC LOSS AVERSION

If we will be quiet and ready enough, we shall find
compensation in every disappointment.

HENRY DAVID THOREAU

The most successful people are those who do not let failure derail their goals and dreams. Our natural instinct is to give up or run away when a situation becomes difficult rather than trying again or attempting to implement a new strategy. We have a tendency to focus on the short-term results rather than our long-term goals, particularly if things don't go as expected initially. Behavioral finance experts call this *myopic loss aversion.*

We coach our children to get back on the bike when they fall off for the tenth time, but we need someone to do the same for us. Even if we understand and agree with an investment strategy, it may be hard to stay the course if the strategy doesn't immediately work, no matter how much we agree it should work over the long run. Investors often want to get out of an asset if it doesn't generate immediate returns.

Understanding the investments you own and their purpose in your portfolio is essential to avoiding myopic loss aversion. Too often, we are caught up in how an investment is performing today without considering its use in the portfolio. Studies have found that investors often set arbitrary time frames for evaluating the effectiveness of an asset or investment strategy; they typically choose to reevaluate at the one-year mark, even if that's not an appropriate reference point for the investment.[83] An intelligent portfolio is structured to have assets that provide their value over time, anywhere from today to ten years (or more) into the future. If you don't need to sell an asset today, its current price is irrelevant.

High-net-worth investors often have a private equity component to their portfolio, which you will learn more about in the next chapter. Some of these investments are expected to start with a negative return in the early phases! Nearly every type of investment has a broad trading range (big fluctuations in price) coupled with unpredictable short-run performance, and yet those same asset classes have fairly predictable long-term performance. To control the myopic loss aversion instinct, be aware of this! So long as your needs haven't changed and your portfolio composition is still aligned with your goals, give your investments the time they need to deliver their value.

---

83   Checking your investments every hour is not an effective way to evaluate the effectiveness of your portfolio.

NEGATIVITY BIAS

Over and over, the mind reacts to bad things more quickly,
strongly and persistently than to equivalent good things.

JONATHAN HAIDT

Negativity bias refers to our nature as humans to recall negative experiences more vividly than positive ones, as well as the conscious and subconscious actions we take to avoid negative outcomes.

Like loss avoidance, negativity bias is a powerful force. Teresa Amabile and Steven Kramer found that even minor negative setbacks during the workday changed the happiness of professionals twice as much as positive steps forward. According to researchers, we also learn more quickly from negative reinforcement than positive reinforcement. When analyzing our language, researchers have found that 62% of emotional words are negative and 74% of words for personality traits are negative.[84] This doesn't appear to be a learned response, as research shows that negativity bias is apparent in young children. When asked to evaluate whether a facial expression was good or bad, children perceived positive faces as being good, but both negative and neutral faces as being bad. Even babies exhibit the negativity bias, according to researchers.

Given how powerfully we respond to negative events, it should be no surprise that our news feed is full of them. You are far more likely to hear about the latest robbery in your neighborhood rather than its overall decreasing crime rate. And during the political campaign season, a candidate's commercials are almost always negative attack ads directed at opponents rather than focusing on their own virtues. These are blatant attempts to tap into our negativity bias and elicit a more powerful emotional response.

Negativity bias is apparent in the world of investing as well. It is this negatively oriented perspective that causes investors to want to sell

---

84   Negativity bias research is certainly not the most uplifting or inspiring line of work.

during market corrections or bear markets. Going to cash becomes a way for investors to avoid the negative experience of watching their position topple. Succumbing to negativity bias is particularly tempting when recent significant events are still fresh in the mind, which behavioral scientists refer to as *vividness*. For example, after investors experience a severe bear market like the financial crisis in 2008 and 2009, or the coronavirus pandemic, negativity bias can cause them to overreact at the slightest correction and sell to cash in a panic, fearful that another crisis is looming.

Like any other behavioral bias, the key to mitigating the effect of negativity bias is to know that it exists, so you can realize when you are beginning to succumb to it and stop yourself before it can hurt you or your portfolio. Negativity bias is so strong that we dedicated Chapter 1 of this book to overcoming it!

HOME RUN BIAS

I want it all, and I want it now.

FREDDY MERCURY, Queen

We all have a tendency to want the biggest and best results as quickly as possible rather than focusing on incremental changes that add up over time. This is known as a *home run bias*, and fad diets are a great example. We all know the key to sustained weight loss is consuming fewer calories combined with exercise, yet millions try to shortcut the system through pills, juice cleanses, and extreme dieting.[85] Investing is very similar, with investors looking for that home run rather than focusing on *sustainable* long-term returns.

---

85   Like my friend who lost quite a bit of weight on the carrot diet. He literally ate nothing but carrots for an entire week. He did lose weight; unfortunately, he turned orange too. Seriously.

The drawback for investors looking for home runs is no different from baseball players looking for them; you're probably going to strike out more often than not. Instead, players who try to take a good swing every time they're at bat will likely have a better outcome over time (and hit some home runs along the way too). Your investment philosophy should take the same approach: own the assets that are most appropriate for your goals, and take advantage of opportunities when the market provides them. You'll hit your own "home runs" along the way, but you'll also avoid striking out when the "game" (in this case, your financial independence) is on the line.[86]

THE GAMBLER

You've got to know when to hold them, know when to fold them. Know when to walk away, know when to run.

KENNY ROGERS

Some people are *speculators*, treating the market as their own personal casino by placing bets on a handful of stocks, trading options, or timing the market with the hope of winning big or outperforming the rest of the market.[87] Most people prefer to be *investors*, following a repeatable, disciplined strategy that focuses on improving the likelihood of realizing their long-term goals. Many fall into both camps.

The desire to gamble is built into all of us. The gaming industry is built around physiology and psychology: Winning causes our bodies to release endorphins (which make us feel euphoria), prompting our brains to want to keep playing. When we are losing, our brains tell us to keep playing to get those endorphins pumping again and to avoid the emotional

---

86   No more sports analogies, I swear!

87   The latest fad for the gambler is cryptocurrency, which made a handful rich while the majority lost their tails.

pain caused by further losses.[88] Casinos know how to exploit this to their advantage: they pump in extra oxygen to keep you alert and give you free drinks to reduce your inhibitions. They know that the more you play, the more they will win.

We've already discussed how active trading works against you, but it does benefit the house—in this case, brokerage companies. Active trading generates fees, which is revenue for the broker. Consider the advertisements for these firms, which promote free or low-cost trades, encourage you to start picking the winners, and provide access to fancy tools that will give you market "insights." Do you think it's a coincidence that your online trading platform looks and sounds like a casino, with green and red colors, scrolling tickers, flashing images, and dinging sounds?

The gambler in us is not easily suppressed. Over the long term, keeping all your assets invested in a manner consistent with your overall strategy gives you the highest probability of success. But if you can't completely shut off your inner gambler, consider opening a separate trading account with a small amount of funds you can "play" with. This way you can enjoy the thrill of gambling without jeopardizing your financial independence.

POLITICAL BIAS

You may have heard the news that we Americans are somewhat divided when it comes to politics. That division, encouraged by media outlets that feed us only what we want to hear, has gotten far worse over the years. In fact, it's gotten *so* bad that I've now seen many investors cause serious damage to their portfolios by basing important investment decisions on political views. In 2008, when President Obama was elected, much of the financial media went into absolute hysteria, claiming that socialism

---

88   Casinos do so well because gambling feeds into so many of the biases we cover in this chapter. Plus, they often come with free buffets.

was on its way and would destroy the markets. Instead, the market had one of its best eight-year runs in history during his presidency. When President Trump was elected in 2016, the financial media claimed the markets wouldn't be able to handle his unpredictability, that the threat of war would cause a market meltdown, and that his policies would end the market run. Instead, the markets went on to have one of their best years ever, and for the first time, every single month in the year following his election posted a gain.

Here's the deal: the market doesn't care much about who is sitting in the Oval Office. The market only cares about future earnings (company profits). While a multitude of factors go into future earnings, only a few are influenced by who is the US President. These factors are undoubtedly important, but they are usually not enough to compensate for the multitude of other factors over which the President has no control, such as interest rates. Whether you are on the right or the left politically, you are far better served to stay in the middle when it comes to investing. Never make portfolio decisions based on which political party is in power.

FREE YOUR MIND

While this little tangent from the fundamentals of planning and investing may seem like a diversion, I think we've established that is simply not the case. No amount of planning and investing can compensate for a major (and preventable!) behavioral mistake along the way. Like the 1992 En Vogue classic says, "Free your mind, and the rest will follow."

CHAPTER TEN

ASSET CLASSES

On average, 90 percent of the variability of
returns is explained by asset allocation.

ROGER G. IBBOTSON

By this point, we've covered several important parts of the investment land-scape. First, you now understand the market: its ups and downs (and how they are to be expected), its overall growth, and how it can benefit long-term investors. Second, you now understand the type of mental fitness you have to maintain to stay engaged through market turmoil: you can't allow yourself to be distracted by the media, brokers, or your own fear. With that, you are ready to move onto investments themselves. We'll start with a tour of major asset classes, how they work, and their role in an investor's portfolio.

CASH: THE ILLUSION OF SAFETY

The one thing I will tell you is the worst investment you can have is cash. Everybody is talking about "cash being king" and all that sort of thing. Cash is going to become worth less over time. But good businesses are going to become worth more over time.

WARREN BUFFETT

When you think of risky asset classes, you may think of commodities (i.e., gold and oil), real estate, stocks, and even some bonds. Cash may be last on the list. Cash, however, has many inherent risks. First and foremost, it is the worst-performing major asset class in history.[89] Over long periods of time, cash has always underperformed all other major asset classes. The more time you spend with a significant portion of your holdings in cash, the higher the probability is that your portfolio will underperform.[90]

Second, holding cash for long periods of time practically guarantees that you will not keep up with inflation and will lose purchasing power. In essence, your cash becomes worth less each year as the prices of goods go up and your cash remains static. Imagine you put $100,000 in the bank and earn 1% or so a year for ten years. When you withdraw your cash, you may feel pretty good; however, the 1% or so you earned did not keep up with the cost of a stamp, a suit, a candy bar, health care, or higher education. You may think you made money, but really you lost valuable purchasing power.

One reason many "investors" hold cash is to time the market. They want "dry powder" on hand. They do this despite the fact that there has never been a documented, real-world study showing that repeatedly moving from the market, to cash, and back to the market actually works. After all, you need to be right about when to get out *and* when to get in, and then be able to consistently repeat the process. If you get burned just once, your portfolio's performance can be permanently affected. But you already know this, because we spent an entire chapter on it!

Finally, many investors hold cash in the event of financial Armageddon, a situation when the stock market goes to zero, or near zero, and never recovers. In reality, if we live in a world where Amazon, Nike, McDonald's, and the rest of the world's dominant companies go down and never recover, it will likely accompany a default by the US government on Treasury bonds.

---

89   Nice start, right?

90   Professional portfolio managers know this, and they even have a term for it: *cash drag*. Cash drags down returns!

How can the government make its debt payments on its bonds if all the major US companies have collapsed? Who exactly would be working and paying taxes to cover the debt payments? In this event, the FDIC (Federal Deposit Insurance Corporation) guarantee on your bank accounts would essentially mean nothing and cash would become worthless. If you do not believe America's major corporations can survive, then the natural conclusion is that the US economic system itself cannot survive. In that event, cash may be the worst asset to own.[91] Despite all of this, Americans are currently sitting on trillions in cash, the most in history.

Keeping short-term reserves on hand is a good idea; hoarding cash as a long-term investment is not. Eliminate cash as a consideration for your investment portfolio.

BONDS

If we could simply call all bonds "loans," everyone
would understand them a heck of a lot better.
SAYS SOMEONE WHO DOESN'T LIKE HOW COMPLEX
EVERYTHING IN FINANCE HAS BECOME[92]

When you purchase a bond, you are making a loan to a company, government, or some other entity. Bonds are loans. That's it.[93] When you lend money to the federal government, it's called a *treasury bond*. When you lend money to a city, state, or county, it's called a *municipal bond*. When you lend money to a corporation like Netflix or Microsoft, it's called a *corporate bond*. When you lend money to a company that has to pay a higher interest

---

91 And a bunker, powdered foods, and survival kits would suddenly look like brilliant investments.

92 Source: yours truly.

93 Bonds are often made out to be far more complicated than they really are, largely due to the financial services industry doing all it can to make everything as confusing as possible.

rate to attract investors, it's called a *high-yield bond*,[94] more commonly known as a *junk bond*.[95]

Bonds are issued when these entities want to borrow money from the public, placing you in the role of the lender when you purchase a bond. Let's say that Target wants to raise $100 million. There's probably not one individual or institution that wants to take on the risk of loaning that much money to one company, so Target will issue enough bonds in smaller amounts, say in $25,000 increments, to obtain the full amount it needs. This allows more investors to participate in the loan offering. Like any other loan, there will be an interest rate paid to the investor for a set amount of time (known as the *term*). At the end of the term (known as the bond's *maturity* date), the loaned amount ($25,000 in our example) is returned to the investor.

Depending on the entity doing the borrowing, the interest rate will vary. The two main factors that dictate the amount of interest an entity will pay are the credit quality of the loan and the term.

First, let's look at how quality affects the rate. Many consider that loaning money to the US Treasury is the safest investment in the world, which is why you are paid a lower yield than if you were to lend money to a corporation. The odds that a corporation will go out of business and not pay back its bondholders are higher than the odds that the US government will default on their loans.[96] To entice you to lend money to a city, state, foreign country, or corporation, these borrowers must offer a higher after-tax return than the US Treasury. Corporations that are weak must offer an even higher rate of return to entice you to take the

---

94   Industry term.

95   Calling-it-what-it-is term.

96   Some would be quick to insert an end-of-the-world type of scenario here. For our purposes, the federal government is the only bond issuer that can run downstairs and print more dollars to pay for their debts. At least, they're the only ones that can do it legally.

risk of lending to them. Everything else being equal, the higher the yield being offered to you, the greater the risk you are taking. This is known as *credit risk*.

Bonds are rated by agencies that assign a letter score (much like you have a FICO score for your credit rating). Both Fitch and Standard & Poor's use an identical scale (AAA is the top rating, followed by AA+, AA, AA-, etc.), and Moody's uses a different scale to reflect the same information (Aaa is its top rating, followed by Aa1, Aa2, etc.). Any bond rated BBB- or above on the Fitch/S&P scale (or Baa3 and above on Moody's scale) is classified as an investment-grade bond, and any bond rated below is a *speculative grade* (junk) bond.[97]

Let's look at the effect of the term of the loan on the rate. For example, if you were to lend the federal government money over a 10-year period starting today, the government would pay you interest at a very low rate; however, if are you willing to lend the government the same amount of money for a 30-year period of time, the government will pay you a higher rate. This principle applies to municipal and corporate bonds as well: the longer you are willing to lend your money, the higher the rate they will pay you. The reason is straightforward: you take on more *interest-rate risk* the longer you lend the money.[98] It is true that if you hold the bond you purchased to maturity, you'll get all of your money back, along with all of the interest payments along the way; however, there are two things to consider.

First, if you lend money to the federal government for 30 years at a rate of 2.6%, it's highly possible that over that time, interest rates will rise. Let's assume the economy gets a little stronger, and the Federal Reserve

97 The high-yield bond folks really need to hire a better marketing team.

98 As a quick aside, sometimes market participants pay less for longer-term bonds, in which case the yield curve is said to be "inverted." This is often the sign of (1) a pending potential recession as investors are basically saying they are willing to tie up long-term money for less than short-term money, meaning the future doesn't look good and (2) mass hysteria in the financial media.

raises interest rates, eventually offering 10-year bonds at 4%. If anywhere along the way you want to sell your 30-year bond, you would have to sell at a discount. Say after 20 years, you want to sell it. Why would anyone want to pay full price for your now-10-year bond with an interest rate of 2.6%, when there are 10-year bonds they can purchase that have a interest rate of 4%? Second, if you hold your bond to maturity, you've missed out on the higher yield you could have received had you been able to invest in later, higher-yielding bonds.

Once you understand credit and interest rate risks, it becomes easier to understand bond pricing. It is not uncommon to think one bond is better because it's paying a higher yield, when in fact it's usually just riskier, because it is from a lower-rated company or has a longer term.

Bonds are far less risky than stocks because they make guaranteed payments to you. Bond payments are a contractual obligation, meaning the company has to pay you back, whereas stock dividends (which are distributions of profits) are discretionary, meaning the company can stop paying dividends whenever it feels like it. Because of this, if you hold a bond to maturity and the bond issuer does not go bankrupt, you receive your original loan back plus the interest payments. Bonds as an asset class deliver positive calendar-year returns approximately 85% of the time. Note, however, that bonds are a very broad asset class with a very wide range of expected returns. So where do bonds make sense in a portfolio? Short- to intermediate-term, high-quality, diversified bonds make sense for an investor's needs inside of the next two to seven years. Bonds also provide "dry powder" for investors who like to keep funds available for purchases when the stock market goes on sale; owning a highly liquid bond portfolio allows you to quickly raise cash to opportunistically purchase stocks. A diversified bond portfolio can also meet most of the needs of conservative investors who can't tolerate market volatility and have a large enough portfolio of investments that bond yields alone are enough to meet all of their needs.

STOCKS

Behind every stock is a company.

PETER LYNCH

When you purchase a stock, you own actual shares of a real company. You also move from being a consumer to being a shareholder, which is an important shift in mindset. Often financial media give the impression that stocks are like lottery tickets or going to a casino. That's not the case at all. Understand that when you purchase a share of a publicly traded company, *you actually own part of an operating business.* This can help you make better decisions about what you want to buy (and why). As a shareholder, your shares will increase or decrease in value based on the perceived fortunes of the company. Many stocks also pay *dividends*, quarterly distributions of profits to their shareholders.

Historically, stocks earn an average return of approximately 9% to 10% per year, though many pundits believe stocks are more likely to average significantly less going into the near future. Either way, stocks are among the investments with the highest expected rate of return. They are also extremely volatile, and it's not uncommon for them to drop 20% to 50% or more every few years. Stock market investing is not for the faint of heart.

Stocks have an expected long-term rate of return that is higher than bonds because of the *risk premium* concept, which means that the more risk you take, the more reward you expect in return. If stocks didn't have a higher expected rate of return than bonds, no one would ever buy stock. Can you imagine someone calling his advisor and saying, "I'd like to get a bond-like return, but instead, please buy something that can fluctuate in value as much as 50%. That really sounds preferable"?

So where do stocks fit within a portfolio? Over the long run, nothing better reflects economic expansion than the stock market. If you believe that the economy and businesses will be doing better ten years from now than they are today, the stock market is a place to allocate some of your investments. However, over the short run, stocks are incredibly unpredictable.

In fact, they tend to be down approximately one in every four years. It's common for stocks to drop dramatically, sometimes for legitimate reasons but sometimes for no reason at all. Because of this, any money you need to meet short-term goals should *not* be invested in stocks. This is the place to invest money to help you achieve long-term goals, like retirement.

REAL ESTATE

Don't wait to buy real estate, buy real estate and wait.

WILL ROGERS

Investors can turn to publicly traded real estate as well. This is usually done through publicly traded REITs (real estate investment trusts). REITs own commercial real estate (industrial buildings, apartment complexes, and strip malls, for example, as opposed to your home), and other properties that produce income.

Investors like publicly traded real estate because it doesn't behave exactly the way stocks do, but it is important to note that they are still very much in sync[99] with the market and at times do correlate, particularly during a financial crisis. Because REITs behave somewhat differently than stocks do, they help diversify the portfolio. They can also provide excellent diversification within the real estate market itself. Say you have $100,000 to invest in real estate; one option is to buy a small rental property in a small town, and another is to buy shares in a publicly traded REIT and own a small part of thousands of commercial properties across different market segments (apartments, industrial, storage, and so on) all over the country.

REITs often produce more dividend income than stocks do, often double or more, because the net rental income passes through to investors. And who doesn't like getting rent checks without the trouble of being a

99   Not a reference to a boy band.

landlord? Rents also tend to move up with inflation, so REITs can provide some protection from inflation. Finally, publicly traded REITs are liquid, meaning they can be traded just like stocks. Overall, publicly traded REITs can be a wise investment as part of a well-diversified portfolio.[100]

COMMODITIES

A commodity is a raw material or agricultural product that can be bought or sold, such as energy like oil; food like coffee, corn, and wheat; or precious metals like gold, silver, and copper. Commodities don't inherently produce income, are highly volatile, and are often taxed at higher rates than other investments.[101] By way of example, let's look at one of the most popular commodity investments: gold.

> What motivates most gold purchasers is their belief that the ranks of the fearful will grow. During the past decade, that belief has proved correct. Beyond that, the rising price has on its own generated additional buying enthusiasm, attracting purchasers who see the rise as validating an investment thesis. As "bandwagon" investors join any party, they create their own truth—for a while.
>
> WARREN BUFFETT[102]

Many investors worry the global economy will collapse, and gold will be the one true currency (though, of late, cryptocurrencies are stealing a

---

100 Warning: Private "nontraded" REITs have become incredibly popular among brokers because they pay huge commissions. The problem is that they are NOT liquid and you don't have near the same level of transparency. Steer clear of these!

101 So far, not so awesome.

102 Also from Buffett, and more entertaining: "Gold gets dug out of the ground in Africa, or someplace. Then we melt it down, dig another hole, bury it, and pay people to stand around guarding it. It has no utility. Anyone watching from Mars would be scratching his head."

bit of this narrative). Others view it as the safest place to be should we see high inflation that would diminish the value of cash.

Unlike companies, real estate, and energy, the intrinsic value of gold is nearly worthless. Companies and real estate have the potential to create income, and energy companies have the potential to produce income and provide one of the most critical resources in the global economy. But gold produces no income and is not a critical resource. Historically, gold has performed worse than stocks, real estate, energy, and bonds, barely keeping pace with inflation. Every time in history it has done extremely well and surged in price, it has ultimately collapsed. Finally, although gold has proven to dramatically underperform stocks and even bonds, it is still one of the most volatile asset classes over the long run. Gold belongs only in the portfolios of fearmongers and speculators. If you own gold in your portfolio, expect to receive no income, pay higher taxes on your returns, take a more volatile ride than the stock market will give you, and get a long-term return lower than bonds. I'll pass.

Figure 10.1

INFLATION ADJUSTED ANNUAL AVERAGE GOLD PRICES (1914–2018) IN MARCH 2018 DOLLARS

ALTERNATIVE INVESTMENTS

Ask 100 people to define "alternative investments" and you will get 100 different answers. Here, we look at it through two lenses that offer a view into the vast majority of the market. *Alternative investing* most often means "an alternative way to invest in public markets" or, more frequently, "investments that serve as a way to earn returns without investing in the public markets." Hedge funds are the most common investment in the first category (spoiler alert, I'm not a fan).

The most common alternatives to trading in public markets are privately held versions of stocks, bonds, and real estate. There is also a private market for companies that are not publicly traded. Most of these companies are owned by individual entrepreneurs, but others are owned by any one of the thousands of private equity firms that look to buy growing businesses that they believe will increase in value with their support and capital. There are also private real estate funds. Has anyone every pitched you on buying into a local development, strip mall, or apartment complex with them? That's private real estate.

The odds of success are stacked against investors with many alternative investments, while others can greatly help well-educated and qualified investors. I'll demystify all of the options and more in this next section.

Most of these alternative investments require investors to meet certain minimum regulatory requirements to participate in the offerings; some products are available only to *accredited investors*, with a net worth of over $1 million, or *qualified purchasers*, with a net worth of over $5 million.[103]

---

103 This is an intentional oversimplification of the rules, but the moral of the story is that these types of investments aren't available to most people.

Hedge Funds: The Worst Way to Buy Stocks

I want to pay more in fees, pay more in taxes, give up

access to my investment, not know exactly what is going

on with my money, and get below-average returns.

SAID NO ONE, EVER

There are all sorts of hedge funds, but the most common are the ones that invest in stocks. In 2008, Warren Buffett made a ten-year bet with Ted Seides, a partner at the hedge fund company, Protégé Partners. Warren and Ted bet a million dollars,[104] to be paid to the other's favorite charity, with Warren claiming that hedge funds couldn't beat the market or justify their fees and Ted claiming that they most certainly could while at the same time taking less risk. Warren was so confident that he even let Ted choose the hedge funds rather than simply compare the performance of the overall stock market to the overall hedge fund market. In other words, this was a bet between owning the S&P 500, a basket of publicly traded stocks, and five funds from cream-of-the-crop hedge funds, hand-selected by Seides. In a minute, we'll find out how they did.

I am a believer in using multiple asset classes, including stocks, bonds, real estate, and alternative investments; however, there is no place in a portfolio for hedge funds that invest in the stock market. There are a lot of reasons for this, but the main one is simple: *investing in hedge funds is a great way to increase the odds of underperformance.* This goes against most of what you will hear about these investment vehicles, so let's look at the facts.

Hedge funds are private investment funds available to eligible investors who engage in a wide range of activities. Some hedge funds are "event driven," meaning they try to gain an edge on the markets based on major events such as wars, oil shortages, economic events, and so on. Some are long/short funds, meaning they bet on some stocks going up and others

---

104 Quite the bet, considering I get a little tense with $25 on a blackjack table.

going down. Some use derivatives and options, and many use *leverage*, meaning they borrow additional money to invest. This all just scratches the surface of how hedge funds can operate. The main objective of many of these funds is to deliver stock market return, or an even better return, with less volatility. In times of underperformance, like the last ten years, hedge fund managers will claim their job is to reduce volatility in exchange for a lower return. In my experience, the "lower return" part is usually news[105] to the (mostly) nonprofit institutions and endowments that invest in them.

At Creative Planning, we never use equity hedge funds because I'm aware of what drives future performance, and hedge funds start out with a great disadvantage *in every major category*: taxes, fees, risk management, transparency, and liquidity.

First, for high-net-worth individuals, the top indicator of future performance, after asset allocation, is taxes. You should always be actively working to reduce taxes. Hedge funds do the opposite.[106] By actively trading, nearly all hedge fund managers deliver a much larger tax hit than simply investing in a fund that just tracks the market index. Strike one.

Second, most hedge funds have ridiculously high fee schedules, with the typical fee being an annual management fee of 1.5% to 2% whether the portfolio is up or down, plus 20% of the profits over a certain return (if there are profits).[107] Given that fees are a major indicator of future perfor-mance, let's call this strike two.[108]

Third, while we are discussing how hedge fund managers get paid, it is interesting to note that the manager has a great incentive to take huge risks with your money. If the manager gets paid 2% no matter what happens,

---

105 After the fact.

106 Yes, I know, most institutions don't pay taxes. You are probably not an institution.

107 This is a big if. The failure rate for hedge funds is very high. More on that later.

108 If you are an institutional investor, take note, as this and the other strikes do in fact apply to your organization and are probably the reason your investment committee meetings start with your consultant trying to position that somehow the subpar returns are a good thing.

plus a huge percentage of the profits, why not swing for the fences? It is not uncommon for a hedge fund to go up 30%, make the manager a centimillionaire or billionaire, and then blow up a year later, at no negative consequence to the manager save for a little embarrassment he will likely overcome.[109] Strike three.

Fourth, hedge funds do not regularly disclose what they own or what strategies they use; therefore, investors often have no idea what they own or the risks they are exposed to at any given period. With most hedge funds, you simply wait for the statement to see what happened. I am a big believer in transparency; at all times, you should know what you own and how your investments are doing.[110]

Finally, hedge funds lack liquidity. Hedge fund investors usually need to wait for redemption "windows" to open at certain points during the year, so they can withdraw their funds. This is in stark contrast to index funds, which are highly liquid, giving you the ability to exit positions at any given time. There are some investments where giving up liquidity makes sense, like private real estate, but there is no need to take an inherently liquid investment, like publicly traded stocks, and tie it up in an illiquid investment vehicle.

Why in the world would anyone invest in hedge funds when they know they will pay more taxes, pay 100% to 500% higher fees, have less control over their risk, lose transparency, and lose the ability to exit the investment whenever they wish?

The answer is quite simple: investors believe hedge funds will outperform.[111]

---

109 Sailing off the Amalfi coast in your $100 million yacht tends to have that effect on people, or so I hear.

110 Hedge funds as an investment already struck out, so no need to keep counting strikes.

111 And cocktail party bragging rights, as many funds have the manufactured exclusivity of a velvet rope nightclub.

Only one problem: they don't perform nearly as well as investors think they do!

Hedge funds aren't scarce and they aren't special. It may surprise you to know there are more than 10,000 hedge funds, more than double the number of US stocks! The Credit Suisse Hedge Fund Index tracks hedge fund performance, and its comparative data are telling: since the index's inception in 1994, a time frame that includes both bull and bear markets, the S&P 500 outperformed the major hedge fund strategies by about 2.5% on an annualized basis. In addition, most hedge funds perform so poorly they don't survive. A recent study examined 6,169 unique hedge funds (eliminating those not in US currency and those that are funds of funds[112]) from 1995 through 2009. Of these 6,169 that were around in 1995, only 37% (2,252) were still around at the end of the study in 2009.

You may be thinking, "What about the best hedge funds? Are there a few unicorns that have done extraordinarily well for long periods of time?" Yes, but with thousands of hedge fund managers, statistically you'd expect one or two to perform well. But here is a scary fact: the best hedge funds are often the ones that have the most spectacular downfalls. In 1998, Long-Term Capital Management, run by Nobel Prize winners and considered the greatest hedge fund of its time, collapsed overnight and nearly took the markets down with it. Warren Buffett, who has repeatedly stated he finds hedge funds to be ridiculous investments, said of the Long-Term Capital Management fiasco: "They probably have as high an average IQ of any sixteen people working together in one business in the country . . . just an incredible amount of intellect in that group. Now you combine that with the fact that those sixteen had extensive experience in the field they were operating in . . . in aggregate, the sixteen probably had 350 to 400 years of experience doing exactly what they were doing. And then you throw in the third factor: that most of them had

---

112 A fund of funds is yet another layer of fees. These are hedge funds where you pay them to invest in other hedge funds.

virtually all of their substantial net worths in the business. . . . And essentially they went broke . . . that to me is fascinating."[113]

The most recent hedge fund star, John Paulson, predicted the mortgage crisis and used his hedge fund to bet correctly. His investors made huge returns, and he made billions, all in one year. Unfortunately for his investors, he lost 52% in 2011 when the market was up, and since 2011, he has lost over $29 billion of the capital in his funds. But Paulson is not alone; since 2015, more hedge funds have closed every year than have opened.

Hedge fund defenders[114] will say that while the purpose of hedge funds used to be to outperform the market, now the purpose is simply to reduce portfolio volatility and smooth out the ride. However, a study covering 2002 through 2013 looked at the performance of hedge funds that largely attempted to reduce volatility and compared the results to owning a simple 60% stock index, 40% bond index portfolio. Not only did the simple indexed portfolio outperform the hedge funds, *it did so with less volatility*.

Now, back to the bet between Warren Buffett and Ted Seides. At the end of the ten-year bet, the S&P 500 finished up 99%, averaging 7.1% per year. The hedge funds finished with a gain of 24%, just 2.2% per year.

Yes, hedge funds will make someone rich. Just likely not you.[115]

Private Equity

Private equity funds invest capital, usually for years, in private companies in return for an equity interest that is not tradable in the public markets.[116]

---

113   "Fascinating" may be what Warren calls it, but I am pretty sure those that invested in the fund would use an unprintable phrase to describe it.

114   Who are usually the people running them or selling them.

115   But hedge fund managers will continue to laugh all the way to the bank or their yachts. How foolish they must think we all are. And we have given them plenty of reason to think that.

116   Private equity funds can also invest in a public entity, but even then, the fund's stake is not tradable in the public market.

There are three main categories of private equity: venture capital, which many consider to be a separate asset class in and of itself; growth equity; and buyout funds. *Venture capital funds* invest in early-stage companies: think no profits, sometimes no revenue, and sometimes no product. It's not uncommon for venture capital funds to invest in an idea. This is a high-stakes game that's not appropriate for most investors, but one we will examine more closely in this section.

When most people think of private equity, what they are really thinking of is a common subset of the asset class known as *growth equity*. Growth equity funds invest in businesses that are already showing promise in the form of a proven product delivering not only revenues but usually profits. Finally, *buyout funds* are known for buying a majority stake in a business, almost always using leverage.[117]

Let's break it down.

Venture Capital

> We have met the enemy, and he is us.
>
> POGO[118]

San Francisco, 2017. I'm sitting in a café in downtown San Francisco, waiting to meet a very high-profile multibillionaire. He's a tech guy and shows up an hour late, unshaven and wearing a hoodie. At this point, I'm not sure if this is real life or an episode of *Silicon Valley*. He's also cooler and smarter than I imagined, skipping from topic to topic with brilliant insights. He orders from the waiter, and after a brief description of his recent family vacation

---

117   What rich people call "debt."

118   Pogo is not a philosopher or money manager. He is the main character of a comic strip from the 1940s that stayed popular through the 1980s. For readers under 30, a comic strip is a sequence of drawings arranged in boxes to display humor, typically printed in a newspaper. For those under 20, a newspaper is a printed publication consisting of folded sheets containing news, articles, editorials, advertisements, and sometimes comic strips.

on a yacht, he dives right in. He tells me he has several billion dollars in his company's stock and loves investing in start-ups; he's already invested in over 100 of them. His personal family office chief financial officer had sought me out and arranged the meeting to encourage him to diversify his holdings. I went over the reasons he may do better with a diversified portfolio and that he should consider it with some of his funds. He explained that he "fully expects" the vast majority of his venture capital investments to fail, that the few that work out should pay for the others (one of those investments, Uber, was obviously a good example of one that succeeded), and that if they all failed, he didn't care because he had billions of dollars.

And you know what? *He was right.* If you have more money than you could ever possibly need, then you should do whatever you want to do: give it all away, invest in the future, invest in start-ups, or, heck, create your own swimming pool full of cash and jump in like Scrooge McDuck. If not, venture capital likely isn't for you.

Venture capital investments sound about as sexy as you can get. Many of America's greatest companies were born from venture capital funds, including Google, Facebook, Twitter, Dropbox, Uber, and nearly every other unicorn investment you have read about. However, many investors and even institutions have the misperception that venture capital funds produce outsized returns.

The Kauffman Foundation,[119] with its $2 billion fund, is one of the largest endowments in the country. In 2012, it released a groundbreaking paper on its experience with 100 venture capital funds over 20 years, aptly titled: "We Have Met the Enemy . . . and He is Us." I love the subtitle too: "Lessons from Twenty Years of the Kauffman Foundation's Investments in Venture Capital Funds, and the Triumph of Hope over Experience." They found that the majority of venture capital funds underperformed the publicly available small company index (only 4 of 30 venture capital funds outperformed

119 Kansas City shout-out!

the index) and the average venture capital fund "fails to return the capital invested after fees." This is especially troubling since while the companies that venture capital funds invest in are small, they are much, much smaller than small companies that comprise the publicly available index. This puts into perspective how risky venture capital funds actually are. Not only did these funds underperform; they did so with far more risk, higher fees (2% plus 20% of profits is the norm), less liquidity (investments often locked up for as much as a decade or more), and less transparency (What do we really know about what is going on in a private start-up company anyway?).

The conclusion of the report is straightforward: investors are likely better off owning a small company index fund than a venture capital fund. The researchers wrote, "Investors like us succumb time and again to narrative fallacies, a well-studied behavioral finance bias". In other words, investments in venture capital funds are based largely on a fascinating story of the allure of promised high returns.

Assuming you still have an interest in investing in venture capital and are confident your fund will do what the Kauffman Foundation's venture capital funds failed to, note that unlike the foundation, which is a nonprofit, you will owe taxes on any gains. So if you find yourself overcoming the investment return odds, the tax gods will set you back. For most people interested in investing in an asset class that has a high probability of outperforming large company stocks over ten years or more, small company index investing, not venture capital, is the answer.

Growth Equity and Buyout Funds

> Private equity is investing in hindsight.
> Venture capital is investing in foresight.
> GEORGES VAN HOEGAERDEN

Growth equity funds do what their name implies: they pool capital from investors to buy into a small, profitable business and use the fund managers'

Figure 10.2

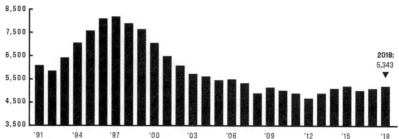

NUMBER OF U.S. LISTED COMPANIES, 1991-2018

expertise to transform it into a larger, even more profitable business. The expectation is that the fund's investors can realize profits when the business is sold in the future at a much higher value or the company goes public. In addition to deploying their investors' capital, growth equity funds frequently use leverage, particularly if it is a buyout fund. By borrowing money to buy businesses, fund managers can maximize the use of their capital and get better returns if the business's fortunes pan out. This asset class is rapidly expanding, and there are now far more private equity funds, nearly 8,000, than there are publicly traded companies.

Figure 10.3

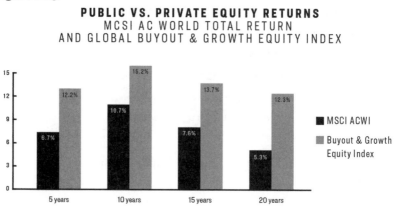

PUBLIC VS. PRIVATE EQUITY RETURNS
MCSI AC WORLD TOTAL RETURN
AND GLOBAL BUYOUT & GROWTH EQUITY INDEX

Money has poured into private equity since the 1980s. Given the proliferation of private equity funds over the last 20 years, the multidecade performance tells a clear story: growth equity has consistently outperformed the public markets.

Over the same period of time, institutions like universities and charities have started to review the historical performance of their alternative investments, mainly in hedge funds and private equity funds. The results are telling: hedge funds have substantially underperformed the stock market, and private equity firms have substantially outperformed. With these data in hand, institutions are reducing or eliminating their allocation to hedge funds and flooding private equity funds with money.

To put all this money to work, private equity firms search for private businesses in which their capital and expertise can generate profits. While some private equity firms simply invest money and monitor their investments, many take an active role in giving advice and helping the business grow. Private equity firms are usually very involved in working with, and sometimes even selecting, the key management of a business in which they invest. This economic setup aligns everyone's interests, with the private equity firm sharing in profits above a certain threshold return, management being incentivized to grow, and the investors typically locking up their money for a period of 7 to 12 years in exchange for anticipated growth.

The outperformance of private equity funds aligns with my personal experience. At Creative Planning, we have an ultra-affluent practice that focuses on a small group of clients with anywhere from $10 million to $500 million or more to invest. How did they get their wealth in the first place? Many of them built businesses that were growing fast or had the potential to grow fast and sold a portion or all of their company to a private equity fund.

Often successful businesspeople are able to come up with a great idea, hire some people, and start to develop their business, but usually don't have the capital or skill set to scale the business. By *scaling*, I mean developing it in a way as to drive dramatically higher revenues and (ultimately) profits. Private equity firms are excellent at scaling and can provide a valuable resource to these businesses. It is common for Creative Planning clients to sell a substantial stake in their business to a private equity fund in one year and sell all their remaining equity three to ten years later for double the amount they received in the first round due to the effectiveness of the fund managers in scaling the business. Private equity firms are also skilled at maximizing the sale price of a business: they have experience selling to all sorts of buyers, including strategic partnerships (another company that can immediately scale the business—think of Facebook buying Instagram), sponsors (like another private equity fund), or completing an initial public offering (see Google or Lyft).

Top private equity firms bring expertise at scaling businesses, funding growth, investing in experienced talent, and imposing discipline. Nevertheless, as an investment, the asset class has its downsides. Investors must lock up their money for many years because the holdings are not publicly traded. No one who needs their money back in the short term should invest in private equity. Your tax return will almost certainly be delayed as you await another Schedule K-1 (tax form). And of course, there is no guarantee the expected performance will be achieved or continue. To the same end, there is no guarantee that stocks will outperform bonds either. Having said all that, the evidence suggests that private equity may continue to offer a premium return to the high-net-worth, long-term, patient investor.

PRIVATE LENDING

A banker is a man who will lend you the short sleeve shirt
off his back and demand a long sleeve one in return.
JAROD KINTZ

If you aren't a bank, you can make money in the private lending category by investing in a private lending fund. There are many kinds of private lending funds, including funds comprising:

- Loans to consumers
- Loans secured by real estate
- Loans to businesses
- Loans for funding just about anything you can think of, from movies to race car drivers

Here, we are focused on middle-market lending funds. If one can liken private equity investing to a private version of the stock market, middle-market lending is the private version of the bond market. Businesses with revenues between $25 million and hundreds of millions in revenue find themselves in a spot where they are too big for small business loans, too small for big bank loans, and, as private companies, unable to access the public bond market to raise funds. To obtain capital to grow, these businesses are left essentially with two choices: they can sell a portion of their company to a private equity fund or borrow money from a middle-market lending fund.

Middle-market lending funds are run much like private equity funds—in the sense that professional investors raise funds and evaluate businesses—but instead of taking an equity position in the company, they simply lend money. The loans may or may not be *secured*, meaning the loan uses some sort of asset, like a building or equipment, as collateral, or they may offer the option for the fund to convert the loan into equity. Because banks don't operate in this space, these funds are able to charge businesses a higher interest rate. As with private equity funds, investors must meet certain qualifications to invest, be willing to lock up their money for a period of time, and deal with extra tax forms and tax preparation extensions. While there is no guarantee a private lending fund will outperform publicly traded bonds, especially given how little history exists in the space, based on the risk profile of loans being made, there appear to be good odds that middle-market lending will deliver better risk-adjusted returns over time. These funds vary widely in terms of management experience and risk profile, so even the most sophisticated investors should proceed with great caution.

PRIVATE REAL ESTATE

He is not a full man who does

not own a piece of land.

HEBREW PROVERB

Private real estate covers a wide spectrum. If you own any investment real estate outside of publicly traded REITs, then you own private real estate. This means that if you lease farmland that you own, you own an alternative investment. Same if you own a townhouse you rent out or a share in an apartment complex. There are all sorts of other private real estate holdings. We have your personal residence (bad news: it's nice you own a home, but it's not really an investment; more on that later). You may own a second home or vacation property as well (sorry, still not really an investment even if you tell yourself that's why you bought it). Or you may own property on your own from which you earn income or have the potential to earn income (this one you can call an investment). You can also invest in a private real estate fund, where you give your money to a professional who uses it to invest in some sort of real estate.

Let's break all these down.

Your Home

In the summer of 2000, my wife and I purchased our first home, and we were thrilled! This was the biggest asset we had ever "invested" in. On our next update to our financial plan, we listed the house on our net worth statement the same way everyone does: as an asset. The mortgage was listed as a liability. In reality, both the house and the mortgage are cash flow "liabilities." With the loan, we pay interest each month. For the house itself, we pay property taxes each year, maintenance costs, and insurance. Even when the mortgage is paid off, all of those property expenses will stay and likely increase over time.

For most of us, the purchase of a home, represents our largest asset. And for many, the forced "savings," from paying off the mortgage every month, results in building equity over time, which can be unlocked when we downsize at some point in the future and the remaining proceeds can help fund retirement. In that sense, owning a home is beneficial because it forces us to save, in a manner of speaking. But make no mistake:, a house is not a great investment. Investing the same amount of money in a boring, diversified portfolio is likely to yield results that are 100% better over the same time it takes to pay off a mortgage. But you have to live somewhere, and for many, owning a home is better than renting, not having forced savings, and not building equity.

Ultimately your choice of a home should be an emotional decision. If it were just about money, we would all choose to live in a room with four walls and invest the difference. But it's not just about money; a home is where we spend most of our time and build many memories. When looking for a home, get one you feel great about and can afford, and allocate the difference into better investments.

Your Second Home

One of the most frequent questions I hear clients ask their Creative Planning wealth manager is, "Is a second home a good investment?" I personally enjoy the conversations around this question because it cuts to the heart of true wealth management. Most scenarios are partially financial issues, such as how to maximize wealth, but also emotional issues, such as the purpose of having wealth. The straight-up financial answer to, "Should I spend my money on a second home?" is almost always a "no." Rarely does a second home (or a first home, for that matter) make a good investment. This is for asset value reasons as well as cash flow reasons.

First, let's cover the asset value gain or loss on a second home. If you purchase a property, say, a condo in Florida or a cabin in Colorado, you may be fortunate to sell it at a gain a decade or two from now. However, when you factor in the negative cash flow, the situation looks much worse than you think.

My in-laws have a condo in Florida on the Gulf of Mexico, and every year, our family of five would vacation there with them. It became quite the tradition, and our kids looked forward to it every year. As our family grew, space in their condo got tighter and tighter. In the middle of the financial crisis, another unit in the building came up for sale. After much deliberation, my wife and I decided to take the plunge and purchase the extra unit for our family. Just over a decade later, similar condos in the building are selling for nearly twice what we paid. We made out like bandits, didn't we? Actually, we didn't. Over that same time period, we had the same types of expenses and costs on the condo you would on any home, which totaled more than the appreciation in market value. We purchased at the market bottom, the current price is near an all-time high, and after paying the ongoing costs, we still haven't made a profit. If we had taken the same money and instead purchased a stock market index, we would have more than doubled our money over the same time frame!

By definition, good investments generate positive cash flow. For example, if you own stocks, you likely collect dividends. If you own bonds, you collect the coupon payments. If you own investment real estate, like a publicly traded real estate fund or rental, you collect distributions or rent. This is beneficial because even as the value of the asset fluctuates, *money is flowing to you*. If you own a second home, *money is flowing away from you*. In general, we would all be better off if we picked anywhere in the world for a vacation and stayed at the Ritz Carlton instead of buying a second home.

But that is just the financial side of the story. For most of us, money is saved and invested to serve a purpose in our lives rather than just accumulating money for the sake of having more of it. *The sole value of money is what it can do for us*. It can enable us to be the family rock, ensuring everyone around us is taken care of. It allows us to make charitable gifts, have an impact on our community, and be able to focus on significance over success. It also allows us to buy a car just because we think it is cool or buy a second home where we can create memories with our family. So while a second home should never be seen as a good financial investment, it can certainly be a worthwhile emotional investment.

That's how I see my family's Florida condo. I am purposefully sacrificing any hope of economic gain in exchange for creating priceless family memories. It's that simple. If you have been considering that second home for emotional reasons and you can purchase it while staying on track for your personal financial goals, by all means, do it!

Private Real Estate

Having exposure to real estate as part of a well-diversified portfolio can definitely add value, but real estate as an asset class is overrated in my opinion. There is a popular narrative that it's somehow a better or safer way to make money than owning stocks. Much like your friend's oft-repeated story of his successful trip to Vegas, you tend to hear only about the "winners" who made millions in the real estate game, not those who went bankrupt. Every investment carries risk, and just because the risks with owning real estate are different from those of the stock market doesn't make it an inherently risk-free investment.

Part of what fuels this narrative is the use of leverage in real estate. As you may recall, in investing, leverage refers to using debt to generate investment capital. In the case of real estate, most investments are not made using 100% cash; instead, investors borrow money against the value of the property to buy it. Let's say you want to buy a $100,000 duplex. You will most likely invest $20,000 of your own money and borrow the remaining $80,000 from the bank. One year later, the same property is worth $120,000, so you decide to sell it. After paying off the $80,000 loan, you pocket $40,000. So although the property increased in value by 20%, your profit was 100%. That's the power of leverage: it amplifies an investor's returns.

The problem is that it works the other way too. If instead, the property value had dropped to $80,000 and you were forced to sell it, there is nothing left after paying off the loan. Instead of losing just 20% on your investment, you lost 100%. This is the reason you see a tremendous number of bankruptcies in real estate; investors can become overleveraged and lose more than the value of the property if it drops substantially. And when things go bad, they can get very bad very quickly. This was on full display during the 2008 financial crisis when families were underwater on their mortgages; real estate values dropped so low in many places that people couldn't get enough from the sale of their house to cover what was owed.

You can, of course, use leverage on almost any investment. If I had a $100,000 investment account, I could borrow $50,000 and purchase more stock. Most people would think that's *extremely risky*, but they have no qualms about borrowing money to buy real estate when, in essence, it's the same thing. Some believe that the inflationary power of real estate is somehow immune to the same rules that govern other asset classes, particularly if you live in an area where you generally observe prices rising over time. However, that myopic view ignores the parts of town that were once desirable but have now declined in value due to decaying infrastructure, a shift in centers of economic production, or changing consumer tastes.

For those where an allocation to private real estate makes sense in a portfolio, there are some benefits. One is that you can choose the types of properties you want to invest in—be it office buildings or single-family rental properties. Investments in development projects in certain economically depressed areas, referred to as *opportunity zones*, can qualify an investor for favorable tax breaks. In many cases, these investments are offered through a private real estate fund, where money is pooled from various investors to fund certain projects, including retail space, hospitals, and apartment buildings. The fund manager's objective is to develop these properties, typically lease them to a tenant, and then sell the property to someone else after about seven years. These investments are still subject to many of the same limitations as other private investments: they can add cost and complexity to filing your tax returns, and your investment capital may be largely inaccessible for a period of years. Typically, these types of funds have specific windows when you may request a withdrawal, but for the most part, your cash is locked up until the property sells.

The Real Estate "Business"

And now a quick note to those of you who are in the real estate business and rolling your eyes. None of what we have covered so far about real estate should be confused with being in the real estate business itself. Let's take home builders, for example; they aren't purchasing income-producing property and owning it as part of a diversified pool of investments. Instead, this is their job. They are putting up capital, creating something of value, and selling it. The returns one can achieve by making real estate their job can be 30% or more; they need to be, or no one would take on the big risks that developers face. Just as there is a difference between owning stock in a publicly traded company and owning a small business, the same can be said of investing in real estate when compared to being in the real estate business. It's investing in the same way starting a small business is investing (i.e., it's risky), and shouldn't be confused with traditional asset classes.

I think the best way to think about private real estate is this: if you could choose only between owning stock in any of the world's greatest companies or owning the building they operate out of, which would you pick? Sophisticated investors would pick the stock every time.

CRYPTOCURRENCIES

I can say almost with certainty that
cryptocurrencies will come to a bad end.

WARREN BUFFETT

Cryptocurrency is electronic money that uses cryptography to make transactions secure, prevent the unauthorized creation of additional units, and verify the transfer of the currency from one person to another. "Investing" in it is all the rage. While there are literally thousands of cryptocurrencies in the world, Bitcoin is all over the media and Internet of late, so we will focus largely on that first. Let's start with some background information.

Much like the dollar, yen, and euro are examples of traditional currencies, Bitcoin is a type of cryptocurrency invented by Satoshi Nakamoto. Get this: no one knows who Satoshi Nakamoto is, or if it is a person or group of people. Satoshi does not like or trust governments and has said that his mission is to cut out governments and create a decentralized monetary system that governments cannot easily attack. He created Bitcoin as the first decentralized digital currency. It is effectively decentralized because Satoshi also invented blockchain (the essential chassis that serves as the "ledger") to ensure each Bitcoin could be verified as legitimate and irreplicable.

Blockchain essentially allows someone to have confidence in a transaction with another party via the Internet. Prior to blockchain, an intermediary would be necessary to accomplish the same transaction. A familiar example would be a real estate transaction. Let's say you decide to sell your house. Most likely, a stranger is going to buy it, and he relies on the local government to provide a centralized ledger or database for deeds and titles to ensure that you are the true owner. This enables the buyer and his lender (if there is one) to purchase the home with confidence. In this example, the centralized database is essential to facilitating the transaction.

The purpose of blockchain is to eliminate the need for a centralized database. With blockchain technology, a group of people each have a copy of the ledger to keep track of transactions. Using our property sale example with blockchain, when you sell your home to Mary Sue, all parties agree the sale happened and update their ledgers. When Mary Sue is ready to sell, the next buyer can instantly confirm she has clear title because it is listed as such across the blockchain. This accomplishes two things. First, the need for an intermediary, in this case the local government, is removed. Second, the transaction can happen instantly. There is no need to involve a lawyer, request records, or validate their authenticity. This is a very real technology that is already changing the way many industries and major corporations operate.

IBM has invested heavily in blockchain. Its former CEO, Ginni Rometty, wrote to shareholders: "Blockchain brings together shared ledgers with smart contracts to allow the secure transfer of any asset—whether a physical asset like a shipping container, a financial asset like a bond or a digital asset like music—across any business network. Blockchain will do for trusted transactions what the Internet did for information." IBM is working with Walmart to use blockchain to track inventory. Walmart said that blockchain trials had helped it narrow the time needed to trace the movement of fruit from seven days to two seconds. Blockchain is in its infancy, but it is here for good.

With blockchain, we may soon live in a world where it's common to have financial records maintained on the historical ledger of a blockchain network, allowing new transactions to be instantly validated. Similarly, while today we, like other countries, count on the federal government to back the dollar and control the currency through central banks, local banks serve as the middlemen for financial transactions. With the invention of blockchain, Satoshi created a platform that eliminates governments and banks from being relevant to cryptocurrency transactions.

Over 1,000 cryptocurrencies now use blockchain technology. Considering there is no cost to launch a cryptocurrency, there just may be 1,000 more right after you blink. Outside of Bitcoin, other popular cryptocurrencies are

Ethereum, Litecoin, EOS, Ripple, and Tron.[120] Blockchain technology is a great idea and will change the way a lot of records, contracts, and transactions are handled. While cryptocurrencies are likely here for good, it is likely over 99% of them will quickly become worthless.

That brings us back to Bitcoin, which has soared from being worth $0 in 2009, to over $20,000 in 2017, and then back to around $5,000 as I write this in 2020. Some people say Bitcoin is worthless because it has no intrinsic value. Unlike real estate that can produce income, bonds that spin off yield, and stocks that pay out dividends, Bitcoin produces nothing. However, a number of investments produce nothing. Investors and collectors purchase paintings, which also do not spin off any income but may rise in value simply because someone is willing to pay more. Bitcoin, though, reminds me of Las Vegas condos in 2008 or Internet stocks in 1999: people were buying both at high prices that had no connection to reality, based on the assumption someone else would pay more for it later because that had happened repeatedly in the months and years prior. It is highly improbable that Bitcoin is going to emerge as a viable long-term currency solution. However, it will most likely end up in finance books a decade or two from now as an intriguing anecdote in a discussion of how investment bubbles form and ultimately collapse, bringing financial ruin to many.

Also, let's put a few things to bed that are out there. First, some say Bitcoin cannot be hacked because it is on the blockchain. In fact, the blockchain can be hacked; investors have already had over $1 billion in cryptocurrency stolen. Second, Bitcoin does not need to be hacked for people using it to lose money (the rise and fall of the market will do that). Third, some argue that governments will stay out of the way of cryptocurrencies. That is likely flawed thinking, as all governments like regulation, control, and taxes.[121]

---

120   Not to be confused with the 1982 Disney movie, *Tron*. No one said cryptocurrency enthusiasts were original.

121   And will most certainly not give up on their ultimate control mechanism: currency.

Yet just because it is improbable that Bitcoin will last doesn't mean it's impossible, and it is this sliver of hope that encourages speculators. Bitcoin is attractive to many because of the elimination of third-party interference (the government can't manipulate it by creating more, for example) and because of the anonymity that comes with it. These same benefits apply to over a thousand other cryptocurrencies. The reality, though, is that most people buying it have no plans to use it. They are buying it purely to speculate.

Ultimately that is what is driving the interest in Bitcoin. *Speculation* is defined as "guesses about something that is not known; activity in which someone buys and sells things in the hope of making a large profit but with the risk of a large loss." This is in contrast to investing, which is defined as "expending money with the expectation of achieving a profit or material result by putting it into financial strategies, shares, or property." Buying an apartment complex that is 90% occupied is investing; buying land on the moon because you think it will be inhabited one day is speculating. Bitcoin has already dropped over 80% on three occasions, but each time it has rocketed to new highs. Last year, "buy Bitcoin with credit card" became a popular search on Google. People are piling on the ship to the promised land.

As with all other bubbles, there will likely be as many people on the ship as possible before it goes down. But the same thing happened with the Internet bubble. Remember Lycos, Excite, and AOL? Did you ever Ask Jeeves? They were all ultimately felled by the competition as an eventual king, Google, emerged. The same may happen here, and any money placed in the cryptocurrency space should be considered highly speculative.

AND IT GOES ON AND ON AND ON

An entire book could be written just about the different types of alternative investments. While we have covered the major alternative asset classes, there are many other types. To give you a sense of how varied this space can be, here are just a few:

- *Reinsurance.* When you purchase an insurance policy, such as homeowner's insurance, the company that sold it to you may transfer the risk to another insurance company. This allows it to reduce risk and write more policies. Think of it as insurance for insurance companies. Some funds invest in these reinsurance pools.
- *Royalty funds.* In the 1990s, David Bowie and his financial team sold the rights to some of the income from his music catalog. These investments were dubbed "Bowie Bonds" and created a way for artists to immediately unlock value from their music income streams. Since then, music (and other forms of entertainment) royalty funds have sprung up, buying rights to artists' catalogs ranging from Mary J. Blige to Eminem, Iron Maiden to Elton John.
- *Life settlements.* The majority of people who purchase permanent life insurance policies end up surrendering them to the insurance company for a fraction of the death benefit. Life settlement funds purchase the policies from their owners for much more, giving the insured a chance to get fair value for their policy. When the policy ultimately pays out, the proceeds are distributed to the fund's investors.

We could go on and on: funds that invest in funding lawsuits in exchange for part of the potential award; funds that invest in only art, cars, or violins; funds that gamble on baseball . . .

Alternatives aren't for everyone. Even if you meet the legal net worth requirements to invest in many of these, they still are not suitable for most investors. For investors with a long-term plan, a strong team to conduct a thorough review of each investment, access to top-shelf invest-ments with lower minimums and at reasonable prices, and a willing-ness to deal with added complexity in their financial management, some alternatives can improve the expected long-term return of a diversified investor's portfolio.

For almost everyone else, though, a simple portfolio of publicly traded stocks, bonds, and real estate is likely all you need to achieve your finan-cial goals.

PART IV
THE CLIMB

CHAPTER ELEVEN

BUILDING AND MANAGING THE INTELLIGENT PORTFOLIO

Remember, diamonds are only lumps of coal that stuck to their jobs.

B. C. FORBES

Putting together a sound portfolio is part art, part science, and certainly never perfect, but it should follow a plan that makes sense for your particular situation. Choosing what to invest in and when can feel overwhelming, but when you are armed with a few helpful strategies, it should be much easier to tackle.

First, *asset allocation* is just a fancy phrase for how much of your portfolio dollars are earmarked for each type of asset class, such as stocks, bonds, and real estate. Which asset class should you invest in? At first glance when reviewing past returns, you might be tempted to go all in and invest just in the stock market, since as you can see in Figure 11.1, investing in 100% stocks has historically had the highest returns. But nothing is that easy. The more you invest just in stocks, the more volatility you introduce into the portfolio, which could cause you undue stress. A 100% stock portfolio has ranged from its best annual return of 54.2% to its worst at -43.1%. That's quite a nauseating ride. But if you balance it out with 60% stocks and 40% bonds, we smooth out the ride significantly, narrowing the range of performance from a 36.7% best year to a -26.6% worst year return.

Figure 11.1

THE PERFORMANCES OF VARIOUS MIXES OF U.S. STOCKS AND BONDS
1926-2018

ASSET ALLOCATION	AVERAGE ANNUAL RETURN
100% bonds	5.3%
10% stocks 90% bonds	5.9%
20% stocks 80% bonds	6.6%
30% stocks 70% bonds	7.1%
40% stocks 60% bonds	7.7%
50% stocks 50% bonds	8.2%
60% stocks 40% bonds	8.6%
70% stocks 30% bonds	9.1%
80% stocks 20% bonds	9.4%
90% stocks 10% bonds	9.8%
100% stocks	10.1%

Most financial advisors and books suggest using your age to determine your asset allocation. If you're 60 years old, your portfolio should be 60% in bonds and 40% stocks, or if you're 70 years old, it should be 70% bonds and 30% stocks. But this generalization is way too broad.

Other advisors and books tell you that your allocation should be based on your risk tolerance. If you're uneasy with your portfolio going down 10%, you shouldn't own any stocks or have an extremely small allocation to them. Such advice, however, is unfortunate and misleading, and it potentially impedes you from achieving your goals. For example, an investor who has a low risk tolerance but doesn't have much saved for retirement will likely

Figure 11.2

THE MIXTURE OF ASSETS DEFINES THE SPECTRUM O
BEST, WORST, AND AVERAGE RETURNS
FOR VARIOUS STOCK/BOND ALLOCATIONS, 1926-2018

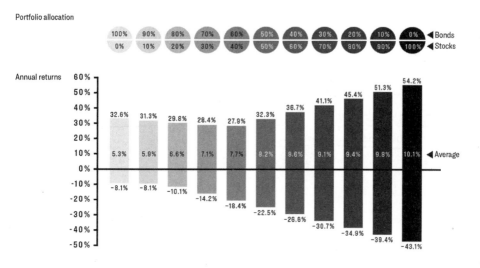

need to take on more portfolio risk to be able to retire soundly. Otherwise, when she's ready to retire, she'll likely have nowhere near enough saved.

All investors' allocations should be determined based on their needs. Therefore, you need a customized plan that aligns with what you're looking to achieve. If you need to earn a specific rate of return over the next 15 years to reach a specific goal, you should be invested in the combination of asset classes that have the highest probability of making that happen. And you know what your needs will be because you have a financial plan! Use this road map. Your financial plan reveals where you are today and what goals you want to achieve, while also showing how much you are able to save and any outside sources of income. Put that all together and you can back into the rate of return you need to be able to accomplish your goals. An investor attempting to achieve an average annual return of 6% to 7% over the next 15 years may be invested in approximately 70% stocks and 30% bonds (and potentially other alternative investments covered in the previous chapter). It doesn't matter if this investor is starting out at age 50 or 60: the need, not the age, determines the allocation.[122]

Studies show that anywhere from 88% to 91% of your portfolio's variance is determined by your asset allocation. Knowing this, you should examine the accompanying volatility (how much everything will move up and down) once you decide on the allocation and determine if you can live with the volatility. If you can't live with it, then you need to adjust the goal (spend less) or the plan (save more) so that a more conservative allocation can still ensure success. The point is that your personal allocation should *always* be pointed toward your goals, with your risk tolerance acting more as a checkpoint and your age having nothing to do with anything.

THE BIG PICTURE

The finance industry spends a lot of time discussing which asset classes are "good" or "bad" when in reality the investor's goals, not the various markets, should be what's driving the exposure[123] to any given asset class. For most investors, diversifying across many different asset classes to achieve various goals makes the most sense. As the saying goes, don't put all your eggs in one basket.

Often the top-rated money managers in any given year have invested in the same asset class as each other, and the worst-performing money managers also have invested in the same asset class as one other (but in a different asset class from the top-performing managers). You might think it's because they're all geniuses or idiots, but take emerging markets for example. Emerging market funds were the top-performing mutual

---

122 Age should, however, be a factor when choosing the length of your shorts, when determining what slang language is acceptable, and, according to my kids, reconsidering my "cool" Fortnite dances.

123 Another fancy investment word that just means "amount."

funds in 2017, and the following year, emerging market funds were the worst-performing mutual funds. The manager doesn't have much to do with returns—the asset class itself drives most of the return. In fact, only 9% to 12% of the return in any given fund is attributable to the manager. So if you owned a fund that was up 8% in a given year, on average only 0.072% to 0.96% of your return was because of their genius. This is why the first major decision of portfolio construction is asset allocation.

Cash is a terrible investment, as we have discussed. It really makes no sense to include cash in a portfolio. Consider an investor who has a million-dollar portfolio with 10% invested in cash. She could expect that $100,000 to earn practically nothing, as well as lose ground to inflation over the remaining decades of her life. Contrast this with bonds, which have never had a negative five-year return—*ever*. If that investor chose bonds instead of cash, which average a few points a year over cash, they will likely earn tens of thousands more over their life. The risk that the market falls out for bonds is the same for cash: if the entire bond market went to zero, a series of events must have occurred that would also make your cash totally worthless. These outlier scenarios, perpetuated by reality TV shows like *Doomsday Preppers*, make the ridiculous seem mainstream. Cash makes sense only to run your household, go to a restaurant, buy a car, and have reserves in place in case of a potential period of unemployment or unexpected shorter-term expenses. It has no place in an investment portfolio.

So do bonds ever lose money? Sure. Bonds deliver a negative calendar-year return about once every five years. But as long as the entity you loan money to stays around, you will get paid back with interest. By contrast, a stockholder never really knows what will happen since the stock can fluctuate all over the place. *At Creative Planning, we never recommend or own bonds on the expectation they will outperform stocks in the long term.*

So if we expect bonds to underperform in comparison to stocks, why in the world would we buy them? Basically, bonds are insurance. *You give up expected return in exchange for dramatically increasing the likelihood your needs can be met in the short and long run.* While stocks are likely to perform well over ten years, there is a lot of precedent for prolonged periods of misery (see 9/11, the 2008–2009 crisis, or the coronavirus pandemic for a refresher). You never want to be at the mercy of the stock market's often random gyrations and be forced to sell stocks when they are down to meet your income needs. Instead, add up the amount of money you'll need from the portfolio during a prolonged down market, minus the portfolio's projected income, to determine the appropriate percentage exposure to bonds.

THE CRYSTAL BALL

Stocks are the subject of ceaseless predictions, when in reality they are the most unpredictable and predictable (yes, both) asset class. First, let's be clear on how we see this at Creative Planning. No one, absolutely no one, can predict the short-term movement of stock prices, and anyone who tells you otherwise is likely a fool or liar. Yes, these are strong words, but with all the noise, it is important to understand the impact of this point of view on your financial future and how much you choose to allocate to this critical asset class. Over the long run, stocks are expected to perform better than any other publicly traded major asset class. The key to profiting from stocks is to remain fully invested through all the seemingly constant corrections, crashes, and day-to-day movements that cause the fainthearted to jump ship at the worst possible time. Ideally you take the opposite approach and embrace these tumultuous times as buying opportunities!

The key to make it through stocks' volatility is to have enough of your income needs met for the next five years so you don't have to worry about the ups and downs of the market. If you are not at the mercy of the market over the next few years—and we know that over the long run, the market has done nothing but go up—getting through the roller-coaster ride becomes far easier. An investor who has more than 10 to 20 years before needing income from this part of the portfolio can invest in subsets of the market that have greater volatility but also a long, equally well-documented history of rewarding investors for patience. This includes mid-cap stocks, small-cap stocks, micro-cap stocks,[124] and emerging markets stocks. The higher volatility should reward investors with a higher return.

Alternative investments can give those with a long time horizon and a high net worth a shot at long-term outperformance. With a portfolio of $5 million, $10 million, or far more, it's common to allocate anywhere from 10% to 30% or more to alternative investments, including subset asset classes like private equity, private lending, and private real estate. Many of my clients have wealth they will never spend or parts of the portfolio they will never touch that they would like the next generation to ultimately benefit from. For these situations, even a 75-year-old could have a significant portion of his portfolio in small stocks, emerging markets stocks, or alternative investments.

While this strategy works well on paper and over time, it is not for the fainthearted. These sub-asset classes can move quickly, both up and down, and can underperform for long periods of time. *A good way to know if these sub-asset classes make sense for you is your reaction to a drop in the markets.* If you get excited at the opportunity to sell off some of your bonds and buy more small-cap stocks and emerging markets stocks while they are getting hammered, these sub-asset classes could work well for you. If you find yourself freaking out about the drops, you will not last in the position long enough for it to work out, and you will cause your portfolio undue harm. In times of turmoil, it pays to know yourself.

---

124 Market capitalization ("cap" for short) refers to the price of the stock multiplied by the number of shares outstanding. Large-cap stocks are typically defined as having a market cap of $10 billion or more, mid-cap stocks have a capitalization between $2 billion and $10 billion, with small-cap stocks being anything below $2 billion. Even small-cap stocks are pretty darn big!

THE FINISHING TOUCHES

You should have a strategic asset allocation mix that assumes
that you don't know what the future is going to hold.

RAY DALIO

Now that you have determined your allocation to stocks and bonds and
have gauged your comfort level with including other investments with
greater expected volatility, it's time to take a hard look at your target allocation. Your target allocation is your ideal recipe, your ideal blend of investments that are defined by your plan *and* your emotional capacity to deal
with the ups and downs.

Take a Global Approach

Consider the following fact: Sweden accounts for approximately 1%
of the world economy. A rational investor in the United States or
Japan would invest about 1% of his assets in Swedish stocks. Can it
make sense for Swedish investors to invest 48 times more? No. [T]his
reflects the well-known tendency of investors to buy stocks from their
home country, something that economists refer to as the home bias.

RICHARD H. THALER AND CASS R. SUNSTEIN

We tend to prefer choices that are close to our home base rather than
seeking options outside of our personal comfort zone, otherwise known
as *home bias*. You likely experience this every day when you frequent the
closest and most convenient grocery store, gas station, or coffee house to
your home or office. On the weekend, you are more likely to go out to
dinner in an area close to home than at a restaurant you love a little farther
away. The majority of US investors focus on US large company stocks
when picking stock portfolios simply because we recognize these names.

Regardless of the industry, nearly every domestic company has a global
counterpart with the potential for equal, if not greater, performance. In

fact, according to a recent forecast from Standard Chartered, by 2030, China and India are expected to become the two largest economies in the world by a significant margin. Therefore, international holdings should be part of your portfolio. Although you might feel more comfortable with household names in your portfolio, you're actually increasing risk by over-concentrating assets in one part of the globe. We live in a global economy, and companies everywhere can and do make money. International hold-ings, however, usually behave slightly differently from US holdings. US and international markets often "take turns" outperforming one another for short and sometimes long periods of time. Consider what happened to the US markets during the "lost decade" of 2000–2009, when the S&P 500 delivered a return of just under 0%, even after accounting for dividends. Investors who had allocated strictly to US large-cap stocks suffered, while globally diversified investors found strong returns in international and emerging markets. Diversifying globally helps reduce volatility in your portfolio while at the same time enhancing long-term performance, since many international economies, especially the emerging market economies, have far higher projected growth rates than the United States does.

As Figure 11.3 shows, home bias is a global phenomenon. Perfectly unbiased investors, global citizens so to speak, would own securities in the same proportion as their global market capitalization. For example, in 2010, the US market represented 43% of the total global market, so perfectly unbiased investors would have 43% of their portfolio allocated to US stocks. The average investor in the United States, however, has a portfolio heavily weighted in US stocks. The same goes for other countries: average investors in the United Kingdom, for example, favor UK stocks by 42%, and Swedes have nearly half their money in Swedish stocks! This plan basically equates to investing all you have ever worked for based on location rather than logic.

Global market capitalization is not the only way to determine how much of your portfolio should be allocated to international investments,

Figure 11.3

RELATIVE MAGNITUDE OF HOME-COUNTRY BIAS

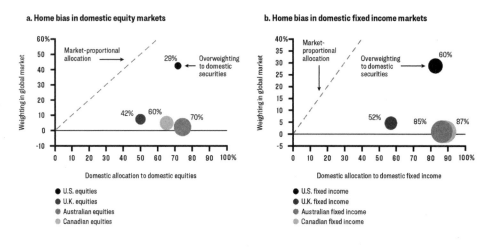

a. Home bias in domestic equity markets

b. Home bias in domestic fixed income markets

- U.S. equities
- U.K. equities
- Australian equities
- Canadian equities

- U.S. fixed income
- U.K. fixed income
- Australian fixed income
- Canadian fixed income

which is largely dependent on your investment goals and risk tolerance. However, don't fall into the trap of discounting the value of global investing only because the company names aren't familiar. You do not need to travel abroad or set up an account overseas to create a global portfolio. By simply purchasing an index fund, an investor can instantly add global exposure. For example, if your plan calls for an allocation of 60 percent stocks, you can easily assign one-third of that allocation to global stocks by buying an international ETF.

Diversify!
The only constant in life is change.
HERACLITUS

For a Greek philosopher, Heraclitus would have made one heck of an investment advisor. He understood the reality that life is in a constant state of motion, and nowhere does that apply more than in the stock market.

Figure 11.4

DOW JONES INDUSTRIAL AVERAGE COMPONENT COMPANIES

1979

3M	Eastman Kodak	Johns-Manville
Allied Chemical	Esmark	Owens-Illinois
Aluminum Company of America (Alcoa)	Exxon	Proctor & Gamble
American Can Company	General Electric	Sears
AT&T	General Foods	Texaco
American Tobacco Company (B shares)	General Motors	Union Carbide
Bethlehem Steel Corporation	Goodyear	US Steel
Chevron	Inco Ltd.	United Technologies
Chrysler	International Harvester Company	Westinghouse
Dupont	International Paper	Woolworth's

2019

3M	Exxon Mobil	Nike
American Express	Goldman Sachs	Pfizer
Apple	The Home Depot	Proctor & Gamble
Boeing	IBM	Travelers
Caterpilar	Intel	UnitedHealth
Chevron	Johnson & Johnson	United Technologies
Cisco	JP Morgan Chase	Verizon
Coca-Cola	McDonald's	Visa
Disney	Merck	Walmart
Dow-DuPont	Microsoft	Walgreens

When you invest in a specific company, anything can happen. The company can perform exceptionally well, a negative event can harm it, or it can even go bankrupt like Enron, Sears, and Toys "R" Us. This risk is often greatly underestimated, since every company has a life cycle before capitalism destroys it and replaces it with something better. Amazon founder Jeff Bezos is well aware that no company lasts forever. He told his employees, "I predict one day Amazon will fail. Amazon will go bankrupt. If you look at large companies, their lifespans tend to be thirty-plus years, not a hundred-plus years."

Check out just how different the Dow 30 looks today compared to forty years ago! As Figure 11.4 illustrates, while a handful of stalwarts have survived over the years, many once-prominent companies have gone out of business, been consumed by other companies, or declined from their positions of prominence since 1979. In 2018, the last company left from the inaugural index in 1896, General Electric, was replaced by Walgreens. Many companies on the 2019 list, like Apple, Microsoft, and Intel, were in their infancy in 1979, and other companies, like Cisco and Verizon, are now the dominant providers of technologies that didn't even exist forty years ago.

Think of it like the restaurant industry. You wonder if some restaurants will be around more than a few months, and some you expect to be around for decades, but very few restaurants will be operating generations from now. No matter what happens to any one restaurant, however, there will always be restaurants. Stocks are the same. By owning a large number of stocks, you aren't betting on any one company but diversifying across many companies. If you own an S&P 500 index fund, you can expect that a few of the constituent companies will go bankrupt or decline substantially every year, but what happens to any one company will not wipe you out or even set you back from achieving your financial goals. Over the long run, the gains from companies that become high-flyers will more than offset the losses.

Another risk that investors take when they invest in the stock market is *industry risk*. Just like you wouldn't want to bet on only one type of restaurant, this is the risk that an entire industry will suffer greatly or be eliminated. Many financial crises start out with an industry meltdown, like we've experienced with recent crises, from the tech bubble and real estate crisis to the financial crisis, and, more recently, the energy crisis. If you own 100 stocks in the same industry and that industry collapses, you may wonder why diversification didn't help you. You must diversify for company *and* industry risk, owning multiple stocks across multiple industries.

Disrupt or Die

When you consider the rate of technological change in today's world—how quickly we've gone from LPs to MP3s, from local video stores to online streaming—we will likely see industries rise and fall even faster than before. Disruption is accelerating in every industry; just ask Kodak, K-Mart, Blockbuster, Yellow Cab, and BlackBerry. Figure 11.5, showing the average company lifespan on the S&P 500 index, provides a powerful illustration of how the rate of change has accelerated: *the average amount of time a company remains listed on the index has dropped almost four-fold*

Figure 11.5

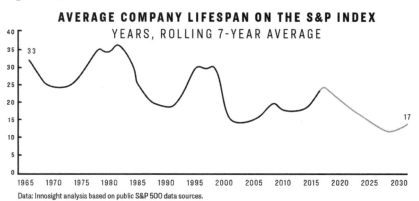

AVERAGE COMPANY LIFESPAN ON THE S&P INDEX
YEARS, ROLLING 7-YEAR AVERAGE

Data: Innosight analysis based on public S&P 500 data sources.

in the past fifty years. This change means that as an investor, you can be positioned to either benefit from the growth of new technologies through proper diversification or suffer from the decline of the old guard. An added benefit of owning an index is that you don't have to worry about which of the constituent companies will be disrupted because the newcomers will simply take their spot in the index, and *voilà!* you are automatically an owner.

The final major risk an investor takes is *market risk* or *systemic risk*: an entire market can sometimes simply go up, or simply go down. We can never eliminate market risk, which is why diversification is essential. For example, you can put all of your money into one duplex apartment and rent it out, and expect to earn 10%. Of course, there's considerable risk in owning just one duplex: if anything goes wrong with this one investment, things can get ugly fast. Let's say instead that you find four duplexes, all of which you expect to earn 10% from, but you can't afford to buy them all. Instead, you partner with three other people to form a company, create a pool of funds, and buy all four duplexes. Now you have the same amount of dollars allocated to the duplexes and your expected return is the same, but your downside risk has been reduced. If something goes wrong with one duplex, it isn't the end of the world. Although buying multiple duplexes reduces the risk associated with owning a single unit, you've not reduced the risk of owning duplexes in general. What if all the renters work for the same company and it goes out of business and they move out of town? You can reduce market risk by being in a variety of markets (or in this case, geographic locations). Proper diversification is about owning a combination of assets where the performance of the positions are not highly correlated with each other. Owning those duplexes in cities across the country reduces your risk.

In simple terms, you want to own assets that respond differently to various economic conditions. This independent movement—with some assets being up more or down less than others at any given time—helps reduce the risk of your portfolio. When stocks drop in value, for example, high-quality bonds tend to increase in value. While most stock markets are correlated, they don't behave in exactly the same way, which is why sophisticated investors include a mix of global assets in their portfolios, as well as a mix of different size companies—small-, mid-, and large-cap stocks—in both the United States and abroad.

Changing economic factors can cause the value of asset classes to move up or down relative to each other, so you want to put your eggs in different baskets to reduce the risk of the portfolio and increase the probability of achieving your goals over the long run. Diversifying to other asset classes, such as real estate, can reduce market risk even further.

DON'T FALL IN LOVE WITH
YOUR INVESTMENTS

Diversification sounds smart, right? But I can't tell you how many clients I've seen over my career watch their net worth plummet because they had refused to diversify away from industry and company risk. Many of our higher-net-worth clients became wealthy by working for publicly traded companies that granted them shares of company stock, and the shares subsequently skyrocketed in value. These clients are often reluctant to diversify, in part because the stock of a single company is the reason they became wealthy. Plus, they worked for the company and know it well, full of fond memories and loyalty to the brand. But remember what Jeff Bezos pointed out: every company eventually dies; it's just a matter of time.

Similar to home bias, I have found that many investors tend to concentrate their stock selection to companies they are familiar with, often leading to industry-specific risk. Many large Canadian companies are involved in commodities and finance, so many Canadian investors have portfolios that are overweight in stocks in those sectors and find themselves vulnerable to price swings in those industries. New clients

Figure 11.6

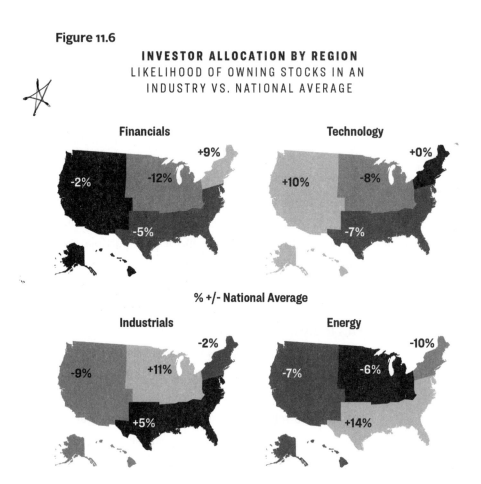

INVESTOR ALLOCATION BY REGION
LIKELIHOOD OF OWNING STOCKS IN AN
INDUSTRY VS. NATIONAL AVERAGE

of Creative Planning often come to us with investments from prominent industries in their backyard: a Texan is likely to own a number of
energy holdings, a northeasterner in financials, a northern Californian in
technology, and an upper midwesterner in industrials. Figure 11.6 illustrates just how susceptible we are to overexposing ourselves to familiar
industries.

If anything, you likely work for these companies and know the industry
well, but that also means you are already overexposed to that industry. If
you are in a position where your retirement plan is subject to its success

and the value of your home can be affected by the cycle of the industry, take a close look at your portfolio to make sure you don't stand to lose even more if it falters.

Taxes Matter

Don't blow out your existing holdings. Know what
you own, and know why you own it.

PETER LYNCH

Once you have determined the right allocation for your portfolio, added international holdings, and diversified away company and industry risk, make sure to account for the existing holdings you bring to the table and the tax consequences for making any changes.

Any investments in tax-deferred accounts like 401(k)s, 403(b)s, IRAs, and the like can immediately be sold and repositioned because there are no tax consequences. Any new money you add to the portfolio can be placed into the new investments as well.

Resist the temptation to sell all the holdings in your taxable account, though. If liquidating your existing holdings will create significant taxable gains, realize you'll be creating a hole for yourself where you will likely need multiple years of strong returns in the markets just to get you back to where you were before selling. By the same token, be very wary of financial advisors who tell you to sell everything, regardless of tax consequences. They are almost certainly causing serious harm to your financial position simply to make managing your portfolio simpler for them. It's also a telltale sign they are throwing your money into a cookie-cutter model portfolio without regard for any tax consequences, which should give you enough pause to consider another advisor. While the tax tail shouldn't wag the dog, we at Creative Planning always consider tax outcomes when designing a portfolio. After all, it's not what our clients earn that matters but what they keep after taxes and fees.

Annuities and Hotel California

You can check out anytime but you can never leave. No, it's not the "Hotel California"; it's the wonderful world of annuities. Many annuities have very high expenses and limited investment options, and they also are subject to *surrender charges* (the ransom you pay if you don't want to be held hostage any longer) if you elect to terminate the contract prior to a certain date.

If these charges are substantial, it may make sense to wait to cash in until the surrender charge expires or if it's low enough to be offset by the savings from a new investment opportunity. One notable exception would be if you are seriously ill. Then surrendering an annuity with a "death benefit" may not make sense because it could pay out a benefit similar to a life insurance policy. In short, while other investments may be better, once you have already purchased an annuity, there are many factors to take into consideration before surrendering the contract.

Too Much of One Stock

I have advised clients to maintain a large position in a single stock that made no sense to hold purely from a target portfolio perspective in certain scenarios. For example, new clients had $3 million of their $3.5 million net worth in one stock. They hired Creative Planning because the husband was dying, and he wanted to help choose an advisor to assist his wife when he was gone. I advised the couple to hold the security in the husband's name until his death. After he died, the stock received a step up in basis, which means that his wife could sell all the stock immediately on his passing with no taxes due, giving us the opportunity to reposition the portfolio into something appropriate for her needs in a cost-effective way. Had the couple worked with an advisor who would have sold everything, they would have stood to lose hundreds of thousands of dollars. Instead, she ended up far better off and was able to remain financially independent.

Sometimes implementing a good investment plan can do more harm than good due to unintended tax or estate planning consequences. Bottom line: be aware of all the implications of repositioning your portfolio before making changes. With customization, your portfolio can often yield a far better after-tax result than moving your entire portfolio immediately into new positions.

Asset Location Matters

By now, I hope you fully appreciate that taxes matter. A lot. Advisors don't talk about them because if you knew the tax bill they generated with all of their trading, you would fire them. (The same goes for mutual funds, hedge funds, and the like.) Most investors don't notice taxes because they aren't paid out of the account. Let's say you have an investment manager who actively trades your $1 million account. At the end of the year, you get a report saying you earned 7%, or $70,000. You are a pretty happy camper. A few months later, you receive a 1099 to use for your tax preparation. If you are like most other people, you probably throw it in a folder, and once all your paperwork is together, you give it to your CPA without looking at it carefully. Now, let's say that the 1099 shows that you owe taxes of $30,000. This will be blended in with the rest of your taxes, and if your CPA asks you to cut a check to pay the IRS, you will. The $30,000 will probably not be paid out of your investment account, and even if it is, the manager's performance report will forever show your rate of return was 7%, when it was in fact only 4% after taxes. Figure 11.7 shows the impact of taxes on actual returns, and the power of compounding with a dollar doubling 20 times. It also reveals the impact of taxes if the gains are taxed each time at 33%.

If you have a mix of tax-deferred and taxable accounts, asset location can mitigate much of the potential damage. What in the world is *asset location*? It's determining which account should own each of your specific investments.

Figure 11.7

IMPACT OF TAXES ON INVESTMENT GROWTH

YEAR	TAX FREE	33% TAX ON EARNINGS
	$1.00	$1.00
1	$2.00	$1.67
2	$4.00	$2.79
3	$8.00	$4.66
4	$16.00	$7.78
5	$32.00	$12.99
6	$64.00	$21.69
7	$128.00	$36.23
8	$256.00	$60.50
9	$512.00	$101.03
10	$1,024.00	$168.72
11	$2,048.00	$281.76
12	$4,096.00	$470.54
13	$8,192.00	$785.80
14	$16,384.00	$1,312.29
15	$32,768.00	$2,191.53
16	$65,536.00	$3,659.85
17	$131,072.00	$6,111.95
18	$262,144.00	$10,206.96
19	$524,288.00	$17,045.63
20	$1,048,576.00	$28,466.20

When building out your portfolio, resist the temptation to make every account look the same. Instead, place the investments that create substantial taxes into your tax-deferred accounts, such as putting investments like taxable bonds and real estate in your IRA or 401(k). Place the investments that do not create a lot of taxes, like large company stocks, in your taxable account. By simply purchasing assets in the most tax-efficient location possible you will substantially lower your tax bill and improve your after-tax return.

Rebalance, Tax Harvest, and Monitor

A lot of advisors discuss rebalancing, but what you aren't likely to hear from them is that *rebalancing* can hurt your returns over the long run. What exactly is rebalancing? Let's say you have a portfolio that is 60% stocks and 40% bonds. If the stocks appreciate in value more than bonds, you will now have a higher percentage of stocks in your portfolio than when you started. While that's hypothetically great from a potential return perspective, you now have much more risk in your portfolio than you originally intended. It's time to rebalance to get back to the intended 60/40 split by selling some of your stocks and buying more bonds. If you never rebalance, you may wake up 20 years from now with a portfolio that is 85% stocks and 15% bonds. Now, there may be a scenario where it makes sense for you to have a more aggressive allocation 20 years from now than you have today, but it's unlikely. By rebalancing, you are keeping the portfolio aimed squarely at the target, increasing your chances of hitting your goal.

Some investors rebalance periodically, such as every quarter or every year. I personally think that's overkill, leaving you with unnecessary costs that can limit the effectiveness of your portfolio's strategy. If a rebalancing trade will result in taxes or multiple transaction costs, consider skipping it until your allocation is totally out of whack. But if the market drops, don't wait! Take the opportunity to rebalance at that time, intentionally increasing your exposure to the weaker asset class, usually stocks, when they are down. If they keep going down, rebalance again. This is called *opportunistic rebalancing*, and it yields a better rate of return over time than periodic rebalancing. If this is just too much to deal with emotionally, confirm that your goals haven't changed, rebalance one to four times a year, and get on with life.

Harvesting Taxes

If you own an investment in a taxable account, let's say an S&P 500 index fund, and the market drops suddenly, the way it did at the end of 2018, you have several options. One, you can sell in a panic, throw your computer out the window, stomp your feet, and cry. But we have made it this far together, and you're too smart for that. Two, you can do nothing. The good news is the index fund you own will likely recover, as it always has, and go on to new highs. No harm, but a missed opportunity. Or three, you can sell the fund while it is down, and replace it with a similar, but not identical investment, like an S&P 100 index fund. When the market recovers, the replacement fund will recover in a similar fashion as the previous investment, but you will be far better off because the loss from the prior sale will be locked in on your tax return and carried forward for life, until it can be used to offset future gains, which will make your portfolio that much more efficient! Now you are really managing your money well.[125]

Finally, monitor your positions. Some investments aren't going to work out no matter how well you plan. Sometimes a lower-cost investment option becomes available, giving you the opportunity to save some money. New investments may present themselves that better serve your goals. Most important, your needs and goals will change over time, so be sure to review your financial plan and make portfolio adjustments as needed to stay on track for your financial goals. Or make sure you have an

125 Let's pause for an imaginary fist-bump here!

advisor who can do the heavy lifting for you and review with him or her once a year. Times change, you will change, your goals will change, and your portfolio should always be focused on helping you fulfill your vision.

HERE WE GO!

Let's recap the steps here to make sure you are on the path to financial freedom:

1. Build a financial plan outlining your goals.
2. Determine the asset allocation most likely to get you the return you need to achieve your goals.
3. Take a global approach to your portfolio.
4. Diversify to avoid company and industry risk.
5. Consider working around your current holdings that have significant taxable gains.
6. Determine which investments to buy in taxable and nontaxable accounts.
7. Rebalance, tax-harvest, and monitor your portfolio.
8. Revisit your financial plan every year, and make adjustments to your portfolio as needed.

If we have done our job correctly, you should never be at the mercy of any asset class at any time, and each asset class should have the room to breathe and run—to do what it is supposed to do. You should also have an allocation in place that gives you the freedom to tax-harvest, rebalance on major drops, and most important, increase the probability that you achieve your goals. In the end, the wealth you have accumulated is a means to an end: freedom and peace of mind. These ingredients will give you the best odds at achieving your vision by incorporating asset classes and sub-asset classes that should always be tied as closely as possible to your goals.

PART V

THE SUMMIT

CHAPTER TWELVE

THE MOST IMPORTANT DECISION OF YOUR LIFE

by Tony Robbins

Most people intuitively know that money does not buy happiness,
but they want the chance to learn that lesson for themselves!

Bo Shao, one of the most successful Chinese tech entrepreneurs, has an incredible life story. In 2019, I asked Bo to share his journey at my Platinum Partners event in Whistler, Canada. While we expected to hear about Bo's many successes, he took a detour in his message to courageously share his heart. He told us the story *behind* the story, and I was deeply touched by his transparency and candor. I'm sure you will be too.

Bo grew up very poor in Shanghai, China. Driven hard by a traditional Chinese father, Bo was taught that performance and achievement were essential to success (while emotion should be a nonexistent factor). His father used a deck of cards to teach him how to rapidly calculate math in his head. By the time he finished high school, Bo had won over a dozen math competitions in what is considered the epicenter of mathematically gifted children.

In 1990, Bo was offered a full-ride scholarship to Harvard—the first full scholarship offered to a mainland Chinese citizen since 1949. He sailed through Harvard, and while working at his first job, at Boston Consulting

Group, he went back and got his MBA from Harvard Business School. At the time, the tech boom was in its relative infancy. Bo decided to return to China to start his first company, EachNet, the self-described Chinese "knock-off" version of eBay. His investment paid off. In 2003, he sold his company to eBay for $225 million. He was 29 years old.

Bo "retired" for a brief time, but boredom set in quickly, so he decided to put the pedal to metal again. He went on to cofound one of the more successful venture capital firms in China that has a long list of investment winners. He has traveled the world with his family, lived in the South of France, bought a beautiful home in the most expensive zip code in California, and "bought a Ferrari with cash." By all accounts, he had settled into his life as a mogul.

But with all that he achieved, with more money than he or his children could ever spend, Bo was miserable. He had fallen victim to the illusion that money, achievement, and accomplishment are fulfilling in and of themselves. He had no community, no friends he could trust, a disconnected relationship with his young children, and a nine-figure bank account. There was a vacuum of meaning in his life. Instead of enjoying all he had accomplished, he had immense anxiety about losing the fortune he had made. "I felt more secure when I was making 50K a year right out of college!" he exclaimed.

If we are honest with ourselves, I think we can all relate to Bo. Sure we may not have sold a nine-figure business, but I am sure you can recall a time in your life where you were obsessed with achieving a lofty goal. Maybe it was a sales figure for your business, a new position at work, or getting a shiny new Bimmer. And when you got it, it felt great for a little while. But quickly, with familiarity, the joy began to fade. The achievement had lost its luster. And so you moved the goal post further and found the next pursuit. I can tell you with 100% certainty that I have seen this movie a thousand times before. It's simply part of the human condition—part of our operating system that seems to be flashing "error" every time we get what we want and start to feel the sense of fulfillment slip through our fingers like sand.

I've had the privilege of working with mega-successful businesspeople, actors, athletes, and politicians. After striving for their entire lives, many reach the summit, only to discover the air is quite thin. Many end up asking the same question: "Is this all there is?" I hate to break it to you, but the same is true with financial freedom. You can implement all the tools and strategies in this book, end up where you aspire to be, and still feel empty—that is, unless you master what I call the **art of fulfillment**.

SUCCESS WITHOUT FULFILLMENT
IS THE ULTIMATE FAILURE

I think we can all agree that when we say we want financial freedom, we don't want piles of paper with pictures of dead presidents. What we ultimately want is to feel the emotions that we associate with money: freedom, security, comfort, joy, satisfaction, and peace of mind. To be able to do whatever you want, whenever you want, and share it with the ones you love. To work and make an impact because you want to, not because you have to. This is financial freedom.

But real wealth, lasting wealth, is much more than money. We need to be emotionally, physically, and spiritually wealthy. Think about a time in your life where you felt unimaginable joy, when you were truly fulfilled. Maybe it was the moment your child was born or when your spouse walked down the aisle and said "I do!" Maybe it was a trip with friends. Maybe it was watching a particularly beautiful sunset and feeling deeply connected to your creator. These are moments of true freedom. We know intuitively that these moments of deep fulfillment often have nothing to do with money and happen far too infrequently. But they don't have to! You don't have to settle for a few moments of fulfillment sprinkled throughout your year. You don't have to wait for your circumstances to change in order for you to feel connected. As you have learned throughout this book, the tools for becoming financially free are not all that complex. You must know the rules of the game, understand how markets work, avoid making poor emotional decisions, harness the power of compounding, and ideally work with an advisor who has your best interest at heart and coaches you along the way.

When there are immutable laws for getting an outcome (e.g., getting in great physical shape or mastering your financial life) this is what I call the **science of achievement**. Bo was a master of the science of achievement. He knew the ingredients for success, and, like a master chef, he knew how to apply them. But despite a track record of crushing it on the business front, Bo had failed to achieve an extraordinary quality of life. Why? Because an **extraordinary quality of life is found only in mastering the art of fulfillment!** Let me repeat: you must master the art of fulfillment because *success without fulfillment is the ultimate failure!*

Here's the great news: you don't have to choose between success and fulfillment. It's possible to have both, but it will take a commitment to the mental work required. It's my sincere wish for you that after this chapter, you will choose to have the financial freedom and peace of mind you deserve, along with the fullness, love, and connectedness of a heart free of suffering.

PAIN IS INEVITABLE; SUFFERING IS OPTIONAL
For as man thinks in his heart, so he is.
PROVERBS 23:7

A few years ago, I decided to take up golf. I am 6'7" and 260 pounds, so watching me play golf is like watching a gorilla swing a toothpick. Like almost everything else in my life, I thought harder and faster had to be better. When I snapped the head off the club my first time at the driving range, I turned to the instructor and said, "I'll need three or four more of these at this rate!" He gently explained that unlike wooden baseball bats, routinely breaking clubs was not a normal part of the game.

If you haven't played golf, it can be an extremely frustrating sport. Harder and faster are *not* always better. It's a game of nuance. One degree can be the difference between setting up a good shot and launching a ball out of bounds or into the lake. It's a game that can never be mastered and requires the patience of Job. After a few lessons, I realized that it was not for me. I don't have time to immerse myself to become halfway decent at golf, and dabbling just made me frustrated. I could find better things to do with my time!

Then on a trip to Mexico, a good buddy of mine, Bert, asked if I wanted to play. I proceeded to tell him my story—my narrative about what golf was to me (slow, frustrating, etc.)—and he quickly stopped me. *"Tony, I know you don't have a lot of time so let's just go play four or five holes?"* I didn't know playing just a few holes was even an option, but I really just wanted to go down to the beach and relax during the short break in my schedule. *"Tony, how about we just play the four or five holes that are right along the ocean ? It's beautiful!"* It was sounding more appealing, but then I realized how truly awful I was. *"Tony, we won't even keep score."* Don't keep score?! What the hell is the point then?!

But I reluctantly agreed, and Bert and I jumped in the golf cart. We pulled up to the first ocean hole, and it was breathtaking. The waves were crashing against the rocks just steps from the green. I hit as many balls as I needed, and I actually had a couple of good shots. I drained a lengthy putt, which felt incredible. Something was shifting inside me. By the end of the hour, we had played all four oceanfront holes and had an absolute blast. We laughed, enjoyed each other's company, experienced nature's incredible beauty, and took in the smell of the salt air.

From that day forth, I made a decision. A decision to not suffer. A decision that when I play golf, I will enjoy every hole. I will enjoy the people I am with, the nature and beauty I get to experience, and my once-in-a-blue-moon good shot. Golfing legend Ben Hogan was spot-on when he said, *"Golf is a game that is played on a five inch course—the distance between your ears!"* Golf is now one of my favorite things to do, and I still don't keep score.

I tell this story because golf was an unexpected teacher on my journey to choosing to live in what I call "a beautiful state." The game of golf didn't change; I changed. I chose to live in a state of mind that created an extraordinary quality of life for myself on that day. Why not do that every day?

A BEAUTIFUL STATE

I visit India almost annually. On my last trip, I was having a great conversation with a friend who has dedicated his life to spiritual growth for himself and others. He shared with me that he believes there are just two mental states that people can be in at any given time. You are either in a low-energy, negative state that he calls a **suffering state** (sadness, anger, depression, frustration, anger, fear) or a high-energy, positive state called a **beautiful state** (joy, love, gratitude, creativity, generosity, compassion).

This conversation was the beginning of a profound shift in my life. I have always believed that the only thing we can truly control in our lives is our internal state. It's what I've taught for decades. We can't control the stock market, the rain, or whether our children or spouse behave the way we want them to. What we *can* control is the meaning we give these events. And the meaning we give these events is what we are going to feel—our emotional experience is indeed our reality. How we feel daily is 100% in our control. As I left India, I was contemplating whether I was truly that way. Was I choosing to live in a beautiful state at ALL times? Was that even possible?

RUNNING HARD

It probably comes as no surprise that I would describe myself as an achiever. I am involved or invested in over 50 companies worldwide and visit over 100 cities every year. My life and schedule have as many moving parts as a Boeing 747. With hundreds of employees across a variety of industries and a travel schedule more packed than the President of the United States, what do you think the odds are that things always go as planned? Answer: zero.

In all honesty, it wasn't unusual for me to get upset, overwhelmed, angry, or frustrated when things went south. Now, if you had asked me if I was suffering, I would have laughed: "I don't suffer! I find a way and break through!" In reality, if I was experiencing these emotions regularly, I was choosing to exist in a suffering state. I had justified these intense emotions as fuel for my fire (as most achievers do), but in reality, they were robbing me of joy and greatly limiting my fulfillment in life.

THE VIRUS OF WHAT'S WRONG

I was suffering because my undirected mind had hijacked my emotions. It was running the show and, like a cork in the ocean, I was at the mercy of its waves. Here is what I now know to be true: you and I have a two-million-year-old brain that is always looking for what's wrong. It's designed for one purpose: to keep us alive. Survival is the name of the game. The brain's software is not designed to make you happy—that's your responsibility! It's *your* job to direct the mind. It's *your* job to look for what is right, what is beautiful, what is loving, what is funny, and what is meaningful in your life. Every minute of every day. And just like any muscle, this takes training.

Once I admitted that I was living in a suffering state, I decided to make the most important decision of my life: That I would no longer live in suffering states and forfeit what I truly want to feel. That for the rest of my life, I would do everything in my power to live in beautiful states. States of love, joy, creativity, passion, fun, playfulness, caring, growth, generosity, and curiosity. It's a decision that has to be made with life-and-death conviction because if you truly want to live, truly want to live a magnificent life of internal fulfillment, you MUST decide that life is too short to suffer!

LOSS, LESS, NEVER

If you give a monkey an apple, he will be incredibly excited. But if you give him two apples and then take one away, he will become furious! Humans aren't much different. Our mind is hell-bent on looking for problems— looking for what we don't have or might lose. **My mantra is as follows: what's wrong is always available, but it takes a directed mind to seek out what is right in any given moment.** So let's explore the triggers for suffering so we can better understand how this software of ours really works, learn how to override this operating system, and take back control.

Trigger #1—Loss. If you believe that you have lost something of value, you will suffer. Even the threat of loss will set off your brain's alarms. It's not usually a loss of something physical (although money is the most common one). It could be the loss of time, love, respect, friendship, or an opportunity.

Trigger #2—Less. Less is not as intense a feeling as a complete loss. Like the monkey that now has fewer apples, if you believe that you will have less of something, you will also suffer. This could be because of something you did or something others did, but if you feel you will have less of something you value, you can suffer mentally and emotionally.

Trigger #3—Never. This is full "Defcon 1" for the brain. The brain's sense of hopelessness tells you that you will NEVER have something that you value. Your brain says if x doesn't happen or y happens, you will never be happy, loved, thin, rich, attractive, or important. This mode of desperation gives way to destructive behaviors that damage both ourselves and our relationships. The brain becomes myopically focused on self.

Often our minds will obsess and suffer over a problem that's *not even real*. Whatever we focus on, we feel—regardless of what *actually* happened. Have you ever thought that a friend did something to hurt you purposefully? You stewed in anger and had numerous imaginary arguments (where of course you triumphed!): *"She will never understand how hurtful she is! She clearly doesn't respect me. I don't know if we can ever salvage this relationship!"* But then you discovered that you were completely wrong. You had entirely misunderstood what actually happened and nobody was to blame. And yet you suffered. All of those negative emotions ran your show and ruined your day, or maybe even your week. Your feelings became your experience. And your experience was some mixture of loss, less, or never.

31 FLAVORS

So here is my question: What is your favorite flavor of suffering? Do you often find yourself angry? Regretful? Cynical? Fearful? Frustrated? What suffering do you bring home to your spouse or children? What suffering do you lug to work like a bag of bricks? What suffering do you allow to pilot that brain of yours?

We all experience a wide range of emotions, but I find that most people have an emotional rut—the place where their mind suffers most often and gets stuck. So how do we take back control? It all starts with the realization that this involves a conscious choice. **Either you master your mind, or it masters you.** If you want to have an extraordinary quality of life, you must decide to take back control of your mind. You must commit to enjoying life when things go your way AND when things don't. When someone hurts you, when you lose money on your investments, when your spouse ticks you off, when your boss or employees don't appreciate you: these are the times when you need to interrupt the pattern and focus on your goal of living in a beautiful state. Life is too short to suffer.

This isn't some positive thinking nonsense. When someone chooses not to suffer despite their circumstances, we are inspired! We write books about them, make movies about their lives, and grant them lifetime achievement awards. We greatly admire someone who has mastered their mind and beat the odds despite unimaginable tragedy or injustice. When someone has endured far greater challenges than our own and maintains an incredible state of mind, we sense that we are being called to a higher standard. We are encouraged to take stock, shift our perspective, and access deep gratitude for the beauty in our own lives. What's right is always there if you are willing to see it.

90 SECOND RULE

Nobody is immune to life's challenges and feeling the emotions of suffering. I am not suggesting you float through life blissfully unaware. This is avoidance, not living. What I am suggesting is that you make a decision to not allow those emotions to drive the ship. Here is a strategy that works for me. I have decided that when my mind goes to an emotion of suffering, whether it's anger, fear, or frustration, I give myself 90 seconds to make a shift and get back to living in a beautiful state. But how exactly?

Let's say I'm having a heated discussion with a team member and find out that there's been a serious error in judgment that caused a host of issues. My undirected brain leaps into action and focuses on everything that is wrong. Lights are flashing and sirens are going off. My brain is practically begging me to get angry, frustrated, and let the suffering begin. That's my cue to take action. First, I gently breathe and slow things down. Changing your physiology is key to breaking patterns. Breathe, walk, do jumping jacks. Do whatever it takes to distract yourself from your emotional remorse.

Then I administer the antidote: appreciation. I have learned that it's impossible to feel fear and gratitude simultaneously. I don't have to appreciate the situation—that would be denying the reality of what actually happened. I simply choose to focus on something that I can appreciate in that moment. I can appreciate my wife who is sitting across the room, my kids whom I see in a picture out of the corner of my eye, or the view of the ocean from my office. Whatever I can appreciate in that moment, I will. In this case, I then choose to appreciate the fact I have a company I love that improves the lives others. I appreciate the fact that this employee is typically a superstar.

When I choose to stop suffering and start appreciating, I am actually rewiring my nervous system and taking back control of my mind. In fact, we can now understand the science and medical benefits of gratitude and appreciation. When I say we can rewire the brain, I'm not exaggerating. Neurons that fire together, wire together. Neuropathways start like a small string, but with repetition end up like a rope. Your capacity for experiencing gratitude is entirely dependent on how often you practice experiencing gratitude.

Once I feel that gratitude is back in the driver's seat, I return to the problem. Then I find another beautiful state, like creativity. Creativity can help me solve the problem in front of me much more quickly. And being in this calm state, I am able to make sure my employee feels appreciated and loved, which creates an environment of understanding and trust.

The point is, there is good in every situation if you allow yourself to see it. What's wrong is always available, but what's right, what's beautiful, and what's important are *also* available to you. It may not be evident in the here and now, but you may need to trust that life is happening *for* us, not *to* us. I grew up in a home with a mother who vacillated between love and abuse. I was forced to raise my brother and sister while she was holed up in her room taking prescription drugs and drinking alcohol. I love my mother dearly, but here is what I know: if my mother were the mom I wanted her to be, I wouldn't be the man I am today. Life happened for me, not to me. That is the meaning I must choose if I want freedom.

Yes, this book is about financial freedom, and that is certainly a worthy goal. But my hope for you is that not only do you achieve financial freedom, whatever that is for you, but that you also choose to create an extraordinary quality of life. Not someday, but *now*. You don't have to wait until you reach some imaginary finish line where you can "finally" feel that you made it. You deserve it. Your loved ones deserve it. Life is too short to suffer!

GRATITUDE: THE BRAIN'S BEST MEDICINE

History's greatest spiritual teachers have known for thousands of years that gratitude is greatest antidote to suffering, but the latest scientific studies show the incredible impact on both the mind and body. Check out these incredible findings!

- Research out of Massachusetts General Hospital by Dr. Jeffery Huffman suggests that positive psychological states, like optimism and gratitude, may independently predict superior cardiovascular health.

- A 2015 study by the American Psychological Association found that patients who kept gratitude journals for eight weeks showed reductions in levels of several inflammatory biomarkers.

- Results of a study on cultivating appreciation and other positive emotions showed lower levels of stress hormones. In those who cultivated gratitude, the study found a 23% reduction in cortisol and 100% increase in DHEA/DHEAS levels, the anti-aging hormone which helps the production of other key hormones like testosterone and estrogen.

- A 2006 study published in *Behavior Research and Therapy* found that Vietnam War veterans with high levels of gratitude experienced lower rates of posttraumatic stress disorder.

- A study reported by Harvard Medical School and done by researchers at the Wharton School of the University of Pennsylvania found that grateful leaders motivated employees to become more productive.

CHAPTER THIRTEEN

PURSUING HAPPINESS

by Jonathan Clements

Note from Peter—As Tony just discussed, money can buy many things, but by itself, it can't buy happiness. Instead, we need to use our money thoughtfully and, if we do, it should enable us to pursue what makes us happy and allow us to enjoy life on our terms. I've asked Jonathan Clements, former *Wall Street Journal* columnist and Creative Planning's Director of Financial Education, to weigh in on the topic of happiness—and how money can play a role in pursuing it.

❧

Ask your friends if they would be happier if they had more money, and most would likely respond with a resounding, "Yes!" And yet there's ample evidence this isn't the case.

Consider the General Social Survey, which has been regularly conducted for almost five decades. In the first survey in 1972, 30% of Americans described themselves as "very happy." Since then, US inflation-adjusted, per capita disposable income has soared 131%, meaning we're now living with more than twice the disposable income we had in 1972. But all that money apparently hasn't done much to improve happiness: in 2018, 31% of Americans described themselves as "very happy," just 1% point higher than 46 years earlier.

Still, I firmly believe money can buy happiness—provided we're thoughtful in how we use our dollars. If we have the wisdom and discipline to follow the advice in the preceding chapters, we should quickly get ourselves on track for a more prosperous financial future. But what can that money buy us? I'd argue that there are three potential benefits—all of which could transform our lives for the better.

FRET LESS

Money's first big benefit: it can ease our financial worries and help us to achieve a greater sense of control over our lives. As I see it, money is sort of like health. It is only when we're sick that we realize how wonderful it is to feel healthy. Similarly, it's only when we don't have enough money that we realize how great it is to be in good financial shape. Heaps of money may not make us extra-happy—but not having money could make us extremely unhappy. We might feel boxed in by our monthly financial obligations, trapped in our current job, and one medical bill away from bankruptcy.

Sadly, this describes life for many Americans. According to the Federal Reserve, four out of ten Americans either couldn't cover a $400 financial emergency or, to do so, they would need to borrow or sell something. Another startling statistic: 78% of American workers say they live paycheck-to-paycheck, according to a CareerBuilder survey. Think about that: we live in the world's most dynamic, most prosperous developed economy—and yet a majority of Americans are living on the financial edge. Maybe it's no surprise that our rising standard of living hasn't boosted happiness.

Yes, we ought to save for retirement, a down payment on a house, and the kids' college education. But these specific goals fall within a broader, overriding financial objective: we want to get ourselves to the point where money isn't something that we regularly fret about or that tightly constrains how we lead our lives. And here's the thing: it may not take much to eliminate many of our money worries. Simply ridding ourselves of credit card debt, paying our bills on time, and stashing a little money every month in a savings account can give a significant boost to our sense of well-being. A study by the Consumer Financial Protection Bureau found that Americans with less than $250 in the bank scored just 41 out of 100 in financial well-being. For those with $5,000 to $19,999 set aside, that number leaps to 59, above the US average score of 54.

By seizing control of our finances, we won't just be better able to cope with the monthly bills and unexpected expenses. We'll also have a greater sense of control over our lives. That's a huge prize—and getting there takes relatively modest sacrifices: A smaller cable package. A little less money spent on clothes. A used car rather than a new one. By giving up just a few material things, we can buy ourselves financial peace of mind. It strikes me as one of life's greatest trades. By living beneath our means, we'll have the extra money to pay down debt and pile up savings, and slowly but surely, we'll escape the financial worry that's a gnawing, daily reality for far too many Americans.

LABOR OF LOVE

What is money's second great benefit? It can allow us to spend our days engaged in activities we love and that we feel we're good at.

Money may seem like our most precious resource, especially when we're younger. But in truth, our most finite resource is time—something that becomes brutally apparent as we age. To have a more fulfilling life, we should use our dollars to make the most of our time. Day to day, that might mean spending our money on pastimes we're passionate about, while freeing up time for those activities by, say, paying others to mow the lawn or clean the house. But there's also a longer-term goal: we want to get to the point where we get to choose what we do all day every day. This goal shouldn't be a distant fantasy, reserved for when we finally have enough set aside to retire, but rather something we ought to strive for throughout our working years.

That brings me to some unconventional advice. When I talk to high school and college students, I don't tell them to pursue their passions. Instead, I tell them to use their first few decades in the workforce to pursue dollars, so they quickly buy themselves some financial freedom—and, with it, far greater control over how they spend their daily lives.

I know, I know: those in their 20s should supposedly pursue their passions before they become burdened by the obligations of family and monthly mortgage payments. This is the conventional wisdom that we as a society have embraced and broadcast endlessly to young people. But it rests on a rarely questioned assumption: that pursuing our passions is somehow more important in our 20s than in our 50s.

I would argue that just the opposite is true. When we enter the work world, it can seem novel and exciting. We're eager to figure out the rules, find our place, and prove our worth. To those in their 20s and 30s, working at a relatively uninspiring job may not seem like such a burden—and it could be a smart financial move if it comes with a fat paycheck that allows them to sock away a healthy sum every month.

But after a decade or two in the workforce, our orientation often shifts. We know the office rules. We have had some success, even if it wasn't as much as we had hoped. We have discovered that the promotions and pay raises—and the material goods they allow us to buy—provide only fleeting happiness. We have grown increasingly cynical about the workplace, with its office politics and frequent layoffs. We're less enamored of the world's material rewards and more concerned with spending our days doing what we find personally rewarding. The good news is that if we have been diligent in saving money through our initial decades in the workforce, we may have the wherewithal to work part-time, swap into a career that's less lucrative but more fulfilling, or perhaps even quit full-time work entirely.

That immediately raises a crucial question: If financial freedom is the ability to spend our days doing what we want rather than being beholden to others, what is it that we should do? "Taking it easy" and "having fun" might come to mind. But I would also focus on doing work that we truly enjoy.

There is a reason the world's gardens are full of benches that nobody ever sits on. As distant relatives of our hunter-gatherer ancestors with their relentless focus on survival, we aren't built for leisure or to relax. Rather, we are built to strive. We are often happiest when we are engaged in activities that we think are important, we are passionate about, we find challenging, and we think we're good at. This is captured by the notion of flow, a concept developed by Claremont Graduate University psychology professor Mihaly Csikszentmihalyi.

Think of a surgeon in the operating room, painters or writers lost in their work, or a sports professional intensely focused on the game at hand. Even everyday activities—cooking dinner, driving to work, doing the taxes—offer the chance for flow, though we are more likely to have these moments if it's a task we are actively engaged in rather than passive activities such as watching television. When we are in the midst of highly challenging activities to which we bring a high level of skill, we can become totally absorbed in what we are doing and lose all sense of time. These moments of flow might not be happy in the conventional sense—we aren't laughing out loud with our friends—and yet they can be among our most satisfying times.

MAKING MEMORIES

Money can allow us to spend our days doing what we love. But it can also allow us to have special times with those we love. That is the third key way that money can buy happiness. Research suggests that a robust network of friends and family is a huge source of happiness. Even dealing with people in passing—the cashier at the supermarket, the parking lot attendant, the barista at Starbucks—can increase our sense of belonging to a community.

We may embrace the American ideal of rugged individualism, viewing ourselves as responsible for our own success and impervious to the opinions of others. But most of us are also social creatures who want to connect with others and care deeply about our reputation. Think about it: Why are we polite to strangers we will never see again? Why do we leave a tip at restaurants we may never go back to?

One academic study looked at the daily lives of 909 women in Texas who worked outside the home. They were asked to list and assess their daily activities. Commuting ranked at the bottom in terms of daily happiness. Work also didn't rate well. Which activities did bring happiness? Only 11% of the women mentioned engaging in what the researchers delicately referred to as "intimate relations." On average, these intimate relations lasted just 13 minutes. But they topped the charts in terms of happiness.

The second-highest-ranked item was more significant—at least in terms of its broad impact on happiness. The women gave "socializing after work" high marks, and it took up an average 69 minutes of the day. Make no mistake: spending time with friends and family is a key contributor to happiness. But we don't need an academic study to tell us that. Not many of us would choose to eat alone in a restaurant when we could be eating with others. Ditto for watching a movie, shopping, cleaning up the yard, and a host of other activities.

Friends and family aren't just good for happiness. They are also good for our health. A 2010 study pulled together data from 148 earlier studies that contained information on the connection between mortality and the frequency of interaction with others. The authors found that the boost to longevity from a strong network of friends and family was roughly equal to the boost we get by quitting smoking.[126]

---

126 What if you insist on smoking? Based on the studies, it seems you should never, ever smoke alone!

There's ample research that we get greater happiness from experiences than from possessions. To squeeze additional happiness from these experiences, be sure to include friends and family. When you go for a hike, go with somebody else. Get concert tickets for you and a colleague. Take the kids on a cruise. Arrange a family reunion. Go out to dinner with friends. Fly across the country to see the grandchildren.

To be sure, a family meal out or attending a concert might last just a few hours, and yet it will likely cost more than, say, a tablet that lets you answer emails, read e-books, watch movies, listen to music, and surf the Web. Possessions are often a bargain, while experiences tend to be expensive. Moreover, paying for all those restaurant meals and family vacations will leave less wealth to bequeath to our children.

Still, creating great family memories strikes me as one of the best ways to spend money. There have been 44 past US presidents.[127] No doubt all of them thought they had achieved some measure of immortality. Yet you would be hard-pressed to find anyone who can name all 44 presidents, let alone tell you much about each. If immortality is proving elusive for US presidents, there isn't much hope for the rest of us. Five or ten years after we are gone, most of us will be forgotten except by family and close friends. We will live on in their memories. That's the closest any of us will ever get to immortality, at least on this earth. My advice: use your money to make sure those memories are good.

---

127   Note to quibblers: We're only counting Grover Cleveland once, though he did serve two nonconsecutive terms. As of 2019, there have been 45 U.S. presidencies, but just 44 presidents.

CHAPTER FOURTEEN

ENJOY YOUR JOURNEY AND
SAVOR YOUR TIME AT THE PEAK

I have found that many of my clients spend their first few months in retirement suffering from a great deal of anxiety around their wealth. Blackrock conducted a study asking people what caused the most stress in their lives: 56% said money causes the most stress! Money finished higher than health at 38%, family at 37%, and work at 34%.[128] (Figure 14.1) This result is largely because people who don't have enough money are stressed they can't make ends meet or retire and those with enough money stress about not losing it or running out of it!

Figure 14.1

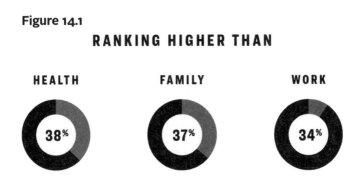

RANKING HIGHER THAN

HEALTH	FAMILY	WORK
38%	37%	34%

128   I suspect this is highly dependent on who is in your family.

"COMPARISON IS THE THIEF OF JOY"

We always feel that we don't have enough. This is because we are constantly doing what humans do: comparing ourselves to others. It's easy for us to fool ourselves sometimes, telling ourselves we are smarter or funnier than those around us, but money is an emotional hot button for many because it's a comparison that usually tells the truth quickly. While we can trick ourselves into believing we stand out in our social networks in many ways, money is something we usually can't fake. That's one reason many of us use it as a measuring stick. We even refer to our balance sheet as our net worth in a way that it sounds like we mean our "personal net worth" when in fact money has little do with what makes up each of us. But this constant emphasis on money and its comparative nature makes it hard to take a step back in the game by making withdrawals. The answer here? Set your priorities straight, and get over it. No one gets an award for being the richest person in the graveyard.

The first months of retirement can be particularly stressful for even a highly successful saver for five key reasons:

1. *You have spent your entire adult life working.* That meant if something went wrong, you could keep working and overcome any setbacks. The idea you "can't make it again" causes market pullbacks to become more stressful than ever.

2. *Markets move faster than ever before.* The speed with which markets pull back and rise is faster than ever. It's not just your imagination: markets are more volatile than they used to be. This is because the market is more efficient than ever, constantly repricing securities based on the future outlook. This speed can be unsettling for many.

3. *You now have time to notice all this!* While you were working, you weren't watching the market week by week, day by day, or hour by hour. You were too busy. Now that you have time on

your hands, you find yourself checking the markets a lot, and are more susceptible to getting sucked into short-term market narratives that can entice you to make a mistake.[129]

4. *People tend to be less optimistic as they grow older.* Studies have shown that people in general believe that their lives are in gradual decline, and they become less optimistic about their future as they age.[130]

5. Finally, and most important, for the first time in your life, you are withdrawing money! The number 1 question I get from clients who have hit the age to begin mandatory distributions, and legally must start drawing from their retirement accounts, is related to how to avoid taking their required distributions. They are so used to putting money away that they can't get themselves to take money out!

All of these things conspire against even the most disciplined investors, making them feel unsettled right when they are supposed to be relaxing and doing everything they want. So much for a carefree retirement!

Well, it doesn't have to be that way. Remember, you have a financial plan. And that plan isn't just to get you to retirement; it's to keep you there. If you planned properly, your portfolio should be established in a way that is built to last: where you are never at the mercy of the market and all your income needs can be met from your first day of retirement until you go to the Great Beyond. So leaving you with the peace of mind that comes from having a plan in place, let me get to what I really want you to focus on: YOU!

---

129 I sometimes wonder how much money people permanently lost trading their accounts during the coronavirus pandemic with everyone sitting at home for weeks with nothing on TV but pandemic coverage and financial media.

130 I hope this chapter and Chapter 1 have you envisioning a future bursting with possibilities instead!

UNCOMPLICATE YOUR FINANCIAL LIFE

I have seen many clients invest in all sorts of "deals," piling up small interests in various properties, businesses, and homes. Many spend the first half of their adult lives accumulating different things and the last half trying to unwind them. The triggering event for many is the death of a friend or relative, and the subsequent realization that all that complexity created tremendous stress for the surviving spouse, kids, or other heirs. Money is here to serve us, not the other way around.

YOU'RE THE ONE

Life is what happens while you are busy making other plans.

JOHN LENNON

In 1970, my dad, who is a physician, was offered some free advice by one of his patients, a prominent politician. "Alex," he said, "I have all the money in the world, but I never enjoyed it. Make time to enjoy yourself." My dad took the advice to heart and expanded his vacation schedule.

I have observed the wisdom in this advice throughout my career. While I lead an investment committee, I am also a CERTIFIED FINANCIAL PLANNER™ and an estate planning attorney. Creative Planning regularly works with clients throughout their lives, through incapacity and with their families on their passing. I get the up-close and personal look at both functional and dysfunctional relationships with money and the mind.

Many of these very successful people have done a great job of saving a good amount of wealth and never messing things up along the way. These are two very difficult things to achieve. I have seen that these people certainly don't deprive themselves, but they are not really enjoying their position to their fullest. Many of these folks got where they are by being thrifty and diligent, and they can't flip the switch and stop worrying about every penny.

Let me tell you something about your money.

Know that it makes no difference whether your heirs inherit $250,000 instead of $300,000, $600,000 instead of $800,000, $1.2 million instead of $1.4 million, or $10 million instead of $11 million, so enjoy yourself and the wealth you have spent your life creating and preserving.

After preparing a net worth statement, a client once said to me, "I would like to die and come back as my kids." Your estate on death isn't just your investment account. It is also the value of your home, insurance, cars, and so on. All will likely be liquidated, thrown into a pot, and split up. That's a cold hard fact. I have seen it hundreds of times.

And let me tell you a secret, none of us are getting out of here alive!

If you are financially independent, let me contradict just about everything you hear from financial advisors when I tell you to get that extra-tall cup of expensive coffee, quit driving that ten-year-old car,[131] and upgrade your next vacation. Believe me when I tell you that your kids will! I have seen kids buy new cars and homes within days of receiving an inheritance from their frugal parents.

If you are charitably inclined and financially independent, go ahead and experience the pleasure of giving now. *Enjoy it!* Why wait until you are dead? It's far more fun to give with a warm hand than a cold one. If you intend your wealth to go your kids and grandkids, start transferring it now. Enjoy seeing the beneficial impact to your family today rather than them receiving larger checks when you are no longer around.

The bottom line is this: *It's your money.* You busted your butt for it, you saved it, and you preserved it. So long as you are not jeopardizing your financial security, ***enjoy yourself.*** Give away what you want, loosen up a bit, and experience the fruits of your labor.

---

131 Seriously, get a new car! You know, one with current technology and safety features! If it's ten years old, you aren't even protecting yourself. This is your life we're talking about here! You don't use a ten-year-old computer, do you? Oh my goodness! If you do, get a new computer too! Geez!

At Creative Planning, I coach my team to make sure our clients know that money is there to serve them and their priorities, not the other way around. You should take the same approach with your money as well. By laying out a plan before you head up the mountain, plotting your path, choosing to go it alone or with a trusted guide, and keeping your emotions in check, you can take time to enjoy your progress to the summit. The joy is in the journey. If you can let go and enjoy it, fulfillment is at the peak.

NOTES

CHAPTER TWO: THE WORLD IS BETTER THAN YOU THINK

"every group of people thinks": Hans Rosling, *Factfulness: Ten Reasons We're Wrong About the World—and Why Things Are Better Than You Think* (New York: Flatiron Books, 2018).

In 2005, compared to 1955: Matt Ridley, *The Rational Optimist: How Prosperity Evolves* (New York: Harper, 2010).

Dr. John Grable of the University of Georgia: John E. Grable and Sonya L. Britt, "Financial News and Client Stress: Understanding the Association from a Financial Planning Perspective," *Financial Planning Review* (2012).

"They were convinced that no one": James Estrin, "Kodak's First Digital Moment," *New York Times*, August 12, 2015, https://lens.blogs.nytimes.com/2015/08/12/kodaks-first-digital-moment/, accessed April 28, 2019.

"Companies are already developing 'lab grown meat'": Matt Simon, "Lab-Grown Meat Is Coming, Whether You Like It or Not," *Wired*, February 16, 2018, https://www.wired.com/story/lab-grown-meat/, accessed April 16, 2019.

"AI is one of the most important things": Catherine Clifford, "Google CEO: A.I. is more important than fire or electricity," *CNBC*, February 1, 2018, https://www.cnbc.com/2018/02/01/google-ceo-sundar-pichai-ai-is-more-important-than-fire-electricity.html, accessed April 16, 2019.

CHAPTER FOUR: CHOOSING A GUIDE FOR YOUR JOURNEY

About half of Americans use a financial advisor: Sherman D. Hanna, "The Demand for Financial Planning Services," *Journal of Personal Finance*, 10 (1), pp. 36–62.

"Despite what many consumers have been led to believe": The National Association of Financial Planners, "Key Policy Issues and Positions," NAPFA.org, https://www.napfa.org/key-policy-issues, accessed May 2, 2020.

Nine out of ten Americans agree: CFP Board, "Survey: Americans' Use of Financial Advisors, CFP® Professionals Rises; Agree Advice Should Be in Their Best Interest," CFP.net, September 24, 2015, https://www.cfp.net/news-events/latest-news/2015/09/24/survey-americans-use-of-financial-advisors-cfp-professionals-rises-agree-advice-should-be-in-their-best-interest, accessed April 16, 2019.

In a recent survey of American's perception: Ibid.

"[Fiduciary duty is] a combination of care and loyalty": Berkeley Lovelace, Jr., interview with Jay Clayton, "SEC chairman: New regulations will force brokers to be 'very candid' with investors," CNBC.com, https://www.cnbc.com/2019/06/06/sec-chairman-clayton-new-rules-will-force-brokers-to-be-very-candid.html, accessed May 2, 2020.

The regulation expressly permits firms : Securities and Exchange Commission, 17 CFR Part 240, Release No. 34-86031; File No. S7-07-18, RIN 3235-AM35, "Regulation Best Interest: The Broker-Dealer Standard of Conduct," June 5, 2019.

According to the Wall Street Journal: Jason Zweig and Mary Pilon, "Is Your Advisor Pumping Up His Credentials?" *Wall Street Journal,* October 16, 2010, http://online.wsj.com/article/SB10001424052748703927504575540582361440848.html, accessed April 17, 2019.

There are over 650,000 "financial advisors": Financial Industry Regulatory Authority, "2018 FINRA Industry Snapshot," *FINRA.org,* October 2018, https://www.fi.org/sites/default/files/2018_finra_industry_snapshot.pdf, accessed April 17, 2019.

Brokerages and advisers should have: Sital S. Patel, "Madoff: Don't Let Wall Street Scam You, Like I Did," *MarketWatch,* June 5, 2013, https://www.marketwatch.com/story/madoff-dont-let-wall-street-scam-you-like-i-did-2013-06-05, accessed April 17, 2019.

The Financial Industry Regulatory Authority, the governing body of brokers: Financial Industry Regulatory Authority, http://www.finra.org/investors/professional-designations, accessed April 17, 2019.

Researchers found that some years added: Francis M. Kinniry Jr., Colleen M. Jaconetti, Michael A. DiJoseph, and Yan Zilbering, "Putting a Value on Your Value: Quantifying Vanguard Advisor's Alpha," *Vanguard,* September 2016, https://www.vanguard.com/pdf/ISGQVAA.pdf, accessed April 28, 2019.

CHAPTER SIX: MANAGING RISK

Forty percent of individuals who reach age 65: Christine Benz, "40 Must-Know Statistics About Long-Term Care," *Morningstar,* August 9, 2012, https://www.morn ingstar.com/articles/564139/40-mustknow-statistics-about-longterm-care.html, accessed April 18, 2019.

The cost of a nursing home: Genworth, "Cost of Care Survey 2018," *Genworth,* October 16, 2018, https://www.genworth.com/aging-and-you/finances/cost-of-care.html, accessed April 18, 2019.

Given that just 44% of the population: Benz, Ibid.

However, if we look deeper: Ibid.

CHAPTER EIGHT: HOW MARKETS WORK

over a 20-year period: DALBAR, "2018 Quantitative Analysis of Investor Behavior Report," *DALBAR,* 2018.

Economists Jerker Denrell and Christina Fang: Jerker Denrell and Christina Fang, "Predicting the Next Big Thing: Success as a Signal of Poor Judgment," *Management Science* 56 (10), pp. 1653–1667.

"about 3 or 4 times out of 10": Tim Weber, "Davos 2011: Why Do economists Get It So Wrong?" BBC.co.uk, January 17, 2011, https://www.bbc.com/news/business-12294332, accessed April 19, 2019.

"I can't point to any mutual fund": Diana Britton, "Is Tactical Investing Wall Street's Next Clown Act?" *Wealthmanagement.com,* December 1, 2011, https://www.wealth management.com/investment/tactical-investing-wall-streets-next-clown-act, accessed April 19, 2019.

In 1994, John Graham and Campbell Harvey: John R. Graham and Campbell R. Harvey, "Market Timing Ability and Volatility Implied in Investment Newsletters' Asset Allocation Recommendations," February 1995, available at SSRN: https://ssrn.com/abstract=6006, accessed April 19, 2019.

Mark Hulbert's own research shows: Kim Snider, "The Great Market Timing Lie," *Snider Advisors,* July 22, 2009, http://ezinearticles.com/?The-Great-Market-Tim ing-Lie&id=2648301, accessed April 19, 2019.

"George Soros: It's the 2008 Crisis": Matt Clinch, "George Soros: It's the 2008 Crisis All Over Again," *CNBC,* January 7, 2016, https://www.cnbc.com/2016/01/07/soros-its-the-2008-crisis-all-over-again.html, accessed April 19, 2019.

"Is 2016 the Year When the World": Larry Elliott, "Is 2016 the Year When the World Tumbles Back into Economic Crisis?" *Guardian,* January 9, 2016, https://www.theguardian.com/business/2016/jan/09/2016-world-tumbles-back-economic-crisis, accessed April 19, 2019.

"Sell Everything Ahead of Stock Market Crash": Nick Fletcher, "Sell Everything Ahead of Stock Market Crash, say RBS Economists," *Guardian,* January 12, 2016, https:// www.theguardian.com/business/2016/jan/12/sell-everything-ahead-of-stock-mar ket-crash-say-rbs-economists, accessed April 19, 2019.

"Here Comes the Biggest": Chris Matthews, "Here Comes the Biggest Stock Market Crash in a Generation," *Fortune,* January 13, 2016, http://fortune.com/2016/01/13/analyst-here-comes-the-biggest-stock-market-crash-in-a-generation/, accessed April 19, 2019.

"These Are Classic Signs": Amanda Diaz, "These Are Classic Signs of a Bear Market," *CNBC,* January 20, 2016, https://www.cnbc.com/2016/01/20/these-are-classic-signs-of-a-bear-market.html, accessed April 19, 2019.

"The First Big Crash": Harry Dent, "This Chart Shows the First Big Crash Is Likely Just Ahead," *Economy & Markets,* March 14, 2016, https://economyandmarkets.com/markets/stocks/this-chart-shows-the-first-big-crash-is-likely-just-ahead/, accessed April 19, 2019.

"Clear Evidence That a New Global": Michael T. Snyder, "The Stock Market Crash of 2016: Stocks Have Already Crashed In 6 Of The World's Largest 8 Economies," *Seeking Alpha,* June 17, 2016, https://seekingalpha.com/article/3982609-stock-market-crash-2016-stocks-already-crashed-6-worlds-8-largest-economies, accessed April 19, 2019.

"Citigroup: A Trump Victory in November": Luke Kawa, "Citigroup: A Trump Victory in November Could Cause a Global Recession," *Bloomberg,* August 25, 2016, https://www.bloomberg.com/news/articles/2016-08-25/citigroup-a-trump-victory-in-november-could-cause-a-global-recession, accessed April 19, 2019.

"Stocks Are Inching Closer": Michael A. Gayed, "Stocks Are Inching Closer to the Second Correction of 2016," *MarketWatch,* September 7, 2016, https://www.marketwatch.com/story/stocks-inch-closer-to-2016s-second-correction-2016-09-07, accessed April 19, 2019.

"Reasons for a 2016 Stock Market Crash": Money Morning News Team, "Reasons for a 2016 Stock Market Crash," *Money Morning,* September 26, 2016, https://moneymorning.com/2016/09/26/reasons-for-a-2016-stock-market-crash/, accessed April 19, 2019.

"Economists: A Trump Win": Ben White, "Economists: A Trump Win Would Tank the Markets," *Politico,* October 21, 2016, https://www.politico.com/story/2016/10/donald-trump-wall-street-effect-markets-230164, accessed April 19, 2019.

"We Are Very Probably Looking": Paul Krugman, "We Are Very Probably Looking at a Global Recession with No End in Sight," *The New York Times,* November 8, 2016, https://www.nytimes.com/interactive/projects/cp/opinion/election-night-2016/paul-krugman-the-economic-fallout, accessed April 19, 2019.

"Economist Harry Dent Predicts": Stephanie Landsman, "Economist Harry Dent Predicts 'Once in a Lifetime' Market Crash, Says Dow Could Plunge 17,000 Points," *CNBC,* December 10, 2016, https://www.cnbc.com/2016/12/10/econo mist-harry-dent-says-dow-could-plunge-17000-points.html, accessed April 19, 2019.

"Now Might Be the Time": Laurence Kotlikoff, "Now Might Be the Time to Sell Your Stocks," *The Seattle Times,* February 12, 2017, https://www.seattletimes.com/business/new-voice-on-raising-living-standard/, accessed April 19, 2019.

"4 Steps to Protect Your Portfolio": John Persinos, "4 Steps to Protect Your Portfolio from the Looming Market Correction," *The Street,* February 18, 2017, https:// www.thestreet.com/story/13999295/1/4-steps-to-protect-your-portfolio-from-the-looming-market-correction.html, accessed April 19, 2019.

"The US Stock Market Correction": Alessandro Bruno, "The US Stock Market Correction Could Trigger Recession," *Lombardi Letter,* March 1, 2017, https://www.lombardiletter.com/us-stock-market-correction-2017/8063/, accessed April 19, 2019.

"Three Key Indicators Are Saying": Michael Lombardi, "3 Economic Charts Suggest Strong Possibility of Stock Market Crash in 2017," *Lombardi Letter,* March 28, 2017, https://www.lombardiletter.com/3-charts-suggest-strong-possibility-stock-market-crash-2017/9365/, accessed April 19, 2019.

"Critical Warning from Rogue": Laura Clinton, "Critical Warning from Rogue Economist Harry Dent: 'This is Just the Beginning of a Nightmare Scenario as Dow Crashes to 6,000,'" *Economy & Markets,* May 30, 2017, https://economyand markets.com/exclusives/critical-warning-from-rogue-economist-harry-dent-this-is-just-the-beginning-of-a-nightmare-scenario-as-dow-crashes-to-6000-2/, accessed April 19, 2019.

"Why a Market Crash in 2017": Money Morning News Team, "Stock Market Crash 2017: How Trump Could Cause a Collapse," *Money Morning,* June 2, 2017, https:// moneymorning.com/2017/06/02/stock-market-crash-2017-how-trump-could-cause-a-collapse/, accessed April 19, 2019.

"The Worst Crash in Our Lifetime Is Coming": Jim Rogers, interview with Henry Blodget, *Business Insider*, June 9, 2017, https://www.businessinsider.com/jim-rogers-worst-crash-lifetime-coming-2017-6, accessed April 19, 2019.

"It's Going to End 'Extremely Badly' ": Stephanie Landsman, "It's Going to End 'Extremely Badly,' with Stocks Set to Plummet 40% or More, Warns Marc 'Dr. Doom' Faber," *CNBC*, June 24, 2017, https://www.cnbc.com/2017/06/24/stocks-to-plum met-40-percent-or-more-warns-marc-dr-doom-faber.html, accessed April 19, 2019.

"Three Reasons a Stock-Market Correction": Howard Gold, "Three Reasons a Stock Market Correction Is Coming in Late Summer or Early Fall," *MarketWatch*, August 4, 2017, https://www.marketwatch.com/story/3-reasons-a-stock-market-correction-is-coming-in-late-summer-or-early-fall-2017-08-03, accessed April 19, 2019.

"The Stock Market Is Due": Mark Zandi, "Top Economist: Get Ready for a Stock Market Drop," *Fortune*, August 10, 2017, https://finance.yahoo.com/news/top-economist-ready-stock-market-162310396.html, accessed April 19, 2019.

"Brace Yourself for a Market Correction": Silvia Amaro, "Brace Yourself for a Market Correction in Two Months," *CNBC*, September 5, 2017, https://www.cnbc.com/2017/09/05/brace-yourself-for-a-market-correction-in-two-months-invest ment-manager.html, accessed April 19, 2019.

"4 Reasons We Could Have Another": David Yoe Williams, "4 Reasons We Could Have Another October Stock Market Crash," *The Street*, October 2, 2017, https:// www.thestreet.com/story/14325547/1/4-reasons-we-could-have-another-october-crash.html, accessed April 19, 2019.

"Stock Market Crash WARNING": Lana Clements, "Stock Market Crash WARNING: Black Monday Is Coming Again," *Express*, October 7, 2017, https://www.express.co.uk/finance/city/863541/Stock-market-crash-dow-jones-2017-Black-Monday-1987-forecast, accessed April 19, 2019.

"Morgan Stanley: A Stock Market Correction": Joe Ciolli, "Morgan Stanley: A Stock Market Correction Is Looking 'More Likely'," *Business Insider*, October 17, 2017, https://www.businessinsider.com/stock-market-news-correction-looking-more-likely-morgan-stanley-2017-10, accessed April 19, 2019.

"Chance of US Stock Market Correction": Eric Rosenbaum, "Chance of US Stock Market Correction Now at 70 Percent: Vanguard Group," *CNBC*, November 27, 2017, https://www.cnbc.com/2017/11/27/chance-of-us-stock-market-correction-now-at-70-percent-vanguard.html, accessed April 19, 2019.

"Stock Market Correction Is Imminent": Atlas Investor, "Stock Market Correction Is Imminent," *Seeking Alpha*, December 19, 2017, https://seekingalpha.com/article/4132643-stock-market-correction-imminent, accessed April 19, 2019.

"Consumer confidence surveys found to be 'useless' ": Dean Croushore, "Consumer Confidence Surveys: Can They Help Us Forecast Consumer Spending in Real Time?" *Business Review— Federal Reserve Bank of Philadelphia*, Q3 (April 2006), pp. 1–9.

To test those who say they can invest perfectly: Mark W. Riepe, "Does Market Timing Work?" *Charles Schwab*, December 16, 2013, https://www.schwab.com/resource-center/insights/content/does-market-timing-work, accessed April 22, 2019.

CHAPTER NINE: IT'S ALL IN YOUR HEAD

"If you can grit your teeth": Justin Fox, "What Alan Greenspan Has Learned Since 2008," *Harvard Business Review*, January 7, 2014, https://hbr.org/2014/01/what-alan-greenspan-has-learned-since-2008, accessed April 22, 2019.

"overconfidence has been called": Scott Plous, *The Psychology of Judgment and Decision Making* (New York: McGraw-Hill, 1993).

the enormous impact of the overconfidence effect: K. Patricia Cross, "Not Can, But *Will* College Teaching Be Improved?" *New Directions for College Education*, 17, 1977, pp. 1–15.

A study relating to the character of students: David Crary, "Students Lie, Cheat, Steal, But Say They're Good," Associated Press, November 30, 2008, https://www.foxnews.com/printer_friendly_wires/2008Nov30/0,4675,StudentsDishonesty,00.html, accessed April 23, 2019.

Finance professors Brad Barber and Terrance Odean: Brad M. Barber and Terrance Odean, "Boys Will Be Boys: Gender, Overconfidence, and Common Stock Investment," *The Quarterly Journal of Economics* 116 (1, February 2001), pp. 261–292.

James Montier asked 300 professional fund managers: James Montier, *Behaving Badly* (London: Dresdner Kleinwort Wasserstein Securities, 2006).

Andrew Zacharakis and Dean Shepherd discovered: Andrew Zacharakis and Dean Shepherd, "The Nature of Information and Overconfidence on Venture Capitalists' Decision Making," *Journal of Business Venturing*, 16 (4), 2001, pp. 311–332.

Richards Heuer researched the behavioral biases: Richard J. Heuer, Jr., *Psychology of Intelligence Analysis* (Washington, DC: Center for the Study of Intelligence, Central Intelligence Agency, 1999).

"The anchoring heuristic appears": Todd McElroy and Keith Dowd, "Susceptibility to Anchoring Effects: How Openness-to-Experience Influences Responses to Anchoring Cues," *Judgment and Decision Making* 2 (1, February 2007), pp. 48–53.

the "anchoring" effect, research: Daniel Kahneman and Amos Tversky, "Choices, Values, and Frames," *The American Psychologist* 39 (4), 1984, pp. 341–350.

In a fascinating experiment: Brian Wansink, Robert J. Kent, and Stephen J. Hoch, "An Anchoring and Adjustment Model of Purchase Quantity Decisions," *Journal of Marketing Research* 35 (February, 1998), pp. 71–81.

Psychologist Ellen Langer, who named this effect: Ellen J. Langer, "The Illusion of Control," *Journal of Personality and Social Psychology* 32 (5), 1975, pp. 311–328.

In one of their studies, they split people: Daniel Kahneman, Jack L. Knetsch, and Richard H. Thaler, "Anomalies: The Endowment Effect, Loss Aversion, and Status Quo Bias," *Journal of Economic Perspectives* 5 (1), 1991, pp. 193–206.

"Since the conscious mind can handle": Jonah Lehrer, "The Curse of Mental Accounting," *Wired*, February 14, 2011, https://www.wired.com/2011/02/the-curse-of-mental-accounting/, accessed April 22, 2019.

the impact of mental accounting: Kahneman and Tversky, Ibid.

mental accounting is the reason tax refunds: Hal R. Arkes, Cynthia A. Joyner, Mark V. Pezzo, Jane Gradwohl Nash, Karen Siegel-Jacobs, and Eric Stone, "The Psychology of Windfall Gains," *Organizational Behavior and Human Decision Processes*, 59, pp. 331–347.

the principle even applies to how those: Viviana A. Zelizer, *The Social Meaning of Money: Pin Money, Paychecks, Poor Relief, and Other Currencies* (New York: Basic Books, 1994).

even minor negative setbacks during the workday: Teresa Amabile and Steven Kramer, "The Power of Small Wins," *Harvard Business Review* 89 (5), pp. 70–80.

Even babies exhibit the negativity bias: J. Kiley Hamlin, Karen Wynn, and Paul Bloom, "Three-Month-Olds Show a Negativity Bias in Their Social Evaluations," *Developmental Science*, 2010, 13 (6), pp. 923–929.

CHAPTER TEN: ASSET CLASSES

Warren Buffett made a ten-year bet with Ted Seides: Carl J. Loomis, "Buffett's big bet," *Fortune*, June 9, 2008, http://archive.fortune.com/2008/06/04/news/newsmakers/buffett_bet. fortune/index.htm, accessed April 23, 2019.

the S&P 500 outperformed the major hedge fund strategies: Credit Suisse, "Liquid Alternative Beta and Hedge Fund Indices: Performance" January 2, 2020, https://lab.credit-suisse.com/#/en/ index/HEDG/HEDG/performance, accessed February 16, 2020.

A recent study examined 6,169 unique hedge funds: Peng Chen, "Are You Getting Your Money's Worth? Sources of Hedge Fund Returns" (Austin, TX: Dimensional Fund Advisors, LP, 2013).

In 1998, Long-Term Capital Management: Kimberly Amadeo, "Long-Term Capital Management Hedge Fund Crisis: How a 1998 Bailout Led to the 2008 Financial Crisis," *The Balance*, January 25, 2019, https://www.thebalance.com/long-term-capital-crisis-3306240, accessed April 23, 2019.

Unfortunately for his investors, he lost 52%: Nathan Vardi, "Billionaire John Paulson's Hedge Fund: Too Big to Manage," *Forbes*, December 21, 2012.

since 2011, he has lost over $29 billion: Joshua Fineman and Saijel Kishan, "Paulson to Decide to Switching to Family Office in Two Years," *Bloomberg*, January 22, 2019, https://www. bloomberg.com/news/articles/2019-01-22/paulson-plans-to-decide-on-switch-to-family-office-in-two-years, accessed April 23, 2019.

since 2015, more hedge funds have closed: Nishant Kumar and Suzy Waite, "Hedge Fund Closures Hit $3 Trillion Market as Veterans Surrender," *Bloomberg*, December 13, 2018, https://www. bloomberg.com/news/articles/2018-12-13/hedge-fund-closures-hit-3-trillion-market-as-veterans-surrender, accessed April 23, 2019.

Not only did the simple indexed portfolio: Morgan Housel, "The World's Smartest Investors Have Failed," *The Motley Fool*, January 27, 2014, https://www.fool.com/investing/ general/2014/01/27/the-worlds-smartest-investors-have-failed.aspx, accessed April 23, 2019.

The hedge funds finished with a gain of 24%: Loomis, Ibid.

In 2012, it released a groundbreaking paper: Diane Mulcahy, Bill Weeks, and Harold S. Bradley, "We Have Met The Enemy . . . And He Is Us: Lessons from Twenty

Years of the Kauffman Foundation's Investments in Venture Capital Funds and the Triumph of Hope Over Experience," *Ewing Marion Kauffman Foundation*, May 2012, https://ssrn.com/abstract=2053258, accessed April 23, 2019.

Bitcoin is a type of cryptocurrency: Bernard Marr, "A Short History of Bitcoin and Crypto Currency Everyone Should Read," *Forbes*, December 6, 2017, https://www.forbes.com/sites/bernardmarr/2017/12/06/a-short-history-of-bitcoin-and-crypto-currency-everyone-should-read/#1b5223393f27, accessed April 23, 2019.

"Blockchain brings together shared ledgers": Adam Millsap, "Blockchain Technology May Drastically Change How We Invest," *The James Madison Institute*, March 7, 2019, https://www.jamesmadison.org/blockchain-technology-may-drastically-change-how-we-invest/, accessed April 23, 2019.

Walmart said that blockchain trials had helped: Michael Corkery and Nathaniel Popper, "From Farm to Blockchain: Walmart Tracks Its Lettuce," *The New York Times*, September 24, 2018, https://www.nytimes.com/2018/09/24/business/walmart-blockchain-lettuce.html, accessed April 23, 2019.

Over 1,000 cryptocurrencies now use blockchain technology: "All Cryptocurrencies," *CoinMarketCap*, https://coinmarketcap.com/all/views/all/, accessed April 23, 2019.

In fact, the blockchain can be hacked: Michael Kaplan, "Hackers are stealing millions in Bitcoin—and living like big shots," *New York Post*, April 13, 2019, https://ny post.com/2019/04/13/hackers-are-stealing-millions-in-bitcoin-and-living-like-big-shots/, accessed April 23, 2019.

In the 1990s, David Bowie and his financial team: Ed Christman, "The Whole Story Behind David Bowie's $55 million Wall Street Trailblaze," *Billboard*, January 13, 2016, https://www.billboard.com/articles/business/6843009/david-bowies-bowie-bonds-55-million-wall-street-prudential, accessed April 23, 2019.

CHAPTER ELEVEN: BUILDING AND MANAGING
THE INTELLIGENT PORTFOLIO

The top-performing mutual fund managers of 2017: Andrew Shilling and Lee Conrad, "Which Mutual Funds Are YTD Leaders?" *Financial Planning*, November 29, 2017, https://www.financial-planning.com/slideshow/top-mutual-funds-in-2017, accessed April 23, 2019.

the worst-performing money managers of 2018: Andrew Shilling, "Worst-Performing Funds of 2018," *Financial Planning*, December 12, 2018, https://www.financial-planning.com/list/mutual-funds-and-etfs-with-the-worst-returns-of-2018, accessed April 23, 2019.

by 2030, China and India are expected to become: Will Martin, "The US Could Lose Its Crown as the World's Most Powerful Economy as Soon as Next Year, and It's Unlikely to Ever Get It Back," *Business Insider*, January 10, 2019, https://www.businessinsider.com/us-economy-to-fall-behind-china-within-a-year-standard-chartered-says-2019-1, accessed April 23, 2019.

"I predict one day Amazon will fail": Eugene Kim, "Jeff Bezos to employees: 'One day, Amazon will fail' but our job is to delay it as long as possible," *CNBC*, November 15, 2018, https://www.cnbc.com/2018/11/15/bezos-tells-employees-one-day-amazon-will-fail-and-to-stay-hungry.html, accessed April 23, 2019.

CHAPTER TWELVE: THE MOST IMPORTANT
DECISION OF YOUR LIFE

Research out of Massachusetts General Hospital: Jeff Huffman, et. al., "Design and Baseline Data from the Gratitude Research in Acute Coronary Events (GRACE) study," *Contemporary Clinical Trials*, Volume 44, pp. 11–19.

A 2015 study by the American Psychological Association: Paul J. Mills, Laura Redwine, Kathleen Wilson, Meredith A. Pung, Kelly Chinh, Barry H. Greenberg, Ottar Lunde, Alan Maisel, Ajit Raisinghani, Alex Wood, and Deepak Chopra, "The Role of Gratitude in Spiritual Well-Being in Asymptomatic Heart Failure Patients," *Spirituality in Clinical Practice*, 2015, Vol. 2, No. 1, pp. 5–17.

In those who cultivated gratitude: Rollin McCraty, Bob Barrios-Choplin, Deborah Rozman, Mike Atkinson, Alan D. Watkins, "The Impact of a New Emotional Self Management Program on Stress, Emotions, Heart Rate Variability, DHEA and Cortisol," *Integrative Physiological and Behavioral Science*, 1988, April–June, 33 (2), pp. 151–170.

Vietnam War veterans with high levels of gratitude: Todd B. Kashdan, Gitendra Uswatte, Terri Julian, "Gratitude and Hedonic and Eudiamonic Well-Being in Vietnam War Veterans," *Behavior and Research Therapy*, 2006, 44 (2), pp. 177–199.

grateful leaders motivated employees: "In Praise of Gratitude," *Harvard Mental Health Letter*, November 2011, https://www.health.harvard.edu/newsletter_article/in-praise-of-gratitude, accessed April 23, 2019.

CHAPTER THIRTEEN: PURSUING HAPPINESS

Consider the General Social Survey: The General Social Survey is conducted by NORC, which used to be known as the National Opinion Research Center and which is headquartered on the University of Chicago's campus. The original data can be found at gssdataexplorer.norc.org.

30% of Americans described themselves as "very happy": Bureau of Economic Analysis, U.S. Department of Commerce.

four out of ten Americans either couldn't cover: Federal Reserve, *Report on the Economic Well-Being of U.S. Households in 2017* (May 2018).

78% of American workers say they live: CareerBuilder, *Living Paycheck to Paycheck is a Way of Life for Majority of U.S. Workers* (Aug. 24, 2017).

Americans with less than $250 in the bank: Consumer Financial Protection Bureau, *Financial Well-Being in America* (September 2017).

paying others to mow the lawn or clean the house: Ashley V. Whillans, Elizabeth W. Dunn, Paul Smeets, Rene Bekkers and Michael I. Norton, "Buying Time Promotes Happiness," *Proceedings of the National Academy of Sciences*, vol. 114, no. 32 (Aug. 8, 2017).

This is captured by the notion of flow: Mihaly Csikszentmihalyi, *Flow: The Psychology of Optimal Experience* (Harper & Row: 1990).

One academic study looked at the daily lives: Daniel Kahneman, Alan B. Krueger, David Schkade, Norbert Schwarz and Arthur Stone, "Toward National Well-Being Accounts," *AEA Papers and Proceedings* (May 2004).

A 2010 study pulled together data: Julianne Holt-Lunstad, Timothy B. Smith and J. Bradley Layton, "Social Relationships and Mortality Risk: A Meta-Analytic Review," *PLOS Medicine* (July 27, 2010). PLOS is an acronym for Public Library of Science.

There's ample research that we get greater happiness: Leaf Van Boven and Thomas Gilovich, "To Do or to Have? That Is the Question," *Journal of Personality and Social Psychology*, Vol. 85, No. 6 (2003).

CHAPTER FOURTEEN: ENJOY YOUR JOURNEY AND SAVOR YOUR TIME AT THE PEAK

people in general believe that their lives: Utpal Dholakia, "Do We Become Less Optimistic as We Grow Older?" *Psychology Today*, July 24, 2016, https://www.psychologytoday.com/us/blog/the-science-behind-behavior/201607/do-we-become-less-optimistic-we-grow-older, accessed April 23, 2019.

CREDITS

Annual Savings to Become a Millionaire by 65: Christy Bieber, "The Most Important Retirement Chart You'll Ever See," *The Motley Fool*, November 18, 2018, https://www.fool.com/retirement/2018/11/18/the-most-important-retirement-chart-youll-ever-see.aspx, accessed April 28, 2019.

Spending on Necessities: Human progress, http://humanprogress.org/static.1937, adapted from a graph by Mark Perry, using data from the Bureau of Economic Analysis, http://www.bea.gov/iTable.cfm?ReqID=9&step=1&isuri=1.

Global Well-Being: Historical Index of Human Development: Prados de la Escosura 2015, 0–1 scale, available at Our World in Data, Rover 2016h. Well-Being Composite: Rijpma 2014,p. 259, standard deviation scale over country-decades.

Life Expectancy: Max Roser, "Life Expectancy," *Our World in Data*, https://our worldindata.org/life-expectancy, accessed April 28, 2019.

Extreme Poverty: Max Roser and Esteban Ortiz-Ospina, "Global Extreme Poverty," *Our World in Data*, https://ourworldindata.org/extreme-poverty, accessed April 28, 2019.

Years of Schooling: Max Roser and Esteban Ortiz-Ospina, "Global Rise of Education," *Our World in Data*, https://ourworldindata.org/global-rise-of-education, accessed April 28, 2019.

Dow Jones Industrial Average: 1896–2016: Chris Kacher and Gil Morales, "Human Innovation Always Trumps Fear—120 Year Chart of the Stock Market," *Seeking Alpha*, March 21, 2017, https://seekingalpha.com/article/4056932-human-inno vation-always-trumps-fear-120-year-chart-stock-market, accessed April 16, 2019. Graph 4.1—What to Avoid

Not All Fiduciaries Are Created Equal: Tony Robbins with Peter Mallouk, *Unshakeable: Your Financial Freedom Playbook* (New York: Simon & Schuster, 2017), p. 86.

Types of Home Damage: Insurance Information Institute, "Fact + Statistics: Homeowners and renters insurance," Insurance Information Institute, https://www.iii.org/fact-statistic/facts-statistics-homeowners-and-renters-insurance, accessed February 16, 2020.

S&P 500 Intra-Year Declines vs. Calendar Year Returns: JP Morgan Chase and Co., "Volatility Is Normal; Don't Let It Derail You," *Guide to the Markets*, https:// am.jpmorgan.com/us/en/asset-management/gim/adv/insights/principles-for-invest ing, accessed April 22, 2019.

Investor Cash Flows/Bull and Bear Markets: The Vanguard Group, Inc., "Vanguard's Principles for Investing Success," *Vanguard*, 2017, https://about.vanguard.com/what-sets-vanguard-apart/principles-for-investing-success/ICRP RINC_042017_Online.pdf, accessed April 23, 2019.

Inflation Adjusted Annual Average Gold Prices: Tim McMahon, "Gold and Inflation," *Inflationdata.com*, April 25, 2018, https://inflationdata.com/Inflation/Infla tion_Rate/Gold_ Inflation.asp, accessed April 28, 2019.

Number of U.S. listed companies: Samantha M. Azzarello, Alexander W. Dryden, Jordan K. Jackson, David M. Lebovitz, Jennie Li, John C. Manley, Meera Pandit, Gabriela D. Santos, Tyler J. Voigt, and David P. Kelly, "Private Equity," *Guide to Markets—US*, December, 31, 2019, https://am.jpmorgan.com/blobcontent/1383654213584/83456/MI-GTM_1Q20.pdf, accessed March 17, 2020

Public vs. Private Equity Returns: Samantha M. Azzarello, Alexander W. Dryden, Jordan K. Jackson, David M. Lebovitz, Jennie Li, John C. Manley, Meera Pandit, Gabriela D. Santos, Tyler J. Voigt, and David P. Kelly, "Private Equity," *Guide to Markets—US*, December, 31, 2019, https://am.jpmorgan.com/blobcontent/1383654213584/83456/MI-GTM_1Q20.pdf, accessed March 17, 2020.

The Performances of Various Mixes of U.S. Stocks and Bonds/Historical Returns: The Vanguard Group, Inc., "Foundational Investments," *Vanguard*, 2019, https://advisors.vanguard.com/ iwe/pdf/FAETFCMB.pdf, accessed February 16, 2020.

Mixture of Assets Defines the Spectrum of Returns: The Vanguard Group, Inc., "Vanguard's Principles for Investing Success," *Vanguard*, 2017, https:// about.vanguard.com/what-sets-vanguard-apart/principles-for-investing-success/ICRPRINC_042017_Online.pdf, accessed April 23, 2019.

Relative Magnitude of Home-Country Bias: Christopher B. Philips, Francis M. Kinniry Jr., Scott J. Donaldson, "The role of Home Bias in Global Asset Allocation Decisions," *Vanguard*, June 2012, https://personal.vanguard.com/pdf/icrrhb.pdf, accessed April 23, 2019.

Dow Jones Industrial Average Component Companies: "The Changing DJIA," S&P Dow Jones Indices, LLC, https://us.spindices.com/indexology/djia-and-sp-500/the-changing-djia, accessed April 23, 2019.

Average Company Lifespan on the S&P Index: Scott D. Anthony, S. Patrick Viguerie, Evan I. Schwartz, and John Van Landeghem, "2018 Corporate Longevity Forecast: Creative Destruction is Accelerating," *Innosight*, February 2018, https://www.innosight.com/insight/ creative-destruction/, accessed April 23, 2019.

Investor Allocation by Region: Samantha M. Azzarello, Alexander W. Dryden, Jordan K. Jackson, David M. Lebovitz, Jennie Li, John C. Manley, Meera Pandit, Gabriela D. Santos, Tyler J. Voigt, and David P. Kelly, "Local Investing and Global Opportunities," *Guide to Markets—US*, March 31, 2019, https://am.jpmorgan.com/us/en/asset-management/gim/ adv/insights/guide-to-the-markets/, accessed April 23, 2019.

Ranking Higher Than: Blackrock Global Investor Pulse Survey 2019, https://www.blackrock.com/ corporate/insights/investor-pulse, accessed April 23, 2019.

ACKNOWLEDGMENTS

Thank you to my friend and colleague, Tony Robbins. I have seen few other people who have had such a positive impact on so many. Thank you to Jonathan Clements, whose work had such an impact on me as I was entering the profession and continues to do so today. Thank you to Jonathan Knapp for your tireless contribution to helping me meet an almost impossible deadline. Your fingerprints are all over this book. Thank you to Molly Rothove, Jay Beebe, Bing Chen, Andy Gryszowka, Brenna Saunders, and Jim Williams for your help with brainstorming, sourcing, and editing. Thank you to Josh Robbins for your support and work with the graphics and all of the other key components that go into a book launch. Thank you to all my fearless colleagues at Creative Planning. Not a day goes by without me learning something meaningful from you, and it's not always related to financial planning or investments. I am truly blessed to work with such a passionate, caring, intelligent, and energetic group of people. To my beautiful wife, Veronica, who refused to let me make up another errand to run in an attempt to avoid working on this book, and to my children, Michael, JP, and Gabby, all of whom gave me the very best excuses to take long breaks. All mistakes are my own.